**international
review of
social history**

Supplement 10

De-industrialization: Social, Cultural, and Political Aspects

Edited by Bert Altena and Marcel van der Linden

CAMBRIDGE
UNIVERSITY PRESS

University Printing House, Cambridge CB2 8BS, United Kingdom

Published in the United States of America by Cambridge University Press, New York

Cambridge University Press is part of the University of Cambridge.

It furthers the University's mission by disseminating knowledge in the pursuit of education, learning and research at the highest international levels of excellence.

www.cambridge.org
Information on this title: www.cambridge.org/9780521532167

A catalogue record for this publication is available from the British Library

ISBN 978-0-521-53216-7 Paperback

CONTENTS

De-industrialization:
Social, Cultural, and Political Aspects

Edited by
Bert Altena and
Marcel van der Linden

NOTES ON CONTRIBUTORS

Bert Altena, Vakgroep Maatschappijgeschiedenis, Erasmus Universiteit, Postbus 1738, 3000 DR Rotterdam, The Netherlands; e-mail: altena@fhk.eur.nl

Franco Barchiesi, Department of Sociology and Sociology of Work Unit, University of the Witwatersrand, Private Bag 3, PO Wits 2050, Johannesburg, South Africa; e-mail: 029frb@muse.wits.ac.za, f_barchiesi@yahoo.com

Robert Forrant, Department of Regional Economic and Social Development, University of Massachusetts Lowell, 500 O'Leary Library, Lowell, MA 01854, USA; e-mail: rforrant@external.umass.edu

Stefan Goch, Institut für Stadtgeschichte, Wissenschaftspark, Munscheidstrasse 14, 45886 Gelsenkirchen, Germany; e-mail: stefan.goch@ruhr-uni-bochum.de, dr.goch@gelsen-net.de, Stefan.Goch@gelsen.net

Christopher Johnson, History Department, College of Liberal Arts, Wayne State University, Detroit, MI 48202, USA; e-mail: aa4307@wayne.edu

Chitra Joshi, 129 Uttarakhand, Jawaharlal Nehru University, New Delhi 110067, India; e-mail: chitra17@vsnl.com

Bridget Kenny, Department of Sociology, University of the Witwatersrand, Private Bag 3, PO Wits 2050, Johannesburg, South Africa; e-mail: 029bkenn@muse.wits.ac.za

Darren Lilleker, Centre for Mass Communication Research, The University of Leicester, 104 Regent Road, Leicester LE1 7LT, UK; e-mail: dg14@@le.ac.uk

Marcel van der Linden, Internationaal Instituut voor Sociale Geschiedenis, Cruquiusweg 31, 1019 AT Amsterdam, The Netherlands; e-mail: mvl@iisg.nl

Gregory S. Wilson, Department of History, University of Akron, 208 Olin Hall, Akron, OH 44325-1902, USA; e-mail: gwilson@uakron.edu

IRSH 47 (2002), pp. 1–2 DOI: 10.1017/S0020859002000755

Preface

Bert Altena and Marcel van der Linden

As Christopher Johnson rightly argues in the introduction to this collection of essays, de-industrialization is not a recent phenomenon. It has attracted much interest among historians, but that interest has focused primarily on its economic causes and consequences. The social, cultural, and political aspects of de-industrialization have attracted less attention – perhaps because our discipline is more concerned with the *formation* of social relationships and social movements and less with their disappearance. Do the close ties between social historians and social movements play a role here? Does their involvement blind them to the process of decline? Significantly, the most famous and impressive analysis of an anti-de-industrialization movement sheds little light on that aspect; it was the radical resistance to the parallel process of industrialization that captured the author's imagination.[1]

Whatever the precise reasons for this relative lack of interest in the social, cultural, and political aspects of de-industrialization, it is only recently that social historians have begun to show a strong interest in the subject. Having discovered de-industrialization, they initially focused on the "classic" labour history, concentrating first and foremost on the role of employers, trade unions, and strikes.[2] It did not take long before other aspects began to be studied, and Christopher Johnson's own *The Life and Death of Industrial Languedoc, 1700–1920* (New York, 1995) was a landmark in this respect too.

Three elements in particular seem to have gradually drawn the attention of social historians in recent times. First, the often dramatic consequences for those working-class households affected: gender relations within families could change as a result, as could relations between parents and children. New forms of income had to be found, and, for example, the wives and daughters of men who were previously breadwinners began increasingly to undertake paid work. Sometimes, subsistence agriculture and cattle breeding became more important too. And if these proved

1. E.P. Thompson, *The Making of the English Working Class* (London, 1963).
2. See for example Donald Reid, *The Miners of Decazeville: A Genealogy of Deindustrialization* (Cambridge, MA, 1985), and John P. Hoerr, *And the Wolf Finally Came: The Decline of the American Steel Industry* (Pittsburgh, PA, 1988).

insufficient, individual family members, or entire families, might sometimes even have to migrate to forge a new future elsewhere.[3]

Secondly, politics was an important element. What role did local authorities play in the process of de-industrialization? What determined their policy and room for manoeuvre? And where political parties existed with the support of labour, what influence did de-industrialization have on their supporters and the political functioning of these parties?

A third key aspect is the industrialized and de-industrialized region as a whole. Demoralization, impoverishment, and migration might lead to the potential for recovery in de-industrialized regions being compromised, as is painfully evident in a number of areas throughout the world. Long-term unemployment can encourage defeatism or xenophobia. Migration leads to depopulation and an ageing of the population that remains. Sometimes the sociocultural character of a region is altered for a very long time.[4]

None of these aspects can be considered outside the regional, and often even the global context. In the course of time, capital has moved farther and farther across the globe. Industrialization and de-industrialization are therefore two sides of the same coin. If the value of a concept like "global labour history" is apparent anywhere, it is here, in research into de-industrialization. De-industrialization also means that the vicissitudes of groups of labourers in different parts of the world are connected in complex ways.[5] The great challenge to historians now seems to be to link the local (material *and* cultural) aspects of de-industrialization with the "larger picture" of ongoing transnational capital mobility. We hope that the essays presented here will help in preparing the ground for such an analysis.

3. Shireen Moosvi, "De-industrialization, Population Change and Migration in Nineteenth-Century India", *Indian Historical Review*, 16 (1989–1990), pp. 149–162; June Nash, "Global Integration and Subsistence Insecurity", *American Anthropologist*, 96 (1994), pp. 7–30; Thomas Dublin, "Working-Class Families Respond to Industrial Decline: Migration from the Pennsylvania Anthracite Region since 1920", *International Labor and Working-Class History*, 54 (Fall 1998), pp. 40–56.

4. David Washbrook, "Economic Depression and the Making of 'Traditional' Society in Colonial India, 1820–1855", *Transactions of the Royal Historical Society*, 3 (1993), pp. 237–263; Geoffrey Beattie, *Hard Lines: Voices from Deep within a Recession* (New York, 1998).

5. A pioneering study that reveals some of these connections is Jefferson R. Cowie, *Capital Moves: RCA's Seventy-Year Quest for Cheap Labor* (Ithaca, NY, 1999).

IRSH 47 (2002), pp. 3–33 DOI: 10.1017/S0020859002000767

Introduction: De-industrialization and Globalization

Christopher H. Johnson

THE RELATION BETWEEN DE-INDUSTRIALIZATION AND GLOBALIZATION

The problem of de-industrialization has undergone a decisive transmutation in the past two decades, roughly from the moment when it was linked to proto-industrialization at the Budapest Economic History Conference in 1981.[1] Also interacting with the remarkable efforts of Immanuel Wallerstein and his colleagues who dated the formation of a "world economic system" from the expansion of European conquest and trade in the fifteenth and sixteenth centuries, its place in historical and sociological analysis rapidly transcended local concerns (such as the warmly received 1982 study by Bluestone and Harrison of the American "rust belt") and has become an element in the overall problematique of global capitalism.[2] Only very recently, however, have the necessary studies (and hence theoretical perspectives) formed an appropriate critical mass to integrate the concept of de-industrialization fully into the long-term history of economic globalism. We are coming to understand that the phenomenon at the tip of the tongue of every head of state and the source of massive (and lethal) protest that came to be termed "globalization" in ordinary

1. See Franklin Mendels, "General Report, Eighth International Economic History Congress, Section A.2: Proto-industrialization: Theory and Reality", Budapest, August 1982, and attached papers (photocopied reproductions). An excellent collection of articles selected from these papers appeared as Carlo Poni (ed.) *Protoindustria*, a special issue of *Quaderni strorici*, 52 (1983). Also central to the proto-industrialization debate was Peter Kriedte, Hans Medick, and Jürgen Schlumbohm, *Industrialization before Industrialization* (Cambridge, 1981).
2. Immanuel Wallerstein, *The Modern World System: Capitalist Agriculture and the Origins of the European World Economy in the Sixteenth Century* (New York, 1974); *idem*, *Mercantilism and the Consolidation of the European World Economy* (New York, 1980); and *idem*, *The Second Era of Great Expansion in the Capitalist World-Economy* (San Diego, CA, 1989); Barry Bluestone and Bennett Harrison, *The Deindustrialization of America* (New York, 1982). An excellent analysis of the shortcomings of localized approaches appeared early in Robert Kuttner, *The End of Laissez-Faire: National Purpose and the Global Economy after the Cold War* (New York, 1991). More recently, the sober overviews of Robert Gilpin contest the extent to which globalization has overpowered national economic policy and national markets: Robert Gilpin, *The Challenge of Global Capitalism: The World Economy in the 21st Century* (Princeton, NJ, 2000) and *idem*, *Global Political Economy: Understanding the International Economic Order* (Princeton, NJ, 2001). He nevertheless understands "de-industrialization" as an aspect of more general market shifts.

parlance around 1990 is hardly new and, most importantly, not simply a one-way street originating in the West.

An array of recent studies have demonstrated the remarkable variety of sophisticated practices and vast geographic scope of integrated trade networks that look suspiciously "capitalistic" pervading the borderlands of the Indian Ocean and the western Pacific from Kilwa to Kaifeng at a time when Europeans were just beginning to "invent" capitalism.[3] The idea of "parallel development" between China and Europe for much of the second millennium, best argued by Kenneth Pomeranz and R. Bin Wong, seriously challenges Eurocentric notions of the origins of the modern economy. Particularly in terms of "extensive" agricultural growth and population balance, the vitality of international trade, the quality of handicraft manufacturing, and even technological inventiveness, there would be no way to predict, say in 1700, whether Europe or China would lead the way toward the industrial breakthrough. For Wong, the European advantage arose above all from the happy circumstance of accessible mineral-based energy production, while Pomeranz stresses the broader advantage of European New-World domination and its multiple consequences.[4] And new work on India has definitively shown that the economy of the subcontinent, particularly the cotton textile region of the south, was booming in the later seventeenth and eighteenth centuries, stimulating not only British interest in tapping into its trade throughout the Indian Ocean-East Asian region, but also the British indigenous cotton industry – that famous "engine of modernization" – the pre-industrial organization of which was remarkably similar to the Indian business (which dwarfed the *entire* British textile manufacture until the nineteenth century). The Indian cotton industry was certainly harmed and its laborers impoverished by growing British colonial dominance, but it can hardly be said that India fell into a state of pure "dependency" as the interactive

3. Janet Abu-Lughod, *Before European Hegemony: The World System AD 1250–1350* (New York, 1989) attracted the most attention. See also the ambitious Braudelian study by K.N. Chaudhuri, *Asia Before Europe: Economy and Civilization of the Indian Ocean from the Rise of Islam to 1750* (Cambridge, 1990) as well as his earlier work, *Trade and Civilization in the Indian Ocean* (Cambridge, 1985). The pioneering work of Philip Curtin, *Cross-Cultural Trade in World History* (Cambridge, 1984), and Marshall Hodgson, *Rethinking World History: Essays on Europe, Islam, World History*, Edmund Burke III (ed.) (Cambridge, 1993) should not be forgotten. A good collection is James Tracy (ed.), *The Rise of Merchant Empires* (Cambridge, 1990). On European primacy, see E.L. Jones, *The European Miracle* (Cambridge, 1987) and David Landes, *The Wealth and Poverty of Nations: Why Some Are So Rich and Some So Poor* (New York, 1998). See also the balanced analysis of Patrick Verley, *L'échelle du monde: Essai sur l'industrialisation de l'Occident* (Paris, 1997).

4. Kenneth Pomeranz, *The Great Divergence: Europe, China, and the Making of the Modern World Economy* (Princeton, NJ, 2000); R. Bin Wong, *China Transformed: Historical Change and the Limits of European Experience* (Ithaca, NY [etc.], 1997). For a solid analysis of this new historiography, see Gale Stokes, "The Fates of Human Societies: A Review of Recent Macrohistories", *American Historical Review*, 106 (2001), pp. 508–525.

process of colonial contact enhanced opportunities for many Indian merchants, and indigenous entrepreneurs benefited from imported technologies in modernizing "traditional" industries, so offsetting to some extent the deluge of British imports. Similar arguments have been made for the (less intrusive) Dutch encounters with Chinese and Muslim merchants and indigenous landowners and rulers in Indonesia.[5]

The central argument in the new history of globalism is that while the European presence and military dominance clearly rerouted many economies of Asia, the latters' *prior* sophistication and scope was for the most part encroached upon rather than transformed, and that while some elements in those working populations were indeed more greatly exploited, others, mainly from the merchant and professional castes and classes, continued to do well and creatively integrated their earlier practices with those of the Europeans, while the latter did the same. This is not to say that these elements became stooges for the colonizers – and indeed we know well where the leadership of the anticolonial movements came from – but that they created a parallel economy, sometimes integrated with the European, sometimes not (the latter often emphasizing "traditional" methods and goods) and maintained their own trading networks, if often at the behest of Europeans. From this perspective, the "Asian miracle" of the second half of the twentieth century (though led indeed by the one nation that successfully resisted Western incursion), and an even brighter twenty-first century as China and India fully enter the global economy, seem less miraculous. Some, such as André Gunder Frank, even argue that the West's 200 years of power will, in the long run, seem like a mere blip on the historical radar screen.[6]

It will be noted that the previous discussion concerns Asia. Similar arguments cannot be so easily sustained for encounters with Europeans in the Americas and most of Africa, as disease in one and the slave trade in the other permanently undermined pre-existing, often vital economies.

5. Prasannan Parthasarathi, *The Transition to a Colonial Economy: Weavers, Merchants, and Kings in South India* (Cambridge, 2001); Claude Markovits, *The Global World of Indian Merchants, 1750–1947* (Cambridge, 1999); Tirthankar Roy, *Traditional Industry in the Economy of Colonial India* (Cambridge, 2000); Peter Harnetty, "'Deindustrialization Revisited': The Handloom Weavers of the Central Provinces of India, c. 1800–1947", *Modern Asian Studies*, 25 (1991), pp. 455–510; Kristof Glamann, *The Dutch Asiatic Trade, 1620–1740* (The Hague, 1981); Charles Boxer, *The Dutch Seaborne Empire, 1600–1800* (New York, 1965); Maurice Aymard (ed.), *Dutch Capitalism and World Capitalism* (Cambridge, 1982). On China, see Michael Godley, *The Mandarin Capitalists from Nanyang: Overseas Chinese Enterprise in the Modernization of China, 1893–1911* (Cambridge, 1981) For the notion of the "indigenization of modernity", see Marshall Sahlins, "Goodbye to *Tristes Tropes*: Ethnography in the Context of Modern World History", *Journal of Modern History*, 65 (1993), pp. 1–25.

6. Frank is the most extreme revisionist and overstates his case, but is very much worth reading: André Gunder Frank, *ReOrient: Global Economy in the Asian Age* (Berkeley, CA, 1998).

Although the peoples of the preconquest western hemisphere often constructed huge trading areas and developed marvelous production techniques (think of Cahokia near the confluence of the Ohio and Mississippi rivers trading Keweenau copper goods for Gulf shell products or the vast Inca Empire connected by paved roads), they obviously never participated in a world economy, and indeed, insuperable barriers prevented anything close to continental integration. As for Africa, certainly the northern and eastern coastal regions were vital elements (and key connectors) of the Muslim world systems of the Mediterranean and Indian Oceans, while powerful West African states provided the gold, via Arab traders across the Sahara and the Sudan, that allowed Europeans and others to buy coveted goods such as silks and porcelains from the East and contributed mightily to (especially) Chinese economic growth during the Yuan and early Ming. But all that changed after the disastrous sixteenth century. The survivors entered relationships with Europeans that *were* transformative and dependent, even for the most successful, such as the fur traders of the American north or the slave traders of Asante and Dahomey.[7] And indeed, as noted, Pomeranz, in his search for advantages of Europe over China, sees New World dominance and its consequences for Africans on both sides of the Atlantic as the critical difference. There does remain something to be said for dependency theory, but its applications are specific and its scope too narrow to stand as a general theory of the global economy.[8]

What has all this to do with de-industrialization? In understanding its causes and place in history, a great deal, in understanding its consequences, less perhaps, though for its victims to confront seriously its inequities and mount meaningful protest, the globalist framework seems to me essential.

Is it legitimate to include prefactory instances of industrial decline under

7. On the deep historical advantages of Eurasia vis-à-vis the rest of the world see Jared Diamond, *Guns, Germs, and Steel: The Fates of Human Societies* (New York, 1997). In a vast literature, see Eric Wolf, *Europe and the People without History* (Berkeley, CA, 1982); Stuart Schwartz (ed.), *Implicit Understandings: Observing, Reporting, and Reflecting on the Encounters Between Europeans and other Peoples in the Early Modern Era* (Cambridge, 1994); Alvin M. Josephy, Jr (ed.), *America in 1492: The World of the Indian Peoples Before the Arrival of Columbus* (New York, 1992); Alfred Crosby, *Ecological Imperialism: The Biological Expansion of Europe, 900–1900* (Cambridge, 1986); Walter Rodney, *A History of the Upper Guinea Coast, 1545–1800* (Oxford, 1970); Robin C.C. Law, *The Impact of the Slave Trade on a West African Society* (Oxford, 1991); Ira Berlin, *Many Thousands Gone: The First Two Centuries of Slavery in North America* (Cambridge, MA, 1998).

8. Pomeranz, *Great Divergence*, ch. 6; the classic theoretical statement of dependency appeared in André Gunder Frank, *Capitalism and Underdevelopment in Latin America* (New York, 1969). The economics of dependency are studied with insight by Daniel Headrick, *Tools of Empire* (Oxford, 1981) and *idem*, *The Tentacles of Progress* (Oxford, 1988), though recent research on India needs to be integrated with this work, which states the theme too baldly, perhaps.

the rubric "de-industrialization"?[9] I will argue, and hope to demonstrate via examples given below, that it is not only legitimate, but essential if one is to integrate the notion into general economic theory. The word itself seems to be a recent one and originally referred to quite active steps taken to reduce or eliminate the industrial base of regions and countries by the Nazis. It was then picked up by the Allies in discussing possible postwar retribution against Germany. As a term for a conjunctural, structural process, according to the Oxford English Dictionary, it enters British usage in the 1970s as the discussion of massive plant closings and regional collapse of Fordist industries, not only in the UK but on the continent, preoccupied the public. US usage for the same quickly followed, and was canonized by Bluestone and Harrison's *Deindustrialization of America* in 1982. In French, use of *désindustrialisation* for a structural process may well have been coined by Raymond Dugrand in 1963 in his classic study of the rise of the vine and its consequences for urban life in Languedoc in the later nineteenth and twentieth centuries. The term was thus originally established to describe the decline of *modern*, factory industry and generally in relation to the limits in the West of mass production as competition from elsewhere and plant relocation overwhelmed superannuated, high-wage industries and specific sites.[10]

But, by the early 1980s, in laying out the theory of proto-industrialization, Franklin Mendels, Pierre Deyon, and the Göttingen team of Hans Medick, Peter Kriedte, and Jürgen Schlumbohm were speaking of areas with previous industrial concentration based in handicraft production that failed to make the transition as "de-industrialized". Such regions have in fact turned out to be so numerous that the "theory" of proto-industrialization (if not the reality of industrial ruralization in Europe *and* India and China from the late Middle Ages to the eighteenth century) predicting the conditions for machine-industrialization has proven unconvincing, though what a pot it stirred! D.C. Coleman, in the initial foray against the theory, pointed out that of the ten British regions (though he also challenges the very idea of "region") where large amounts of textiles were produced by hand mainly by rural people, a majority, six, did not make the transition, or as he mockingly puts it, they

9. Incidentally, American usage has suppressed the hyphen, thus elevating the term, in the language of the Oxford English Dictionary, to an "older and more important word", something the OED was not prepared to do in 1989. I have continued the British usage here. See D.C. Coleman, "Proto-industrialization: One Concept Too Many?", *Economic History Review*, 36 (1983), pp. 435–448.

10. Oxford English Dictionary (2nd edn), Compact (Oxford, 1989), p. 392; Raymond Dugrand, *Villes et campagnes en Bas-Languedoc* (Paris, 1963). Discussions of India during the colonial period also use the term and predate these examples. Daniel Thorner, "'De-industrialization' in India, 1881–1931", in *Contributions, Communications: First International Conference of Economic History, Stockholm, 1960* (Paris [etc.], 1960), pp. 217–226.

"deprotoindustrialized".[11] German historians, in sorting out regional economic trajectories in the nineteenth century, opted in the 1970s for the term "*Reagrarisierung*" to describe such transitions – a phenomenon that happened in many places where, while the shift back to the land might have been hard on certain highly concentrated industrial localities, the new commercially oriented agriculture provided sufficient livelihoods for the bulk of the population in the long run, and even encouraged in-migration, as was, for example, the case in Languedoc.[12]

There are more than enough similarities between modern and early modern industries in both town and country (non-European as well) to include them in the history, and the possible theorization, of de-industrialization. And, as the integrated approach of the Germans cited above and our work on Languedoc show, exactly where the line between handicraft industry and factory industry lies is difficult to ascertain. Indeed, as we now know, there were so many "alternatives to mass production" throughout the history of "modern industry" that "coexistence" rather than a dominant form may well have been typical. Agriculture itself can be a spur to industrial growth, both small- and large-scale, as the history not only of re-agrarianized regions but of entire nations, demonstrates.[13] So the variables multiply. The reasons for including the entire industrial experience of Eurasia from 1200 on (even earlier to include the Abbasid economic network centered in Baghdad) in the assessment of de-industrialization seem straightforward. As in the modern (and "postmodern") era, the essence of widespread systems was a substantial trade in manufactured goods whose rhythms of productions responded to market fluctuations far and near: fluctuations in demand, to be sure, but also in capital and labor markets, and punctuated as well by crises generally based in agricultural price increases (food was the "energy" of hand production – the equivalent of modern fossil fuels) but also in goods overproduction and financial market panics.

11. Coleman, "Proto-industrialization", pp. 445–447.

12. On German historiography, see W.R. Lee, "Economic Development and the State in Nineteenth-Century Germany", *Economic History Review*, 41 (1988), pp. 346–367; P. Fried, "Reagrarisierung in Südbayern seit dem 19. Jahrhunderts", in Hermann Kellenbenz (ed.), *Agrarisches Nebengewerbe und Formen der Reagrarisierung im Spätmittelalter und 19/20. Jahrhunderts* (Stuttgart, 1975); H. Kreiswetter, "Erklärungsversuche zur regionalen Industrialisierung in Deutschland im 19. Jahrhundert", *Vierteljahrschrift für Sozial- und Wirtschaftsgeschichte*, 67 (1980), pp. 305–333. On Languedoc, see Dugrand, *Villes et campagnes*; Leslie Page Moch, *Paths to the City: Regional Migration in Nineteenth-Century France* (Thousand Oaks, CA, 1983); Christopher H. Johnson, *The Life and Death of Industrial Languedoc* (Oxford, 1995).

13. Charles Sabel and Jonathan Zeitlin, "Historical Alternatives to Mass Production", *Past and Present*, 108 (1985), pp. 133–176. Alan Kulikoff, *The Agrarian Origins of American Capitalism* (Charlottesville, VA, 1992); Thorkild Kjaergaard, *The Danish Revolution, 1500–1800* (Cambridge, 1994); Kristoff Glamann, "Industrialization as a Factor in Economic Growth in Denmark since 1700", *Stockholm Conference, 1960*, pp. 115–128.

De-industrialization, as today, might be stimulated by crises, but, as today, had more profound roots. The most typical pattern would seem to have the following features: declining demand due to shifts in the perceived price/quality ratio as coupled with a range of cultural factors, including the slippery one of taste. High prices would have to do with wage levels; productivity shortfalls with worker dissatisfaction or ennui; decline of quality and/or lack of innovation could be linked to manufacturer and marketer decisions to stick with "tried and true" techniques that spelled success in the past, thus failing to respond to shifts in taste; increasing costs of raw materials (even in labor-intensive manufacturing, supply costs outweighed labor, especially in textiles) could be the result of price-fixing or gouging by capitalists, and also withdrawal of capital resources by outside investors (usually a second-tier response after sales decline was under way, but could also occur with the emergence of much more attractive investment opportunities). Another element in the gravity of de-industrialization for a region is its overspecialization in one product. Remaining in the purely economic realm, none of these factors would necessarily lead to decline of a product or region, if competitive goods did not exist. These might not even be in the same product line (cotton's victory over linen is the readiest example). But in the world-trading systems under discussion, competition is always present: it is, by definition, its lifeblood. The competitors, of course, would possess advantageous conditions regarding most of these economic factors.

If the foregoing could be a description of what happened in the American automobile industry in the later twentieth century, it works equally well for Flemish woolens in the earlier fourteenth, diverse north Italian industries in the mid-seventeenth, Dutch papermaking in the later eighteenth, or the dual (pre-machine/post-machine) decline of lower Languedoc in the later eighteenth and then mid-nineteenth centuries. It also works for earlier machine-industrial de-industrializations, the British "climacteric" of the later nineteenth century, and the decline of New England textiles in the earlier twentieth, thus fully demonstrating the relevance of the concept of de-industrialization to pre-machine industry experiences. We should also consider the fate of the early modern Indian cotton industry in this same context. These examples were all enormously successful in their heyday. Just as market forces within a world system made them, they also contributed to breaking them.

But, this is not, was not, and will not be a pure Smithian world. Competition is always modified by politics. It is ironic that the putative fathers of economics as a natural science, the names beloved by contemporary neoliberals, called their work "political economy"; unlike their latter-day disciples, they understood that policy and economy could not be untangled. *How* they are tangled was their concern and is (should be) what economic historians must seek to understand. The *politics* of de-industrialization were as critical to the handicraft industrial world as to the machine or informational ages. The most obvious influences from the political realm are conquest, war, and diplomacy, having both conscious and unintended effects. More difficult to ascertain, however, are the effects of political negotiations and day-to-day decisions of sovereign authorities bearing upon regions already threatened by "natural" shifts in the economy. Several of the papers in this collection deal brilliantly with precisely this issue and my own study of nineteenth-century Languedoc is subtitled "the politics of de-industrialization". Were politics important in earlier de-industrializations? Indeed, and perhaps even more so. In an age where, in the words of Josiah Child, "power and profit ought jointly to be considered" and the notion of laissez-faire was yet undiscovered, political decisions by sovereign authorities could not only enhance industrial decline, but precipitate it.[14]

A third, and more problematic, factor influencing the fates of industrial economies can be termed "ecological". At the most basic level, this refers to the availability of resources, natural and human, and hence the significance of disease in history (as it attacks both human and non-human life), the role of climatic change, and, of course the overutilization of finite (and/or harmful) resources. This is an area of intense historiographical interest today that goes far beyond the subject at hand, but we are indeed reminded of its significance for both the trajectory of the world economy and the power of politics to alter it as we watch the current American administration, in this age of threats to US hegemony, back away from *all* the international accords envisioning control of such potential disasters.

The historical record is, of course, full of instances where ecological catastrophes precipitated economic decline. But, with the notable excep-

14. On Child, see Barry Supple, *Commercial Crisis and Change in England, 1600–1642* (Cambridge, 1964). The American experience is often cited as a prime example (versus, say, France or Prussia) of economic growth due to "hands off" policies of government. This may well have been the case with regard to regulation for social protection, but government subsidization of growth is as American as apple pie (unless you are a *Native* American). Witness selective, often two-faced, tariff protection throughout US history; the great land giveaways of the Homestead Act and railroad construction; the "GI Bill of Rights"; or the interstate highway system. For trenchant analysis of the role of the state in American economic growth, see the works of Robert L. Heilbroner, especially the overviews, *The Making of Economic Society*, 5th edn (Englewood Cliffs, NJ, 1975) and (with Aaron Singer), *The Economic Transformation of America: 1600 to the Present*, 2nd edn (San Diego, CA, 1984). On the origins of "big business", see Alfred D. Chandler, *The Visible Hand: The Managerial Revolution in American Business* (Cambridge, MA, 1977). See, for Europe, Betty Behrens, "Government and Society", in E.E. Rich and C.H. Wilson (eds), *The Cambridge Economic History of Europe*, vol. 5, *The Economic Organization of Early Modern Europe* (Cambridge, 1977), pp. 549–620; and Gregory Clark, "The Political Foundations of Modern Economic Growth: England, 1540–1800", *Journal of Interdisciplinary History*, 26 (1996), pp. 563–588.

tion of history's greatest victory of germ over human, the "American holocaust" of the sixteenth century, most have served in the long run for renewal and reoriented growth. European economic historians thus couple the horrible "solutions" to fourteenth-century overpopulation (the falling temperatures and the Black Death) with the end of serfdom in the West, increased yields, and the agrarian stimulation of growth of trade and manufacturing. Early modern deforestation in western Europe threatens shipbuilding and metals refining only to advance the American timber industry (the colonies' biggest export) and lead to coal-coking technology. The *pébrine* causes the collapse of the French silk industry, but gets Lyon off its single track to a multifaceted economic renaissance that continues to this day (not to mention intense interest in a certain area of southeast Asia). The phylloxera ravages European vines and stimulates, via the use of American rootstock, one of the great economic success stories of the twentieth century.[15] In general, then, one must be skeptical of arguments that privilege ecological factors in the history of de-industrialization, though obviously demographic disaster, the mining out of resources, natural catastrophes, and the like can have significant short-run effects.

THREE CASES OF EARLY DE-INDUSTRIALIZATION

Let us now examine three cases of early de-industrialization with an eye toward parallels with examples in this volume and other contemporary instances, to return finally to perhaps America's most famous modern story, the Detroit automobile industry. The purpose of this exercise is to explore the comparability of the phenomenon over time.

The earliest major (European) case of regional economic decline occurred in the great Flemish woolen industry during the late thirteenth

15. David Stannard, *American Holocaust: The Conquest of the New World* (Oxford, 1992). On the issue of the significance of the Black Death in the late medieval "crisis of feudalism", one must take care not to fall into demographic determinism, but there can be no doubt that it was a contributing factor in the restructuring of economy and society in western Europe during the fourteenth and fifteenth centuries. In the enormous literature, see Wilhelm Abel, *Agrarian Fluctuations in Europe from the Thirteenth to the Twentieth Centuries* (New York, 1980); Guy Bois, *La crise du féodalisme* (Paris, 1976); T.H. Ashton and C.H.E. Philpin (eds), *The Brenner Debate: Agrarian Class Structure and Economic Development in Pre-Industrial Europe* (Cambridge, 1987); R.G. Albion, *Forests and Sea Power: The Timber Problem of the Royal Navy* (Hamden, CT, 1926, repr. 1965); John McCusker and Russell Menard, *The Economy of British America, 1607–1789* (Chapel Hill, NC, 1985); G. Hammersly, "The Charcoal Industry and Its Fuel, 1540–1750", *Economic History Review*, 26 (1973), pp. 593–613. Yves Lequin, *Les ouvriers de la région lyonnaise (1848–1914)*, 2 vols (Lyon, 1977); Marcel Lachiver, *Vins, Vignes et vignerons: histoire du vignoble français* (Paris, 1988); Harry W. Paul, *Science, Vine, and Wine in Modern France* (Cambridge, 1996).

and fourteenth centuries.[16] By the early thirteenth century, the flourishing cities of Flanders had developed an excellent fulled broadcloth produced in an urban putting-out system dominated by great merchants who nevertheless had to negotiate agreements with producer guilds (above all the "blue-nailed" weavers). The industry's success was rooted in a far-reaching trade system, drawing its raw wool from the best source available, England (especially its monasteries), processing it in the humid Flemish lowlands, and shipping it through the fairs of Champagne via exchange with Italian merchants (mainly Genoese) who then distributed the cloth throughout the Mediterranean and trading again, in the east, with Arabs who sold it throughout their vast "world system". The sources of its decline, which in terms of overall sales only dates from the 1310s but can be traced more deeply, include elements of all three factors – economic conjuncture, politics, and ecology – and seem impossible to grid into a causal pattern. But all resonate with contemporary experience. Flanders, like the midwestern American auto industry centered in Detroit, received its raw materials from elsewhere, benefiting due to its location from cheap maritime transport of bulky goods as well as inland trans-shipment of lighter materials.[17] This vulnerability exposed the industry to competition

16. The classic study, of course, is Henri Pirenne's *Belgian Democracy* (1915). The edition consulted here is *Early Democracies in the Low Countries*, J.V. Saunders (transl.) with an introduction by John H. Mundy (New York, 1963). Pirenne has been revised significantly, largely along the lines suggested by Mundy: "Was the corporatist and statist economy of the late middle ages and early modern times quite as uninventive and reactionary as Pirenne described it? [...] May one properly suppose [...] that economic enterprise, when free and unregulated by princes, government or social corporatism, necessarily provides the principal or sole means for the advancement of human liberty?" (p. xxvi). These remarks reflect the beginning of a massive rethinking of the history of capitalism that had a difficult row to hoe because both liberals *and* most Marxists, who dominated twentieth-century historiography until fairly recently, subscribed to this vision. One of the main themes of my analysis in this essay is its emphasis on the political, social, and cultural variables that always interact with economic forces to shape human life, whether positively or negatively. Another relevant interpretation that one still sees in textbooks is E.M. Carus-Wilson's (*Medieval Merchant Venturers*, London, 1954) explanation of emerging English competitive advantage vis-à-vis Flanders in the woolen cloth business supposedly caused by the fulling mill, an argument canonized by Jean Gimpel in *The Medieval Machine: The Industrial Revolution of the Middle Ages* (Harmondsworth, 1977). Recent work has criticized her studies by pointing out that the areas of the West Country where she found so many mills in the thirteenth century produced precious few cloths. The whole argument needs to be pushed forward a century and one needs to understand that, technically, water pressure is a matter of correctly constructed weirs and sluices, not (necessarily) fast-flowing streams. This does not mean, however, that English policy on wool as well as woolens competition *and* continental military action did not figure as factors in Flemish decline in the fourteenth century.

17. Until the 1950s, most of Detroit's materials came from US areas largely accessible by water. Ford, of course, made his cars at the Rouge plant from scratch: ore from northern Minnesota, coal from Pennsylvania, wood from the (largely his own) forests of the Upper Peninsula (a significant component until the 1930s), leather from mid-Western tanneries, while the other companies bought steel from local mills as well as Pittsburgh, Cleveland, and Gary and semifinished components from innumerable suppliers in metropolitan southeastern Michigan

from the supplier itself and England did not disappoint, beginning its shift to woolen production in qualities directly competing with Flemish cloth by the mid-thirteenth century, and accompanied by a certain "buy English" mentality. The general prosperity of the international cloth trade and the weakness of the English crown kept the potential threat at bay. But in the early 1270s, Prince Edward, later King Edward I, unfurled a policy seeking to revitalize England's continental power that focused centrally on weakening Flanders and specifically on ending the "Flemish ascendancy", the inordinate power of Flemish merchants in England over the wool market. This involved a protracted struggle of seizures and bans, culminating in 1274–1275 in a ban on all exports of wool, since plenty of wool reached Flanders illegally or via non-Flemish merchants and venues. Such policies could not last forever, and Edward and the heir apparent, Count Guy de Dampierre, reached agreement for the reopening of the wool trade and the importation of Flemish cloth (made from English wool, of course). But things were not at all the same, as Italians (along with Cahorsians and English merchants themselves) became increasingly vital middlemen at the expense of the Flemish. The net result was an increase in the price Flemish manufacturers paid for their wool and growing doubts in England about the purchase of Flemish-made goods. Thus, the first important step in the long process of decline seems largely political.[18]

But there also was occurring a shift in Mediterranean and Near-Eastern taste toward lighter woolens and many Florentine traders/bankers sought to develop that city's woolen industry to satisfy it. Simultaneously Italian merchants began to bypass the fairs of France, using the Atlantic route that new shipping technology made more feasible. While this certainly benefited Bruges (whose water access had not yet silted up), the new port of choice was London. As noted, the "Italian ascendancy" in the purchase and shipment of wool begins in the last quarter of the thirteenth century. Italian businessmen also invested heavily in the hinterlands of Flanders, buying cloth directly from Ghent and other industrial city merchant-manufacturers, often unfinished stuff that would then be sent to Florence and elsewhere for upgrading to suit the revolution in taste. Meanwhile, the Flemish patricians, proud of their established product, did little to satisfy new demand and chose instead to capture fully the market in the highest quality *draps*, a strategy that proved successful economically, but, because

and the wider mid-West (e.g. Anderson, Indiana-made batteries and spark plugs). Tires for all (including Ford's recently terminated Firestone connection) came from Akron. The later twentieth century saw an enormous shift to international sources, especially basic steel from Japan. Flanders relied throughout on English wool and on commerce from the south and east for alum and dyestuffs.

18. T.H. Lloyd, *The English Wool Trade in the Middle Ages* (Cambridge, 1977), chs 2 and 3; A.R. Bridbury, *Medieval English Clothmaking* (London, 1982). ch. 3.

of pressures placed on fullers and weavers for ever greater productivity, created conditions leading to the famous social upheavals marking the first decades of the fourteenth century. For some merchants, trimming on quality was another avenue, but this played into the hands of Italians seeking semifinished goods. Through it all, labor costs remained higher in Flanders than in England and Florence. In the former, Flemish imports continued to outcompete town-made English products among the wealthy (for whom even the finest cloth was a lesser expenditure in any case) so the principal problem for the Flemish industry remained the high cost of English wool, much of which passed through Italian hands to reach it. And in the course of the fourteenth century, mechanized fulling, not only in England, but across the continent, did cheapen production costs for good broadcloth and Flemish urban merchant-manufacturers were slow to adapt, leaving them exposed to rural and smaller-town competition even in their own region. Florentine weavers, notoriously, were not allowed to associate, and such "modern" forms of industrial servitude as wage-advances and subsequent debt-peonage were common, assuring that labor costs remained low. In both states, political structures encouraging new exploitative production were in place. As the fourteenth century moved forward, political and ecological forces delivered the *coup de grâce* to an industry losing its bearings as overpopulation and climate combined to drive food prices up relentlessly, (creating not only worker despair but shrinking buying power everywhere) leading to a spiral of upheavals (including rural in the wake of the great famine of 1317–1319) that created precarious conditions throughout the region.[19]

Nevertheless, urban merchant-manufacturers continued to adapt to new market conditions. As noted above, their first move was to emphasize high-quality *draps*, thus searching out a market niche above the Italian competition. At the same time, rural and small-town industry, where labor costs were lower (though it is a Pirennian myth that they were unregulated) and the producers more docile, provided serges and other lower quality woolens that remained competitive. One of the key points of revisionist research is that rural and urban industry became increasingly interactive and complementary as market pressures presented the specter of decline. Clearly the devastating whirlwind of the Black Death immobilized Flemish production, as it did economic life everywhere, for a while (though there is good evidence of surprisingly rapid revitalization

19. The best summary of the Italian role in medieval economic history remains R.S. Lopez, *The Commercial Revolution* (Englewood Cliffs, NJ, 1971); on the impact of climatic change generally, E. Le Roy Ladurie, *Le climat depuis l'an mil* (Paris, 1966) remains essential; see also H.S. Lucas, "The Great European Famine of 1315, 1316 and 1317", in E.M. Carus-Wilson (ed.), *Essays in Economic History*, vol. 2 (London, 1962).

of the English wool trade in the 1350s). But it would be an error to assert, as did Pirenne, that the great textile cities simple rolled over and died, strangled by "medieval" regulations, while industrial survival and finally revitalization occurred in the unregulated countryside, creating the foundation of a "modern" economy. The story of Bruges's survival, based in its role as Flanders' window on the sea and as the region's financial center (with Italian merchants and bankers playing an inordinate role), was long contrasted with the industrial cities, especially Ghent, which supposedly slid into moribund routine. A new generation of scholarship has shown something that might have been expected if one were attuned to global processes, but not blinded by laissez-faire theory: that for every de-industrialization, there is a re-industrialization, especially if rational actors in the economic sphere can find aid in the political sphere (a combination that works particularly well if the elites in both are essentially the same, a common characteristic in most late-medieval cities).

Marci Sortor's powerful analysis of the fifteenth-century successes of Saint-Omer, a large (35,000 population) woolen producer (up to 60,000 bolts) just across the Flemish border in Artois, is instructive. Her main point is that, far from being Pirenne's "commercial dinosaurs" strangled by a medieval mode of production, Saint Omer's cloth merchants adapted to the new market circumstances of the later fourteenth and fifteenth centuries by abandoning their line of fine cloths and moving towards *says*, a serge, and *rays*, a striped fulled *draps* of lesser quality. Undoubtedly the overall income from woolens produced in Saint-Omer was less in 1450 than it had been in 1300, but the town was prosperous again. No longer did their cloth travel south, but now found outlets through Hanseatic traders (via Bruges) to the Baltic and Russia. This turned out to be a more volatile market than those of yesteryear, going through waves of boom and bust. To satisfy such cycles, the industry now relied on a different kind of work force – indigenous weavers were less well and securely paid, and fullers had fewer jobs; moreover, a good number of the urban workers were temporary, migrants from the countryside or other cities ("foreigners" in the parlance of the age) who could be sent home in down time. Most importantly, Saint-Omer maintained complex relationships with woolen production in its countryside, as outworking overseen by urban merchants combined with the direct purchase of cloth from small-time merchants and craftsmen. Such complementarity, Sortor argues, makes much more sense than the image of rural–urban antagonism bequeathed by early fourteenth-century clashes and sustained, until recently, in the historiography for much of the early modern period. Finally, politics. Municipal policy, all in regulating the industry in many ways, proved flexible and adaptable, always with an eye toward promoting the industry and assuring buyers of the quality of goods received. Certainly, the city fathers (also the leading merchants) had to wrestle with the demands of the their lifeline, the Hanse, and thus could not chart a completely independent course, but the town – if not all its inhabitants – did well enough.[20]

Such an overall pattern of de-industrialization and subsequent revitalization on different terms is probably more typical than journeys into industrial oblivion. Capital, rationally administered, always seems to have a way of finding new avenues of investment if the terms – wages, raw materials (Saint-Omer even approved the use of inferior lambs' wool and pretty much abandoned English fine altogether), and property values – are right. Its ability to play "hopscotch", as I once termed it, lies at the very heart of the system.

The seventeenth-century economic decline of northern Italy, Flanders' pre-eminent heir and the next great case of pre-machine de-industrialization, offers similar parallels. Domenico Sella's research challenges much previous scholarship (though not Carlo Cipolla's brilliant 1952 article), presenting a highly nuanced picture that privileges global economic forces while factoring in culture and politics and rejecting monocausal explanation.[21] The old view that the Italian economy was stifled in the course of the sixteenth century by the Turkish presence in the Mediterranean and the opening of the New World and Atlantic routes to Asia was easily dispatched simply by careful analysis of Italian performance records. But, especially after 1620, one can begin to speak of a de-industrialization that affected Florence, Venice, Milan, and Genoa (as well as many lesser towns) more or less equally. Italy was hardly alone

20. Marci Sortor, "Saint-Omer and the Textiles Trades in the Late Middles Ages: A Contribution to the Proto-industrialization Debate", *American Historical Review*, 98 (1993), pp. 1475–1499. See also Yoshio Fujii, "Draperie urbaine et draperie rurale dans les Pays-Bas méridionaux au moyen âge: Une mise en point des recherches après H. Pirenne", *Journal of Medieval History*, 16 (1990), pp. 88–110; and John Munro, "Urban Regulation and Monopolistic Competition in the Textile Industries of the Late-Medieval Low Countries", in Erik Aerts and John Munro (eds), *Textiles of the Low Countries in European History* (Leuven, 1990), pp. 41–52. Although the problem goes far beyond this essay, Sortor's work is representative of an historiographical trend that re-examines the role of cities in the European late-medieval/early modern economy and is unwilling to accept the liberal/Marxist rejection of statist and corporative regulation as inimical to economic growth. In the end, this reinterpretation also makes this period more comparable to Chinese development, a point not lost on Wong and Pomeranz. See the brilliant discussions of this question in Steven Kaplan, *La fin des corporations* (Paris, 2001), especially pp. xiii–xvi and 599–616.

21. Domenico Sella's studies include *Commercio e industria a Venezia nel secolo XVII* (Venice [etc.], 1961); *idem*, *Crisis and Continuity: The Economy of Spanish Lombardy in the Seventeenth Century* (Cambridge, MA, 1979), and his most recent assessment of the problem, *Italy in the Seventeenth Century* (London [etc.], 1997), pp. 19–49. Carlo Cipolla's path-breaking article of 1952, "The Decline of Italy: The Case of a Fully Matured Economy", was reprinted in the outstanding collection, B. Pullan (ed.), *Crisis and Change in the Venetian Economy* (London, 1968), pp. 127–145; it also includes Sella, "The Rise and Fall of the Venetian Woolen Industry", pp. 106–126. Another fundamental collection is Herman van der Wee (ed.), *The Rise and Decline of Urban Industries in Italy and the Low Countries (Late Middle Ages–Early Modern Times)* (Leuven, 1988).

in a crisis that was "general",[22] but its advanced status in manufacturing, commerce, and finance made its fall all the more striking. The northern European powers weathered the storm each in its own way, with the Dutch making the greatest strides, but in fact the reigning notion of seventeenth-century economists that there existed in the world a fixed amount of trade and that it was up to states to deploy noneconomic means to enhance their share of it[23] reflected realities in face of demographic, climatic, and resource-related (silver's depletion) calamities not dissimilar to the fourteenth century. That this second "little ice age" did not lead to total collapse is a tribute to the ability of "modern" states to quarantine, restrict travel, and provide minimal social assistance to offset the ravages of epidemic disease and famine. Ecological forces had a general effect, but cannot explain the specifics of Italy's decline.

Earlier research sought to find the "key" factor behind the process (which affected many industries beyond the core woolen and silk manufactures). One of the most popular was to "scapegoat" (as Sella puts it) the merchant/industrial elites who allegedly now sought to ape the aristocracy in record numbers by abandoning trade to become *rentiers*, urban and rural. "Spanish" cultural influence – hence adding a bit of nationalism – seemed the cause. The latter makes no sense since Spanish domination preceded decline by a half-century and areas free of Spanish rule, such as the Papal States and Venice, suffered as much as or more than those that were not. The simple fact is that three or four generations at the helm of business seem to be enough for most entrepreneurial families wherever and whenever capitalism has flourished, as descendants reorient toward safe investments, public service, and charitable activities (whether founding *hospices* or creating research foundations.) Blaming a *bourgeoisie fainéante* is a favorite historian's (and journalist's) pastime, whatever their politics. Witness liberal David Landes scorning the nineteenth-century French for their country's purported backwardness (a view now totally discredited); Marxist Raymond Dugrand's image of the industrialists and *négociants* of lower Languedoc giving up without a fight to reinvest in the vine; any number of writers on the British "climacteric"; and then the range of Weberian analyses of bureaucratic sclerosis and of ill-advised "diversification" that marked contemporary discourse on American industry in the 1970s and 1980s. This is not to say that businesspeople's decisions are not important, or that they are simply buffeted by forces beyond their control. But it is the *context* in which those decisions are taken that must be understood as central, and in the case of seventeenth-century Italy, the main issue had to be a rational assessment of the

22. See Trevor Aston (ed.), *Crisis in Europe, 1560–1660* (London [etc.], 1965); Geoffrey Parker, *Europe in Crisis, 1598–1648* (Ithaca, NY, 1979).
23. See Joseph A. Schumpeter, *History of Economic Analysis* (Oxford, 1954), pp. 335–376.

profitability of continuation and, for potential new industrial investors (who had always replaced the *rentier*-bound in the past), an assessment of the industrial future. Italy did indeed de-industrialize in the seventeenth and eighteenth centuries, but certainly the universal merchant penchant, as John Hooker put it around 1600, to "creep and seek to be a gentleman" can hardly serve as a sufficient explanation for it.[24]

Another oft-cited internal cause perhaps has greater credence – what might be called the "too much of a good thing" thesis in which the producer guilds, as well as the merchants, having "perfected" their cloth, glass, metalware, etc. are loath to change despite shifts in demand or competitors' price advantage. The problem, of course, is when and how to alter production processes if demand remains strong even though it might be declining (and one always wonders whether the decline is not simply temporary). As we shall see, Italian manufacturers handled the problem poorly and paid dearly for it. Related to this question is the alleged power of the producer guilds and their influence on wage levels (which *were* high relative to Italy's rivals). Although most trades incorporated during the fifteenth and sixteenth centuries and their elaborate regulations remain to bedazzle historians, those which have received detailed study, such as the Florentine weavers, reveal a facade of power on paper, weakness vis-à-vis the merchants in reality.[25] Scapegoating guild resistance is an easy road to follow, but for Italy it is a less viable explanation than in Flanders, where the producers' guilds did indeed have and physically exert their power, clearly affecting overall economic performance. But even there, larger market forces far outweighed their impact. At least one Italian industry – obviously an important one – does seem to have been trammeled by structural inertia, but it had little to do with guild power. Robert Davis's work on the Arsenal, Venice's state shipbuilding enterprise and one of the largest manufacturing complexes in early modern Europe, presents a picture of management domination and subdivision of labor worthy of the Ford Motor Company, but structures of patronage, often cemented by kinship, created a rigidity and high costs of production that ultimately undermined one of Italy's proudest achievements, as the Arsenal was bypassed during the seventeenth century by new shipyards at Chatham, Marseilles, and Livorno.[26] Thus, if not the guilds *per se*, sclerotic work structures could well have been a factor of decline.

24. J.H. Hexter, *Reappraisals in History: New Views on History and Society in Early Modern Europe* (New York, 1961), p. 114.

25. Richard Rapp, *Industry and Economic Decline in Seventeenth-Century Venice* (Cambridge, MA, 1976); Paolo Malanima, *Decadenza di un'economia cittadina: L'industria a Firenze nei secoli XVI–XVII* (Bologna, 1982).

26. Robert C. Davis, "Arsenal and *Arsenalotti*: Workplace and Community in Seventeenth-Century Venice", in Leonard Rosenband and Thomas Safley (eds), *The Workplace before the Factory* (Ithaca, NY, 1993), pp. 180–203.

Sella nevertheless underlines the problem of northern Italy's comparatively high wages, which he attributes not to the power of the guilds, but to the nature of the labor market. A combination of demographic stagnation and the very diversity of the urban economies gave workers the power of exit – the possibility of locating jobs in commerce and service activities (including the burgeoning ranks of domestic servants that every "gentleman" needed to surround himself with) as well as alternative non- or weak-guild manufacturing. Travelers from elsewhere were astounded at the absence of begging and other indicators of surplus labor. Italy's wealth, in other words, though being reoriented away from manufacturing, still allowed the elites and the comfortable to live in ease and hence create jobs (if at lower pay) for most of the common folk. This phenomenon seems common to most contexts of de-industrialization unless the wealthy move out altogether, something that occurred, for example, in many American cities in the later twentieth century. Even if movement was largely nearby, effects could be devastating, especially if punctuated by the factor of race. All papers in this collection touch on the question of re-employment and we shall return to this theme below.[27]

"In the end, therefore, it is to [non-Italian] markets [...] that one must turn to find the key to Italy's woes", argues Sella.[28] He discounts the disjunctions of *mezzogiorno* agriculture as a factor seriously affecting the north, saying that it was not much of a market for northern goods at any time, but rather slides over the fact that prices of southern-supplied raw silk and wool increased with agricultural setbacks (and here climatic changes were important) and thus caused at least temporary pressures before other sources could be found. International markets in the seventeenth century were volatile, to say the least (and not just the Italian world of Europe and the Ottoman Empire, but the Indian Ocean and far-Eastern systems as well). High politics certainly played a role as civil war racked the Ottoman heartland – a key market area – of Syria for much of the first half of the century, and the Thirty Years War devastated German markets. Moreover, mercantilist policies emerged in England and France even early in the century, having a selective impact on exports, especially glass and silk. But the main overall force remained Italians' inability to compete with the new powers of the north, England and the Netherlands (and later in the century, France, especially Languedoc woolens to the Levant). The two great sea powers had better ships and lower shipping costs, and after the Spanish wars ended, could trade unimpeded in the Mediterranean. In general, seventeenth-century customers, wherever they might be and at whatever level of income, operated on tighter budgets, thus

27. See pp. 31–32 below.
28. Sella, *Italy in the Seventeenth Century*, p. 35.

appreciating the lower costs of northern products, even though their quality might be somewhat inferior.

Italians simply failed to adapt to these new market conditions. Why? Their prices remained uncompetitive. Were they pushed up artificially by high taxes? (A lament of businessmen then and now.) This may have been a factor for Venice, but most of the other states placed minimal taxes on business operations and goods. Sella does not perhaps give sufficient attention to raw material prices (which had been central to Flemish decline originally), but zeroes in on wages and manufacturing productivity. The wage issue, already discussed, was intractable due to labor market forces, not the guilds. But in one area the guilds (both the producer and merchant organizations) do bear responsibility: innovation in manufacturing technique was resisted largely on the grounds of eminently successful "tradition". High wages might have been offset by technological change, perhaps combined with different standards of quality, to achieve gains in productivity. But this was not forthcoming. As the Venetian Board of Trade put it in looking back over the century's history in fine woolens: "the true source of its decline is to be found in its reluctance to adapt to modern tastes, steeped as it is in the love of its old ways".[29]

As in Flanders/Artois, industrial collapse was far from total and in the long run reorientations occurred. Some industries, such as Florentine silks, survived unscathed, while others finally developed new products that proved competitive (e.g. Milanese embroidery). The main trend, as in Flanders, was toward ruralization of industry, not only in inherently rural manufactures such as the fine papers of Voltri that found important markets in the Spanish world and, significantly, in England in the eighteenth century, but in textile and metalware production as well. Although some of the latter competed with urban goods, eliciting the obligatory complaints from the towns, others, such as the enormous silk-throwing industry, which gave work to thousands of (mainly female) peasants, were perfectly complementary with urban industry.[30] Thus the themes of adaptation and restructuring in Flanders/Artois and northern Italy, three centuries apart, bear marked similarities. In both, nevertheless, population in the countryside increased at the expense of the cities as industrial opportunities, in addition to agriculture, stimulated growth. Current scholarship stresses that one should not mistake this process with some rural-based "proto-industrialization", but rather see it as an adaptive development in which city, country, and, increasingly, the state interacted for industrial progress.[31]

29. *Idem*, "Rise and Fall of the Venetian Woolen Industry", p. 123.

30. *Idem*, *Italy in the Seventeenth Century*, pp. 41–46.

31. See above all, Herman van der Wee, "Industrial Dynamics and the Process of Urbanization and De-urbanization in the Low Countries from the Late Middle Ages to the Eighteenth Century: A Synthesis", in his *Rise and Fall*, pp. 307–381.

It is in this context that the experience of our third European example, the French region of lower Languedoc, becomes particularly relevant. The Languedocian woolens industry, specializing in good fulled broadcloth, but including an entire array of grades of carded woolen materials, had roots deep in the Middle Ages, but only reached its full potential in the eighteenth century, at which time it had become the largest woolen-producing region in France. Its flagship was a finely worked and relatively light *draps de Levant,* which was exported via jobbers in Marseilles to the *échelles* of the eastern Mediterranean, key ports of the Ottoman Empire. It also possessed a virtual monopoly on cloth for the military, finer stuff for the officers' uniforms and a sturdy *draps* for the men, gained through the good offices of Cardinal Fleury, a native son of Lodève, in 1729. This happy combination meant that the dislocations of war for private commerce were offset by the heightened wartime demand for uniforms.[32]

The role of the state loomed large in the history of Languedocian woolens. The Ministry of War purchased military cloth directly, avoiding subcontracting except during a brief period during the Directory. But *draps de Levant* also benefited significantly from state assistance, having been designated by Colbert as a prime product to enhance French fortunes in foreign trade. Several *manufactures royales*, of which the model *ville ouvrière* conceded to the Maistre family at Villenouvette near the Hérault river was the most famous, set the standards for quality and production technique. Inspectors of Manufactures minutely regulated the cloth's quality, whatever its source, both at the point of production and in Marseilles. The Marseilles shippers also came under state scrutiny, and diplomatic agreements with the Turks oversaw transactions at the other end. Besides creating a documentary bonanza for historians, the policing of this trade contributed mightily to the competitive advantage *draps de Levant* quickly gained over its north Italian and especially English West-Country rivals. It was indeed one of the great success stories of Colbertian economic policy. But oversight of quality, the guarantee that "Languedoc woolens" with the seal of Clermont l'Hérault or Saint-Chinian would have the same length, the same *souplesse* at the hidden interior of the bolt as on the outside, and its grade clearly marked was hardly a new phenomenon. The reputation of virtually all the products discussed so far from the broadcloths of Ghent or the serges of Saint-Omer to the silks of Florence or the glass of Murano found sustenance in the subsidization, regulation, and promotion by their governments, if not perhaps to the same degree as in Colbertian France. And such a role was also hardly limited to

32. Léon Dutil, *Etat économique du Languedoc à la fin de l'ancien régime (1750–1789)* (Paris, 1911) provides a massive overview of the entire economy; Charles Carrière, *Négociants marseillais au XVIII siècle,* 2 vols (Aix-en-Provence, 1977) traces the trade and its practitioners in detail; Christopher H. Johnson, "De-industrializzazione: Il caso dell'industria laniera della Linguadoca", *Quaderni storici,* 52 (1983), pp. 25–56, factors in the military cloth industry.

"pre-industrial" production (one may hope that this term is fading from our vocabulary). All one needs to do is think of the role of the American government in the building of railroads or the aircraft industry or consider the work of the postwar Japanese government in the transformation of the meaning of "made in Japan".[33] Our (brief) Thatcherist age may have revived the ideology of laissez-faire and its condemnation of all who did not practice it, but in fact the long history of capitalism is much more a consideration of "profit *and* power" than it is the triumph of that will-o'-the-wisp called the "free market".

On the other hand, over-regulation was certainly always possible and does figure in the later eighteenth-century difficulties of the Levant trade, especially in the wake of market shifts within the Ottoman Empire caused primarily by the declining buying power of the *rial* (a thoroughly modern problem indeed), a process which introduced growing corrupt practices at both ends (ominously "the Jews" were accused of polluting the markets of Aleppo and Constantinople). As producers and shippers alike cheated on quality to fetch lower prices, the inspectors became more assiduous, causing further consternation and mistrust. The Marseilles jobbers became the scapegoats of this drama, but in fact, market alteration – in this case having little to do with competitive products, though English fabrics from Yorkshire began to attract attention – lay at the base of decline. But if Clermont and Saint-Chinian merchants lost their luster, a new *marque*, that of Bédarieux, burst onto the scene in the 1770s and 1780s – good quality and lower priced goods produced by enterprising merchants who had taken advantage of their previously unprivileged (and hence unregulated) status to find cheaper labor, specifically weavers in the villages down the Orb valley. Clermont, and Saint-Chinian certainly put out work, but mostly to rural spinsters and were tightly regulated as to the number of weaving looms they could employ *extra-muros*. Simultaneously, as James Thomson has documented in his meticulous history of Clermont, merchants there – and well before the crisis – began to retire to become (a now familiar theme) landed *rentiers*, which obviously exacerbated the decline of their city's manufacturing vocation.[34] Similar pressures arose in Saint-Chinian, where the vine also beckoned. Despite the hard work of Bédaricians, the Levant trade did decline by about a third from its peak at mid-century, the victim of global market changes.

33. See my "Capitalism and the State: Capital Accumulation and Proletarianization in the Languedocian Woolens Industry, 1700–1789", in Rosenband and Safley (eds), *The Workplace before the Factory*, pp. 37–62. Robert Kuttner, *The End of Laissez-Faire*, examines the contemporary scene, particularly the Japanese marriage of business and government.

34. James Thomson, *Clermont-de-Lodève, 1633–1789: Fluctuations in the Prosperity of a Languedocian Cloth-Making Town* (Cambridge, 1982). It is hard to sustain it as the key cause of the region's de-industrialization because other towns, especially Bédarieux and Lodève, took up the slack.

Military cloth production flourished, however, and did so with government help – not simply because it bought the product, but because, as a demanding customer, it forced the suppliers of Lodève to become better capitalists. As in the other old towns of the industry, agreements validated by the Estates or the Parlement regulated the number of weavers that might be sought in the countryside. Hence, to increase productivity, the most expeditious mode was to restructure the pay scales in Lodève and encourage immigration of weavers from the countryside who could be engaged outside the guild's oversight. This meant violating previous statutes, thus requiring supportive reports from the Intendancy and statute revision. When this was met with resistance, a simple step was taken (in 1748): abolish the guild! Pareurs, the master cloth-finishers, were similarly treated, their corporate rights diluted. Thereafter, rural weavers flooded Lodève and a rapid re-urbanization of the industry ensued, all with the government's blessing. In the 1780s and especially during the Consulat, officials demanded that bids for army orders be in large-scale units, hence demanding industrial consolidation. Small, and less efficient, cloth manufacturers saw themselves cut out of the business. Later, the government consistently favored *fabricants* who modernized their equipment, and offered subsidies to those who mechanized. The growth of large and productive firms in the defense industry also stimulated imitation in the export sector.[35]

Overall, then, it is not possible to speak of de-industrialization in the later eighteenth century because military cloth production more than made up the losses in the export trade, which became worse during the Revolutionary era. And later, when peace returned and army demand fell, export sales of *draps de Levant* revitalized to restore the equilibrium. Together, the two products went on to new heights by around 1840, selling in the range of 130,000 to 160,000 bolts (*pièces*) for the Department of the Hérault alone, with each accounting for about half, surpassing anything achieved in the eighteenth century. Before my studies,[36] historians tended to see the de-industrialization of the Midi as a straight line from the difficulties of the later eighteenth century as new fabrics (cottons) and new ways of working wool (combed-wool "*nouveautés*") reduced the demand for broadcloth, while that product received a new finesse from producers in Sedan and Amiens. The vital north overwhelms the moribund south as the industrialists in the latter, tails between their legs, follow the

35. Johnson, "Capitalism", and *idem*, "Artisans vs. Fabricants: Urban Protoindustrialization and the Evolution of Work Culture in Lodève and Bédarieux, 1740–1830", *Mélanges de l'Ecole française de Rome*, 99 (1987), pp. 1047–1084.

36. *Idem*, "Il caso", in *idem*, *Life and Death of Industrial Languedoc: The Politics of Deindustrialization* (Oxford, 1995), chs 1–3.

Clermontois into the vineyard, producing an undistinguished wine for the masses.[37]

But what makes the case of Languedoc's de-industrialization interesting is that it is rather a *bridge* between the pre-machine and machine-age phenomena. For, as I show in detail in my book, the woolens towns of the Hérault did mechanize, and the production levels noted above resulted. This "industrial revolution", continuingly stimulated by both a demanding state and market forces, produced social and political consequences that in fact put the modest towns of Lodève and Bédarieux (each had populations of about 14,000 at mid-century) at the forefront of militant trade unionism and socialism. But from the peak in the late July Monarchy, a long phase of industrial decline ensued so that by the turn of the new century "industrial Languedoc" was no more. Mono-crop Languedoc, wine-barrel to the ordinary folks of France and defended by *députés du vin* when prices dipped too low, became its twentieth-century persona.

How this happened and the nature of its human consequences parallel our previous examples from the pre-machine age, and also presage those of the contemporary world examined in this volume. We must begin with markets. The demand for woolens declined relative to cotton in the nineteenth century but was offset by population growth and increasingly global export possibilities.[38] There is no question, however, that felted and shorn broadcloth lost market share within woolens, and within the broadcloth category, the trend was toward lighter and finer material for suits and dresses, whether in Europe or elsewhere. The staple of Languedoc, in other words, was fading as tastes changed. So why not reorient? Bédrarieux did, to some extent, but the Levant business seemed to flourish right down to the Revolution of 1848. Perhaps this niche could be theirs forever. As for the military cloth producers (Villenouvette, no longer "royal", had joined Lodève in the business as had several lesser towns), the army still wanted the staple, so there was not much inclination to innovate. And the government realized that their product's quality/cost ratio was superior to other woolens centers. Lodève held its own in competitive bidding.

The watershed era in the history of industrial Languedoc spanned the years from 1848 to 1868. By the latter date, woolen production had dropped about one-third, and unemployment and out-migration were rife.

37. Serge Chassagne, "L'industrie lainière en France à l'époque révolutionnaire et impériale (1790–1810), in *Voies nouvelles pour l'histoire de la Révolution française. Colloque Albert Mathiez–Georges Lefebvre (30 Novembre–1er Décembre 1974)* (Paris, 1978), pp. 143–167, and Gérard Cholvy, "Histoires contemporaine en pays d'oc", *Annales ESC*, 33 (1978), pp. 863–879 summed up the arguments.

38. Some historians argue that in 1914, the market was more "global" than it is today. Verley, *L'échelle du monde*, pp. 397–615; Herbert Feis, *Europe, the World's Banker* (New York, 1933, repr. 1965); Gilpin, *Challenge of Global Capitalism*, pp. 294–296.

Although the general trends in the market cited above continued, a variety of factors in the social and political realm contributed significantly to the decline. The disappearance of Languedocian manufacturing was anything but "natural". First, there was the power and militancy of the producers, the working class (if we may now use the term) of the two key cities. One of the great ironies in the history of capitalism is that the very power of the producing classes to shore up wages and protect working conditions (including resistance to technological innovation) through association and political action forces capital to look elsewhere for labor and/or find new sources of labor in its industrial region. In the cases of the past already analyzed, the resistance of the producer guilds (and, frankly speaking, labor historians' efforts to distinguish sharply between guilds and trade unions are surely overwrought) clearly played a role in de-industrialization, more in terms of quality control in the case of northern Italy, but to the point of revolutionary dislocation in Flanders. In Lodève and Bédarieux during the July Monarchy, worker trade-union organization (though illegal) grew rapidly, and during the Revolution of 1848 both became beacons of democratic socialism. Both also violently resisted the reaction overseen by Prince-President Louis-Napoleon Bonaparte (including the only assassination of a high public official – in 1849 at Lodève – and the bloodiest response in France to Louis-Napoleon's coup d'état at Bédarieux in 1851), thus generating a shadow of doubt as to the political reliability of the region, despite the profuse declarations of support from the local notability in favor of the Second Empire. I have traced in great detail the relationship between the region and the government during this era – and all historians agree that 1851–1870 saw France's most rapid period of economic growth, a phenomenon stimulated at every turn by the state – and the conclusions seem undeniable.[39] Whether motivated by the desire to promote areas where innovation seemed to result steady growth (mostly in northern France), by the specific interests of powerful figures in or close to the administration, or by a prejudice against a politically questionable region, the Imperial government, in decision after decision, failed industrial Languedoc. Rail concessions, the critical infrastructural contribution of the Second Empire to French economic history,[40] were poorly routed and granted to weak (even corrupt) companies. Despite enormous efforts by the local business community, Lodève was not connected by tunnel to a nearby coal field, thus making coal expensive and seriously inhibiting the introduction of steam power. Equally important, after a brief boom during the Crimean War, the Ministry of War reallocated many orders to Sedan, Châteauroux, and elsewhere, citing –

39. Johnson, *Industrial Languedoc*, chs 4–8.

40. Roger Price, *The French Second Empire: An Anatomy of Political Power* (Cambridge, 2001), ch. 7.

to complete the Catch-22 – their cheaper transport costs specifically. The region did have a powerful agent in Paris to make its case in famed economist Michel Chevalier, but his silence after 1861 finally made sense when he became the first manufacturer (his wife had inherited Barbot & Fournier, the largest firm in Lodève) to "run away", relocating in Sedan. Finally, the market for *draps de Levant* collapsed with the Crimean War and did not recover in part due to government inertia (naughty Bédarieux never regained favor), but also to British competition. Thus it was that social and political forces exacerbated shifting market conditions. Had policy been different, the Languedoc textile industry might have survived. Certainly in our day, sympathetic governments, responding to local action and elected national officials, have mitigated the impact of de-industrialization, as the Chrysler bailout demonstrated for southeastern Michigan. Papers in this volume analyze the vicissitudes of this relationship, from the quite positive national responses to local initiatives in the Pennsylvania anthracite region to the empty lip-service of the South African government towards the East Rand.

It must be said that the bourgeoisie of lower Languedoc did not fade quietly. Their massive (failed) campaign for a rational rail system during the 1850s and 1860s was followed by restructuring of the textile industry towards cheaper goods (including blankets made from shoddy), significant investment in power-looms and steam engines (despite the cost of fuel), and serious efforts to develop the Graissessac hard-coal fields (led by Montpellier Protestant capitalists). But in the end, the reorientation of capital towards the vine made more sense.

In the process, and in the vineyards as well, they sought the cheapest labor they could: a thorough feminization of the workforce in textiles was the first step (which power-looms made possible), followed by the wholesale employment of foreign, largely Spanish, labor whose willingness to accept lower wages and eschew unions fomented xenophobia, a circumstance not unfamiliar in the world today. There were, however, dramatic instances of labor solidarity with women and foreigners, perhaps also a lesson for our times.[41] Still, the politics of the Left drifted increasingly towards a "regional defense", accompanied by Languedocian cultural nationalism. Some distraught workers went to the Right, to the *occitanisme* promoted by Charles Maurras and the Action Française, but the socialists were the main beneficiaries, along with the moderate *bourse de travail* programs stressing the popular linguistic and folkloric traditions of the *félibrige rouge*. Both essentially supported a politics of class

41. C.H. Johnson, "Union-Busting at Graissessac: De-industrialization, Employer Strategies, and the Strike of 1894 in the Hérault Coal Basin", *Journal of Social History*, 19 (1985), pp. 241–260. John Sales's riveting film, "Matewan" (1987), tells a similar story – with an equally unpleasant ending.

reconciliation promoting the wine industry, itself dominated by huge capitalist conglomerates. As is often the case, even progressive political movements seemed to find no alternatives in a context of de-industrialization other than linking their destinies to the best hopes their restructuring economy could provide. Lelliker's paper in this collection analyzes this process brilliantly in assaying the New (post-industrial) Labour Party which, of course, could be Clinton's "new" Democrats, Schröder's Social Democrats, or Jospin's Socialists, etc.

Twentieth-century Languedoc became almost "quaint" in the eyes of northerners who in fact could not imagine the region as one of France's richest and most vital in the fairly recent past. Montpellier (let alone little Lodève and Bédarieux) *was* a dismal town when I started working there in the 1970s. Today, as the whole world knows, it is one of France's miracle cities – insurance, high-tech industries, medical science and pharmaceuticals, luxury commerce, and indeed wine (but now AOC, not plastic-bottled) give it the allure of postmodern opulence, which is visually reinforced by fabulous gentrification of the old city and the new architecture of the Polygone. Clearly a visionary new-socialist mayor, Georges Frêche (assisted by Raymond Dugrand), had something to do with this rebirth, but it is also in the very nature of capitalism to do well by doing good. Low wages, high unemployment, low real estate values in town and cheap land in the suburbs along, of course, with tax incentives and various other public subsidies, made Montpellier, "*ville marchande*" in the eighteenth century, a good place to do business once again and make the residents feel that capitalist investment in their future is almost a matter of *noblesse oblige*. Shiny Pittsburgh, glittery Cleveland, and even Detroit, are experiencing similar rebirths, with capitalists like Mike Illich (Little Caesar's Pizza and sports teams) and Peter Karmanos (Compuware, sports teams, and massive medical charity activities) of Detroit the heroes of the hour.

Although it becomes easier to draw parallels with contemporary de-industrialization (and re-industrialization) as one moves into more recent examples such as Languedoc, the essentials of earlier experiences as recounted above cast shadows of striking similarity. Everywhere, those who paid were the ordinary workers. In dealing with the problem of de-industrialization in a global, macroeconomic context one can become almost callous about the immediate consequences of its processes. But even as we penetrate these effects, there is a certain atmosphere of Greek tragedy afoot. Powerful worker organizations had perhaps contributed to the circumstances bringing about industrial decline. They then found themselves on the defensive: some, as most of the American, European, South African, Languedocian trade-union movements or the *Arsenalotti* of Venice, the Florentine silk guild, and the wool-weavers guild of Saint-Omer did what they could to protect those who kept their jobs or made severance less painful, while fighting against new cheap rural or foreign labor (though sometimes trying to integrate it); others, usually minorities (though in the case of early Flanders, a majority), actually revolted either physically or with massive strikes, saying enough is enough. But to what avail? What was the outcome of the revolt of the blue-nails of the early fourteenth century, Lodève and Bédarieux's gallant struggles of the Second French Republic, the great British miners' strike of the 1980s, or the League of Revolutionary Black Workers in southeastern Michigan in the early 1970s? Repression, recrimination, and indeed further de-industrialization. (Dodge Main, the huge plant that harbored many of the League's most active members, was soon razed; it was replaced, in due time, by a tax-exempt, land-subsidized, two-tiered-wage-based Cadillac plant that has never had the least "labor trouble".)[42] The divided and often desperate workers try to hang on, work sometimes to attract outside political assistance, struggle to organize runaway shop locations or foreign competitors' plants, but mostly look for jobs (or watch their children look for jobs) in less well-paid retail, service, or "independent" activities. And many must move elsewhere. These are themes of most of our papers, but they were also part of the history of Flanders/Artois (recall especially the migratory work force of fifteenth-century Saint-Omer) or of seventeenth and eighteenth-century Italy, where domestic service became a "good job", as well clearly of Languedoc where many industrial workers migrated to larger cities ending up with service or retail positions while Spaniards moved in to fill the increased demand for vine workers.[43] Everywhere, labor organizations lost their potency.

Another theme, emphasized by Barchiesi and Kenny in this collection, is the dynamics of family and gender relations under the impact of de-industrialization. The keys to it are the wage differential between men and women and the patriarchal structure of most households. The family economy becomes burdened and skewed as women tend to keep or find jobs while men have greater difficulty, often forced to migrate temporarily. Whether such situations lead to male psychological distress depends on gender work-role expectations. In contexts where the notion of a male "breadwinner" is firmly established, stress, abuse, divorce, even suicide undoubtedly increase. But this is a rather late phenomenon historically, and some form of family economy where all contribute (usually around a male "head" but widows continued that role[44]) dominates most of the past, and unquestionably still prevails beyond the West. I found little evidence

42. On the League, see Heather Ann Thompson, *Whose Detroit? Politics, Labor, and Race in a Modern American City* (Ithaca, NY, 2000).

43. To my mind the best evocation of the human impact of de-industrialization remains the film by Michael Moore about Flint in the 1980s, "Roger and Me".

44. See Janine Lanza, "Family Making and Family Breaking: Widows in Eighteenth-Century Paris" (unpublished Ph.D. dissertation, Cornell University, New York, 1997).

of serious family disruption even in late nineteenth-century France. Probably more typical historically is the Choletais (western France) de-industrialization studied by Tessie Liu where hand-loom male linen weavers survived in low- and very high-end work, because their women-folk, especially daughters, took in handwork from jobbers operating for the Parisian garment and *articles de Paris* industries, or worked in local factories doing the same. The impact on their lives, their prospects for independence, or for marriage, was significant, but their responses are difficult to document.[45] Families clearly had to make enormous adjustments under the impact of economic restructuring, but those histories, still largely yet to be told, are likely to be as varied as the cultures in which they occur.

CONCLUSION

I am tempted to conclude this essay with another history that I have actually experienced, that of Detroit and its region, but space and my resolve to stress de-industrialization's deep and universal character as an essential element in the functioning of capitalism allow only a brief remark. The wild card in the history of de-industrialization (and globalization) is cultural difference: ethnicity, nationality, religion, race. Determined as we might have been to seek explanations in economics and its history in terms derived from the rationalist traditions of the European Enlightenment, including the accretion of the "political" in the classic notions of political economy, events of our time and their philosophical assessment have forced us to abandon those assumptions. Economic theory (as several recent Nobels attest) has had to search for ways to accommodate decision-making lodged in culture, and while few of us would be willing to subscribe to the more extreme notions of contingency that postmodernism has generated, there is no question that human forces beyond matrix of profit and power animate our existence.[46] One might be able to write the history of racism, or nationalism, ethnic antagonism, and religious hatred, within that matrix, but they have obviously achieved a life of their own that motivates people everywhere very often to act contrary to expected economic interest. However, where economic interest along with apparent technological rationality and cultural interest coincide (at least in the short run), the direction of historical movement can be decisive.

The de-urbanization of the United States since World War II is a case in

45. Tessie Liu, *The Weaver's Knot: The Contradictions of Class Struggle and Family Solidarity in Western France, 1750–1914* (Ithaca, NY, 1994).

46. My own preferences remain with the critics of postmodernism who have nonetheless also abandoned the instrumental rationalism of the Enlightenment: Habermas, Jameson, Harvey, Bourdieu. But Foucault's analysis of the power of "discourse" must be – and is being – integrated with their neostructuralism.

point (and has marked similarities to the history of the East Rand in the 1990s). Thomas Sugrue's *Origins of the Urban Crisis: Race and Inequality in Postwar Detroit* (1996) provides a brilliant analysis of the workings of economics, politics, and race in the process of de-industrialization. What *preceded* the general decline of Fordist manufacturing in the final quarter of the century was the de-industrialization of cities with plant relocation in suburbs; and its human impact was decidedly unequal, with racism softening the blow for most white Americans, whatever their ethnicity,[47] leaving the burden inordinately on African Americans. Arguing against simplistic themes arising in journalistic discussions of Detroit's decline that scapegoated Mayor Coleman Young and his agenda of black political power, Sugrue demonstrates in rich detail that the de-industrialization of the city itself had already occurred well before Young took office in 1973. "Dynamic Detroit", the "arsenal of democracy" during World War II and the heart of the industrial union movement, had provided well-paying jobs and modest home-ownership for working-class citizens unequaled anywhere. And African Americans were part of the story, though as latecomers, they related more marginally. They ranked lowest historically in job quality, but the war and the role of the Fair Employment Practices Commission had improved access. Still, seniority in almost all positions fell to whites, including returning veterans. And housing, already seriously segregated from the early days of Henry Ford's "pro-Negro" policies, remained so during the wartime boom (literally including walls near Eight-Mile road), and mortgage companies, including the Federal Housing Administration and the Veterans Administration,[48] refused to invest in people seen "by nature" as bad risks.

The economic and political conjuncture of the 1950s unfolded in this setting. Although foreign competition was nil, the automobile companies, then many more than the "big three", engaged in possibly the most concerted campaign in history for the allegiance of the American consumer, adding "depth" advertising to pricing policies that sought to include everyone in the car market. Simultaneously, the Eisenhower administration committed unprecedented funds to a limited-access road system without parallel in the world, thus destroying public transport, both long distance and local. In order to meet the competition in the

47. The most interesting study on this topic that I know is Karen Brodkin Sacks, "How Jews became White", in Paula S. Rothenberg (ed.), *Race, Class, and Gender in the United States* (New York, 1998), pp. 100–114, which focuses on the inequalities of the nation's greatest social benefits program, the Veterans' Education, Employment, and Housing Subsidies Act of 1947.
48. Thomas Sugrue, *The Origins of the Urban Crisis: Race and Inequality in Postwar Detroit* (Princeton, NJ, 1996); Sacks, "How Jews became White"; and for the earlier history of ethnicity and race in the city, Olivier Zunz, *The Changing Face of Inequality: Urbanization, Industrial Development, and Immigrants in Detroit, 1880–1920* (Chicago, IL, 1982).

satisfaction of the consumer mania for "wheels",[49] the companies realized that they needed much more streamlined production facilities than the old, multi-floored plants of the city could provide. During the war, new suburban defense plants laid out on vast terrains with a continuous line on a single floor had proved remarkably efficient,[50] and served as models for the massive building projects on semi-rural, relatively inexpensive land. As huge auto assembly and drive train plants relocated, suppliers and tool and dye shops followed them out of the city. Suburban housing did the same. The construction industries prospered, and workers streamed northeast to Warren and Sterling Heights, south to Taylor and Woodhaven, northwest to Novi and Milford. Warren, bordering Detroit, became the second largest city in Michigan, and everywhere, "metro"-Detroit's population surged at the expense of the city, which from its peak population approaching two million in the late 1950s came in at under one million on the 2000 census. By the late 1960s, the main lines of economic change were clear: not only was production being dispersed throughout the region of southeastern Michigan, but many plants still supplying the region had moved to cheap land and labor far away (particularly in rural areas of Indiana and Ohio where farm jobs were evaporating before the onslaught of agro-conglomerates)[51] and entire new production complexes sprang up in other regions of the country where population was exploding and trade unions weak. Everywhere, new technology ate into employment despite ever-growing sales. Jobs in southeastern Michigan had not yet begun to dry up significantly, and immigrants (now especially from the Middle East) still came to Detroit for work in auto, as had their predecessors. But if unemployment rates remained between 5 and 7 per cent for the overall population, for black Detroiters it was more than double that, and at least a quarter of young African Americans just coming onto the labor market could not find jobs in auto or anything else.

The reasons were not hard to find. Plant relocation and new technology often meant proportionately lower employment opportunities, and those with the most seniority got the jobs. Those African Americans who could qualify were faced with long commutes, for, unlike their white colleagues, they were unable to obtain mortgages for housing nearer the suburban plants, even, indeed, for a long time within the more desirable

49. See, for the politics of cars and roads, Stephen Goddard, *Getting There: The Epic Struggle between Road and Rail in the American Century* (New York, 1994).

50. The most famous was Ford's Willow Run B-17 plant. See Douglas Likkel, "Willow Run" (M.A. thesis, Wayne State University, Detroit, MI, 2000).

51. Kingsley Haynes and Zachary Machunda, "Spatial Restructuring of Manufacturing and Employment Growth in the Rural Midwest: An Analysis for Indiana", *Economic Geography*, 63 (1987), pp. 319–333.

neighborhoods at the edges of the city which would have put them closer to work.[52] And in the neighborhoods where housing restrictions were less prevalent, mortgages were more expensive due to "red-lining" (a term invented by the FHA) which also affected insurance rates on both homes and automobiles. The latter contributed to the cost of maintaining a car, which was virtually the only mode for most to get to work in the absence of an adequate metropolitan transit service. Sugrue's elaborate analysis of discrimination in the housing market and the step-by-step process by which the Detroit area became the most segregated in the nation is his most important contribution. It interacted with curtailed access to employment to create the conditions of life in "urban America" that are easily comparable to many cities in former colonial nations. Black radicals of the 1970s hardly erred in terming their situation "internal colonialism". Sugrue ends his discussion with what some call the Great Rebellion, but most whites call "the riots" of July 1967, in which more people were killed and injured and more property destroyed than in any other urban conflagration of an era marked by such upheavals.[53] His book explains them.

Assigning responsibility for the unequal outcome of this first round of de-industrialization (in the second, more general round, many sons and daughters of the white working class – in a kind of ethnic hierarchy – paid dearly as well and headed elsewhere, especially to the South) can be tricky. The automobile corporations' economic decisions responded to market changes and opportunities followed rational pathways. Although not immune to racism in their hiring and promotion practices, they did not "conspire" to punish blacks. Nor of course did the Eisenhower administration, even though its promotion of car travel no doubt had something to do with the powerful presence of the auto giants in Washington. But federal agencies such as the VA and the FHA *were* staffed by Eisenhower appointees, who were even more inclined to look away as discrimination occurred in the housing market than had been the case under Truman. Overall, however, "traditional" structures of racial discrimination in union locals (especially in the booming construction trades, but even in the United Auto Workers') and above all the real-estate industry, banks, and mortgage corporations mattered most. After restrictive covenants (actual clauses preventing sales to racial and religious groups, legally recognized, in many deeds) were ruled unconstitutional in 1951, in a case brought by the only racially integrated law firm in Detroit, Goodman, Crockett *et al.*, it was up to private businesses to maintain the boundaries of race. And they certainly did so. Only one Detroit lender, Standard Federal, which

52. See David Riddle, "The Rise of the 'Reagan Democrats' in Warren, Michigan, 1964–1980" (unpublished Ph.D. dissertation, Wayne State University, Detroit, MI, 1998).
53. Sugrue, *Origins of the Urban Crisis*, "Conclusion".

had been founded by Jews to provide mortgages for Jews, served blacks in any significant number.

The Detroit example, with its profound implications for the quality of life not only for the direct victims, but for all who live with the insecurities generated by cultural discrimination and its resultant hatreds, underlines the fact that calm explanation of the economics of de-industrialization, and its place as a critical factor in the history of capitalism made ever more prominent by the forces of globalization, only begins to capture its meaning. For it is in its lived reality, especially as it is first influenced by politics, usually for the worse but sometimes to mitigate its impact, and then, more complexly, by the cultural context in which it arises, that it becomes a phenomenon of human agency – where blame *can* be assigned and where solutions may be sought. This is why the careful case studies in this volume, which assume the larger perspective developed in this Introduction, are so important – they grapple with the specifics of given situations and provide guidelines for action not only in their context, but in comparable situations. But this is also why, whatever its faults, the fascinating manifesto of Michael Hardt and Antonio Negri, simply entitled *Empire* to capture the stateless new power of the global economy, its architects, and its beneficiaries, must be read. It concludes, if vaguely, with a list of "rights" that the victims of the ongoing rhythms of economic restructuring worldwide, whom they term "the multitude", might/will (as neo-Marxists they pleasantly blur the role of agency) actualize in order to universalize its fruits. These include the right of free movement (or "global citizenship"), the right to a "social wage", and, of course, the right of "reappropriation". If the authors' notions of how the struggle is to be waged will sound too Leninist for most ears, their focus on the potential of the international nongovernmental organizations to serve as conduits for this new army of redressers seems on target.[54] Above all, they underline that de-industrialization and the undulations of economic life are quintessentially human issues not to be obscured by "science", or as Foucault would have it, power-knowledge.

54. Michael Hardt and Antonio Negri, *Empire* (Cambridge, MA, 2000), ch. 4 ("The Multitude against Empire"). The use of the title of perhaps E.P. Thompson's most famous chapter (on the Luddites) somehow seems appropriate here.

IRSH 47 (2002), pp. 35–63 DOI: 10.1017/S0020859002000779

From Workshop to Wasteland: De-industrialization and Fragmentation of the Black Working Class on the East Rand (South Africa), 1990–1999

Franco Barchiesi and Bridget Kenny

INTRODUCTION

In 1999 the South African government passed the Municipal Structures Act which established the Ekurhuleni Metropolitan Council and merged the East Rand towns of Alberton, Germiston, Brakpan, Benoni, Kempton Park, Springs, and Nigel under a common municipal authority. The new demarcation created a unified administrative structure for this region of approximately 2.5 million people living east of Johannesburg. It gave formal expression to long-standing processes of socioeconomic development that have defined the East Rand as a highly specific geographical entity. Between the 1950s and the 1970s the East Rand mapped itself on to South Africa's economic terrain as its industrial "workshop", as manufacturing replaced mining as the major contributor to GDP. The administrative unification of the East Rand has taken place, however, at a moment when established patterns of economic and social integration based on manufacturing are undermined by the impact of restructuring encouraged by domestic and global forces.

Important social processes operate within this transformation to question the position of the East Rand's black working class as a factor of social integration based on industrial wage labour and strong traditions of unionization and militancy. Ironically, these challenges are emerging at a moment when the role of organized labour in establishing post-apartheid democracy has gained institutional recognition and influence. While central to policy processes for reconstruction, unions have had to face the detrimental impact of the new government's adoption of neoliberal macro-economics.

This paper examines worker attitudes and responses to the dynamics of de-industrialization on the East Rand in this context. This includes the ways in which unionized labour has experienced manufacturing decline, how this restructuring has affected forms of solidarity and subjectivity, how it has related to alternative conceptualizations of life strategies, and how the expansion of low-wage, vulnerable service employment has further reconfigured collective responses.[1] Issues relevant to determinants of worker identification, in particular the relations between class and race motifs, are addressed.[2]

Evidence presented here shows that the decline of large-scale manufacturing on the East Rand mirrors a generalized crisis of the sector both in terms of contribution to growth and in levels of employment. At the same time, a transformation is apparently underway in neighbouring Johannesburg. Innovative industries and finance-driven new economy enclaves are expanding around the growth poles of Johannesburg's northern suburbs and Midrand, stretching to Pretoria. The East Rand, conversely, supports no new-growth industries to compete with this "high-tech" region, now delineated distinctly by new municipal borders that include it in Greater Johannesburg. Economically and symbolically, these boundaries exclude the older industrial hub from hopes of participation in the "new economy". The resulting industrial crisis detaches workers from historically entrenched forms of collective identity. Their demands are therefore increasingly diversified to challenge union representivity and strategy.

DE-INDUSTRIALIZATION AND THE CHANGING TEXTURE OF PRODUCTION ON THE EAST RAND

International literature on the concept of de-industrialization provides various pointers useful to contextualize the decline of East-Rand manufacturing beyond a mere measurement of the sector's contribution to growth and employment. Early debates on the concept[3] probably overemphasized the role of managerial rationality and corporate decision-making in analyses of "downsizing". At the same time, however, these contributions usefully emphasized that the concept of "de-industrialization" signalled not simply a trend towards the disappearance of

1. B. Kenny, "From Insurrectionary to Flexible Worker: Fragmentation and Reconfigured Social Networks of Retail Sector Workers on South Africa's East Rand", paper presented at Class, Space, and Community Workshop Conference, Department of Sociology and Social Policy, University of Durham, 6–8 April 2001.

2. The discussion of the engineering industry's workers' experiences is based on semi-structured interviews with union organizers and fifty workers employed in three companies in the engineering sector located in the former Brakpan, Alberton, and Nigel municipalities conducted by Franco Barchiesi in 1999. The experiences of the retail sector workers are based on sixty life-history interviews with shopworkers from one of three supermarkets in Kempton Park, Boksburg, and Benoni, and who reside in East Rand (black) townships. Retail sector interviews were conducted by Bridget Kenny between 1998 and 2000. Interviews cited by number below apply to two different data sets: engineering and retail workers.

3. B. Bluestone, and B. Harrison, *The Deindustrialisation of America: Plant Closings, Community Abandonment and the Dismantling of Basic Industry* (New York, 1982); B. Harrison, *Lean and Mean: The Changing Landscape of Corporate Power in the Age of Flexibility* (New York, 1994); D. Gordon, *Fat and Mean: The Corporate Squeeze of Working Americans and the Myth of Managerial "Downsizing"* (New York, 1996).

manufacturing industry but, perhaps more insidiously, its transformation within new forms of low-wage economy, casualization of employment, and rising social exclusion. These accounts, therefore, directly focus on social polarization and challenges facing organized labour as the representative of general interests and citizenship projects.

Paradigms inspired by "network" concepts[4] emphasize changes in patterns of capital accumulation to explain shifts from an "old" manufacturing-based economy to a "new economy", characterized by increasing mobility of financial flows and informational content of production. This process is usually coupled with changing forms of labour-market stratification. This perspective also underlines the dynamics of spatial restructuring and urban inequalities linked to shifts between industrial and service activities.[5] In South Africa, this refers to economic globalization and trade liberalization, the management of regional dynamics, and the role of local and provincial government in advancing notions of urban space in the integration of municipalities defined as "unicities" as a strategy geared toward comparative advantage and investor confidence.

However interested in labour-market segmentation and processes of informalization, these authors spend less effort examining the dynamics of resistance that contribute to structure spatial accumulation patterns.[6] The analysis advanced by Michael Hardt and Antonio Negri[7] closely relates strategies of "dematerialization" of production processes in an information-based networked financial capitalism to capitalist responses to worker insurgencies located at the level of "Fordist" manufacturing. In this way the mass representation of worker interests is dispensed with in a process that simultaneously emphasizes flexibility and self-entrepreneurship as new forms of access to rights and powers.

In the South African context, debates on de-industrialization have recently been revived by analyses of the geographical restructuring of capital in a context marked by the decline of the previous industrial structure. Fine and Rustomjee[8] define this as a "mineral-energy" complex, centred on raw material extraction and the production of consumer goods. They argue that in the context of apartheid's import-substitution industrialization, this led to imbalances and valorization problems. In particular, the low-cost input that the mining and energy sectors have

4. M. Castells, *The Rise of the Network Society* (Oxford, 1996).

5. S. Sassen, *Losing Control? Sovereignty in an Age of Globalisation* (New York, 1996); P. Marcuse and R. van Kempen, "A New Spatial Order in Cities?", *American Behavioral Scientist*, 41 (1997), pp. 285–299.

6. See as a notable exception, the work of Neil Smith, for example N. Smith, *The New Urban Frontier: Gentrification and the Revanchist City* (London [etc.], 1996).

7. M. Hardt and A. Negri, *Empire* (Cambridge, MA, 2000).

8. B. Fine and Z. Rustomjee, *The Political Economy of South Africa* (Johannesburg, 1996).

provided to a nascent manufacturing industry was coupled to a racially limited, predominantly "white" consumer market. This prevented the development of Fordist mass production on a full scale and facilitated high levels of dependence on imported capital. At the same time, little incentive has existed to develop a local intermediate goods sector.

The crisis of this model of accumulation in the context of rapid unionization and working-class militancy after the 1970s has led to the search for new avenues with the re-insertion of the country into international markets. At the same time, the abandonment of import-substitution industrialization, the adoption of a liberalized, export-orientated approach to growth, and large scale privatization have tended to shift resources towards foreign investment, the financial sector, urban speculation, and activities related to information and communication technology. In this light, the manufacturing decline of the East Rand is also a product of the dynamics of "uneven development"[9] that followed the end of apartheid-era policies of protectionism and massive investment in state-owned companies such as Sasol (chemicals), Eskom (energy), and Iscor (steel). This, at the same time, implied a transnationalization of these companies and a loosening of linkages with their previous manufacturing base, as in the case of the East Rand. Mirroring similar processes that have affected other countries that experienced shifts from import-substitution priorities, and most developing countries in Southern Africa, South Africa has undergone a generalized de-industrialization process in the past fifteen years. This has seen manufacturing contribution to total output growth reduced by more than 40 per cent since 1985 (one of the highest rates of decline in the semi-industrialized world) while contribution to employment growth has declined by 35 per cent.[10]

It is, however, important not to read these developments as the mere product of financial capitalist planning rationality without considering the decisive role played by black working-class militancy in the area. Understanding worker responses to this scenario, which displaces not only their work but also the centrality of their "selves" to economic development, implies looking at the consequences of restructuring not only in terms of shifting workplace power relations and rising unemployment, but also of broader impacts on community life, relationships between production and reproduction, and the definition of alternative worker strategies in a postwaged employment context.

Emerging as a cluster of mining towns linked by rail to Johannesburg

9. P. Bond, *Cities of Gold, Townships of Coal: Essays on South Africa's New Urban Crisis* (Trenton, NJ, 2000); cf. N. Smith, *Uneven Development* (Oxford, 1984).
10. U. Pieper, "Openness and Structural Dynamics of Productivity and Employment in Developing Countries: A Case of De-industrialization?", *ILO Employment and Training Papers*, 14 (Geneva, 1998).

and the West Rand, between the 1950s and the 1970s East Rand towns experienced a tumultuous growth in manufacturing activities that saw the share of the workforce employed in the sector rise from 27 per cent in 1950 to 52 per cent in 1970, while the sector overtook mining to become the most important contributor to the GGP.[11] By the 1980s, the former Transvaal province came to provide 66 per cent of the country's metalworking (40 per cent of manufacturing output) with the East Rand accounting for the largest proportion of this.[12] The availability of cheap land, and linkages with apartheid's massive infrastructural and heavy-industry projects (Eskom, Sasol, railways) facilitated a move of large companies to the East Rand from neighbouring areas. Small engineering companies, foundries, and jobbing firms in precision tools persisted nonetheless due to limited-scale economies.[13] Germiston rose to particular prominence, contributing the absolute majority of manufacturing output in the sector, particularly concentrated in the metal and chemical industries.

However, the manufacturing crisis of the 1980s, linked to intensified worker struggles and the economic recession of the apartheid regime, affected largely the smaller establishments. Government protection sustained large conglomerates in a process that led to further capital intensity, concentration of ownership, and labour-saving restructuring. These characteristics proved a decisive impediment in the more competitive and liberalized environment that followed the 1990s democratic transition. High costs and tougher market conditions, in particular, led to negative growth between 1991 and 1997, in a context marked by the contextual decline of mining, rising job losses, and the relocation of many heavy industries to the coast or overseas to take advantage of more competitive locations.[14]

More recently, areas westward have been designated new growth points for investment. The area of the Midrand in particular has attracted a large

11. P. Cockhead, "The East Rand: A Geographical Analysis of the Transition of the Economic Base of the Region from Gold Mining to Manufacturing, and its Effects Upon Future Economic and Spatial Development", unpublished Ph.D. dissertation, University of the Witwatersrand, Johannesburg, 1970; M. Drake, "The Iron and Steel, Metal and Engineering Industry in the Pretoria–Witwatersrand–Vereeniging Region", unpublished M.A. dissertation, University of the Witwatersrand, Johannesburg, 1971.

12. A. Sitas, "African Worker Responses on the East Rand to Changes in the Metal Industry, 1960–1980", unpublished Ph.D. dissertation, University of the Witwatersrand, Johannesburg, 1983, pp. 4–5.

13. Sitas, "African Worker Responses"; E. Webster, *Cast in a Racial Mould: Labour Process and Trade Unionism in the Foundries* (Johannesburg, 1985).

14. G. Smith and M. Futter, "Revitalisation: Changing Roles and Economies in the Germiston-Daveyton Activity Corridor", paper presented at the International "Urban Futures" Conference, Johannesburg, 7–14 July 2000.

number of multinational corporations and activities in rapidly growing financial, information, and communication sectors. The phenomenal growth of Midrand is reflected by a 224 per cent increase in industrial planning activity between 1995 and 2000, with office-space demand that has risen 33 per cent between 1997 and 2000.[15]

While industry was declining on the East Rand, trade and services, particularly in towns such as Boksburg, Benoni, Kempton Park, and Germiston, have grown throughout the 1990s. In 1998 trade contributed, with 16 per cent, the second largest percentage after manufacturing to regional GGP, followed by government services (12.1 per cent) and business and financial services (10.7 per cent).[16] This was also reflected by developments in retail space, particularly in shopping areas and more recently in mega-shopping/entertainment complexes focused around casinos. The East Rand is home to some of the "largest shopping centres in Southern Africa".[17]

The rise of the tertiary sector has brought with it low-waged and insecure employment in the form of casual and subcontracted labour. Retail trade in food, beverages, and tobacco in specialized stores account for the highest percentage of trade (20 per cent) and of employment in trade (13 per cent) in the region.[18] Research at three large food retailers on the East Rand indicates that very little new permanent employment is available; instead, casual and contract jobs bring workers into tenuous employment.[19] Also there is speculation that large retailing developments are saturated, and retail property analysts support moves to smaller convenience centres, which suggests even more tenuous conditions and security for workers.

The transformation of the East Rand's economy from a strong manufacturing centre has not heralded a healthy, diversified economy. Rather, the growth of services has introduced further casualized, low-wage employment to the region's already fragmenting industrial base. This changing economic context has had a profound effect on workers' organization and subjectivities. In particular the East Rand's history of militant worker organizations linked to community activism has been affected by the changing economic situation.

15. Johannesburg Housing Investment [hereafter JHI], "The Midrand Miracle", unpublished report, 2000.

16. Urban-Econ, *Eastern Gauteng Services Council: Volume 1: Economic Development Perspective* (Germiston, 1999), p. 86.

17. *Ibid.*, p. 117.

18. *Ibid.*, p. 119.

19. B. Kenny, "Selling Selves: Control, Resistance and Detachment on South African Supermarket Shopfloors", paper presented at the 19th Annual International Labour Process Conference, School of Management, Royal Holloway College, University of London, 26–28 March 2001.

A WORKING-CLASS VANGUARD: LABOUR ORGANIZATION ON THE EAST RAND

The East Rand became one of the main sites of militant trade-union activities after the 1973 Durban strikes, which marked the resumption of working-class struggles following a decade of harsh repression. The first organizing networks in the area were started with the help of student activists, black consciousness-aligned structures, "dissidents" from established "white" unions, and unions operating in the Durban area (especially the Metal and Allied Workers' Unions and the Chemical Workers' Industrial Union). It has been argued that unionization in this region responded to specific methods, strategies, and cultural dynamics. In particular, the role of trade-union grassroots structures challenged symbolic and discursive patterns of authority on the shopfloor and in the segregated "compound". In a context marked by coercive labour migration practices, unions managed to advance worker organization as an alternative to ethnic and linguistic hierarchies.[20] Black migrant workers constituted a decisive support base for union activities and provided the most militant sections of the area's working class. The presence of large factories in the metal, chemical, and food sectors facilitated organizing and the diffusion of strike actions, which could be strategically focused on companies that assumed a particularly relevant role in the definition of employer policies, or multinational companies.

A further important issue emphasized by black trade unions in the region concerned the dynamics of territorial organizing. After the initial repression of the post-1973 resurgent unions, new factory organizations arose, coordinated across the East Rand. In particular, the 1981 and 1982 strike waves were articulated by structures such as the Germiston shop-steward council.[21] These processes, although largely related to workplace issues such as union recognition, unfair dismissals, and the improvement of wages and working conditions, also allowed broader exchanges between different workplaces, sectors, and segregated black townships. These interactions focused on the brutality of racist management and at the same time heightened workers' sensitivity to the denial of political and social rights.

Indeed, escalating insurgency in the townships targeted the redesign of apartheid urban policy, which recognized the need for a greater stabilization of sections of the black manufacturing working class, while restating the discriminatory nature of access to residence and property. This was translated into mass movements for the boycotts of rents and transport fees and against the demolition of informal settlements.

20. Sitas, "African Worker Responses".

21. J. Baskin, "Growth of a New Worker Organ: The Germiston Shop Stewards' Council", *South African Labour Bulletin*, 7 (1982), pp. 42–53; Webster, *Cast in a Racial Mould*.

Township struggles sparked a lively debate inside trade unions on whether to take part in the activities of rising civic organizations. In fact, the Federation of South African Trade Unions (FOSATU) had maintained a strong workplace orientation that made its leaders suspicious of the motives of student, church, and residents' groups where allegedly "petty bourgeois" elements such as shop owners and taxi entrepreneurs had gained influential positions.

The territorial structure of trade-union organization facilitated political interactions that defined shop-steward councils as areas of community and political engagement beyond workplace issues.[22] Indeed, leadership of local structures helped to form civic organizations, such as the East Rand People's Organization (ERAPO), and supported township protests.[23] This process led to confrontations inside trade unions, and the role played by "white intellectuals" in leading FOSATU was stigmatized from the grassroots, not so much as an issue of racial polarization but as a form of critique towards leaders that in pursuing a narrow production-orientated agenda were preventing these broader patterns of solidarity developing between workplaces and community.[24] As Swilling (1984) convincingly argued, rank-and-file union members engaging in these forms of joint mobilization retained a sense of the peculiarity of trade-union organizations and of their organizing methods. The trajectory of union–community activism in the East Rand, and of the divisions and conflicts inside the unions that this generated, has been for a long time analysed from a dominant "workerist" perspective[25] as a the product of "spontaneist", "Jacobin" grassroots pressures that ultimately resulted in the "ungovernability" of union structures. When viewed in hindsight, however, the links between union and community organizing forged an alternative collective order grounded in an expansive notion of citizenship rights that brought together the struggle against racism with an organized claim for socioeconomic equality.[26]

Arguments based on an alleged incompatibility between worker consciousness and popular uprisings have recently resurfaced from different angles. Like previous ones, these analyses are largely concerned with stigmatizing "ungovernability". They deny the relevance of class

22. K. Von Holdt, *Trade Unions, Community Organisations and Politics: A Local Case Study on the East Rand*, Sociology of Work Programme, Labour Studies Research Report 3 (Johannesburg, 1987); M. Mamdani, *Citizen and Subject: Contemporary Africa and the Legacy of Late Colonialism* (Princeton, NJ, 1996), pp. 248–249; P. Bonner and N. Nieftagodien, *Kathorus: A History* (Johannesburg, 2001).

23. Von Holdt, *Trade Unions.*

24. G. Ruiters, *South African Liberation Politics: A Case Study of Collective Action and Leadership in Katorus, 1980–1989* (n.p., 1995); Mamdani, *Citizen and Subject*, p. 241.

25. M. Swilling, "Workers Divided: A Critical Assessment of the Split in MAWU on the East Rand", *South African Labour Bulletin*, 10 (1984), pp. 99–123.

26. See also Mamdani, *Citizen and Subject*; Ruiters, *South African Liberation Politics.*

dynamics in township insurgency by arguing that the racialized identities of marginal groups were rather at the core of "millenarian" revolutionary expectations in the anti-apartheid struggle.[27] Such a reading tends to oppose "orderly" political processes of articulation of collective interests in a politics of "responsible" opposition – allegedly represented by trade unions among others – to the chaotic, magmatic community insurrectionism of the "deviants". This latter is seen as largely driven by pre-political forces and characterized by the impossibility of institutional mediation. However, this analysis suffers from a fundamental flaw, deriving from its imposition of normative priorities (in the form of a concern with order and governability), which leads to unproven assumptions. In particular, it reifies the cultural and symbolic expressions of revolt that are univocally assumed as indicators of deep sociopsychological disruptive predispositions. This method of analysis sacrifices the need for a grassroots-orientated research agenda that focuses on processes of subjectivity formation that creatively reshape and articulate diverse motifs and appellations (of class, community-based, and racialized kinds). These define political strategies that link the immediate, visible causes of oppression to more systemic socioeconomic and political determinants. By expelling community activism to the margins of the political this approach arbitrarily excludes the relevance of daily strategies of survival and resistance, social movements, and even "millennial" visions in defining political identities and programmes. Robin Kelley's suggestion[28] is therefore particularly useful in this regard:

> Writing "history from below" that emphasizes the infrapolitics of the black working class requires that we substantially redefine politics. Too often politics is defined by *how* people participate rather than *why* [...]. By shifting our focus to what motivated disenfranchised black working people to struggle and what strategies they developed, we may discover that their participation in "mainstream" politics [...] grew out of the very circumstances, experiences, and memories that impelled many to steal from their employer, join a mutual benefit association, or spit in a bus driver's face. In other words, I am rejecting the tendency to dichotomize people's lives, to assume that clear-cut "political" motivations exist separately from issues of economic well-being, safety, pleasure, cultural expression, sexuality, freedom of mobility, and other facets of daily life [own emphasis].

From this point of view, we argue that processes of subjectivity formation on the East Rand, nurtured in the encounter of working-class and community activism, defined a new discourse of social citizenship. The

27. B. Bozzoli, "Why Were the 1980s 'Millenarian'? Style, Repertoire, Space and Authority in South Africa's Black Cities", *Journal of Historical Sociology*, 13 (2000), pp. 78–110.
28. R. Kelley, "Writing Black Working-Class History from Way, Way Below", in R. Kelley, *Race Rebels: Culture, Politics and the Black Working Class* (New York, 1994), p. 9.

demand for social citizenship as a goal to be achieved in a future democratic society was expressed in acts of seeming ungovernability, as in the case of boycotts and attacks on city councillors. It brought together issues of worker rights and powers with the insistence on decommodified social services practised through rents and services nonpayment. Far from expressing polarized categories, discourses of race and class could largely coexist to articulate different levels of opposition to the apartheid state and the capitalist social order. Working-class organization has, therefore, to be analysed in terms of its contribution to shaping this articulation of meanings, as rights and powers won inside the workplace provided content to the specific demands of rising social citizenship discourses.

Our critique also stands vis-à-vis recent work suggesting the increasing relevance of class identities over race in defining black experience.[29] Authors that support this view cite the widening gap in intraracial income distribution,[30] and claim a deepening social divide within black townships between a "core working class" and a largely unskilled, unemployed "underclass".[31] This leads to suggestions that social inclusion follows from mere access to waged employment, even in unskilled and casual jobs.[32] While post-apartheid policies and practices certainly uplifted a stratum of "black bourgeoisie" into full citizenship rights, while breeching the working poor, we, however, argue that the class reductionism involved in this kind of argument conflates income or occupational categories to workers' experiences in ways that seriously oversimplify the analysis of the latter.

On the contrary, this paper contends that looking for forms of consciousness, either race- or class-based, as inherently "pure" or more authentic is a fruitless exercise in the South African case. More productive would be to explore the formation of collective subjectivities in the mutable interplay of diverse and largely overlapping forms of identification as they emerge in the dynamics of solidarity and struggle. To invert Roediger's emphasis, "to reduce race to class is damaging", and "[t]o set race within social formations is absolutely necessary".[33] In the sections that follow, we show the structural changes in the East Rand's labour market and their impact on black workers' sense of themselves and the parameters of possible social citizenship.

29. O. Crankshaw, *Race, Class, and the Changing Division of Labour Under Apartheid* (London [etc.], 1997), pp. 199–121; N. Nattrass and J. Seekings, *From Race to Class: Inequality, Unemployment and the Social Structure in South Africa* (Oxford, forthcoming).
30. Crankshaw, *Race, Class, and the Changing Division.*
31. J. Seekings, "Is There an Underclass in South Africa?", paper presented at the annual conference of the South African Sociological Association, University of the Western Cape, July 2000.
32. *Ibid.*
33. D.R. Roediger, *The Wages of Whiteness: Race and the Making of the American Working Class* (London [etc.], 1991), p. 8.

RECENT TRENDS IN MANUFACTURING IN THE EAST RAND: AN EXPANDING RUSTBELT

The past two decades have witnessed a marked and constant decline of manufacturing industry on the East Rand, in a context of sluggish economic growth during the 1980s (see Table 1). In fact, only Benoni, Brakpan, and Kempton Park show significant growth performances, while the "far East Rand" area shows signs of a dramatic decline. The case of Kempton Park (whose growth rates become negative, in any case, at the beginning of the 1990s) is peculiar, given that this city is more closely connected than others in the area to the Johannesburg-Midrand-Pretoria corridor of rapid expansion.[34] The first half of the 1990s is characterized by a stabilization, where the most acute decline trends of the previous decade seem to be levelling out, while the relatively successful experiences enter a phase of relative stagnation. The Tress Index of all the towns indicates a high degree of specialization (with the possible exceptions of Nigel and Heidelberg) around manufacturing as the dominant activity. However, specialization tends to be reduced between 1981 and 1991, with the exception of Germiston and Springs, the two most important manufacturing towns, where it remains unchanged. Therefore, on the one hand, the region retains a strong manufacturing-based profile, notwithstanding the general economic difficulties. In fact, it has to be noticed that the positive results by Benoni and Brakpan in terms of "mixed contribution effect" indicate that manufacturing output is still closely correlated to overall growth in these cities. Conversely, the negative trend of this indicator in Kempton Park shows that this is the only area of the region where growth seems to depend on economic diversification, which confirms the already noticed peculiarity of Kempton Park in the context of Gauteng's nascent "new economy".

On the other hand, however, developments in the direction of a greater diversification seem to follow two broad directions. There are, in fact, situations (such as Nigel) where the relative loss of importance of the manufacturing industry has not defined other relevant growth sectors. In other cases (Brakpan and Alberton) there are signs of a more successful diversification of economic activities. These figures seem to underline the rise of intraregional economic disparities inside the territory currently under the jurisdiction of the East Rand metropolitan authority.[35] Behind the uniform image of an area characterized by traditional manufacturing industries, therefore, there are signs of long-term trends towards a new socioeconomic stratification based on differences in terms of diversification and change of economic structures.

34. P. Kok, *South Africa's Magnifying Glass: A Profile of Gauteng* (Pretoria, 1998), p. 195.
35. Cf. C.M. Rogerson and J.M. Rogerson, "Industrial Change in a Developing Metropolis: The Witwatersrand, 1980–1994", *Geoforum*, 30 (1999), pp. 85–99.

Table 1. *Growth and manufacturing indicators for East Rand towns, 1981–1991*

	Alberton	Benoni	Boksburg	Brakpan	Germiston	Heidelberg	Kempton Park	Nigel	Springs
Manufacturing % share on GGP	46.2	44.1	47.9	31.6	47.5	31.3	45.7	23.9	54.7
GGP % growth rate 1981–1991	0.5	1.1	−0.3	1.0	−1.3	−2.3	1.1	−4.0	−1.6
GGP growth rate 1981–1991 (as % of 1981)	4.7	11.2	−2.7	10.0	−12.6	−21.1	11.6	−33.3	−15.2
GGP % growth rate 1991–1993	−0.4	11	−0.3	1.0	−0.7	−1.7	−0.6	0.0	−1.0
Tress Index 1981	0.76	0.71	0.69	0.59	0.69	0.58	0.74	0.58	0.73
Tress Index 1991	0.70	0.70	0.66	0.51	0.69	0.56	0.73	0.47	0.73
Mixed effect contribution 1981–1991 as % of 1981	−2.3	2.9	−12.5	4.2	−4.8	−0.0	−1.7	−0.7	−3.6

Tress Index of specialization: 0 = perfect diversity (same size for all sectors); 1 = perfect specialization (only one sector).
Mixed effect contribution: growth rate that would have been achieved in Gauteng if manufacturing in the town had grown at the provincial manufacturing rate. Positive values indicate the town is over-represented in manufacturing growth.
Source: Kok, *South Africa's Magnifying Glass.*

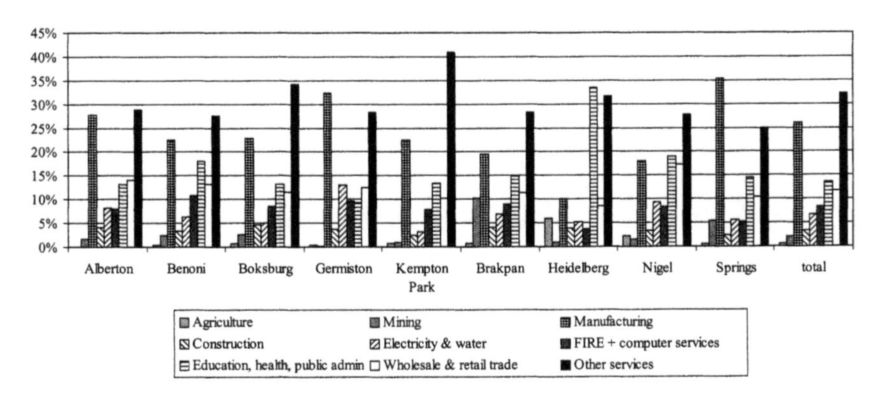

Figure 1. Sectoral contribution to GGP, 1999.
Source: Wharton Econometric Forecasting Associates [hereafter WEFA].

It is, however, in the following decade that the decline in the economic relevance of manufacturing industry becomes spectacular (Figure 1). In fact, during this period the sector loses its predominance in all the towns of the region, with particularly apparent downturns in the manufacturing strongholds of Germiston (from 47.5 per cent in 1991 to 31 per cent contribution to GGP in 1999) and Springs (from 54.7 per cent in 1991 to 36 per cent in 1999) (Table 1 and Figure 1). In terms of contribution to the GGP, however, this shift does not imply a re-evaluation of FIRE (finance–insurance–real estate) or information-technology activities comparable to developments in the nearby Johannesburg–Pretoria corridor. In fact, in 1999 these two sectors combined contributed only 8.4 per cent to the GGP, with relatively limited variations between towns. Notwithstanding national policies of public-sector spending containment, especially after the introduction of the Growth, Employment and Redistribution (GEAR) Policy in 1996, the sphere of education, health, and public administration retains a significant contribution to the GGP (13.5 per cent), as does retail and wholesale trade (11.8 per cent). These data seems to confirm an impression of deepening economic stagnation accompanying manufacturing decline, and an uncertain, to say the least, restructuring towards "new-economy" activities.

These conclusions are supported by employment indicators (Figure 2) which still confirm the relative predominance of manufacturing industry in 1999, but also indicate signs of a rising tertiarization of the economy in an overall employment share of 44.3 per cent in the combination of FIRE and computer services (3.6 per cent), public administration, health and education (16.2 per cent), and wholesale and retail trade (14 per cent).

The dynamics of total manufacturing employment in the region (Figure 3) show that the decline of manufacturing industry has been constant over

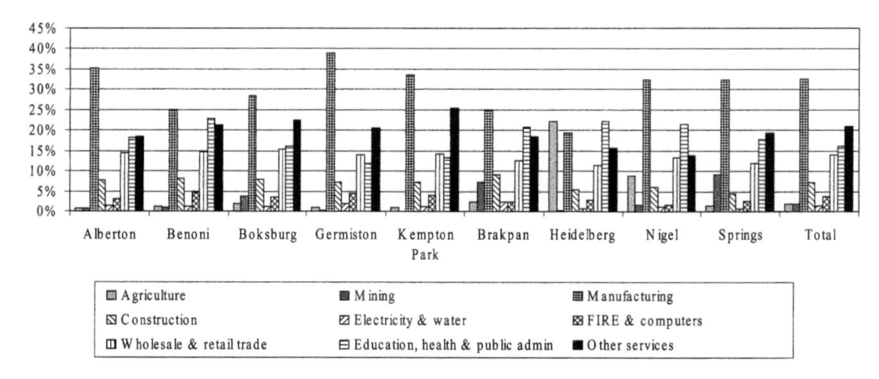

Figure 2. Employment by sector, 1999.
Source: WEFA, 1999

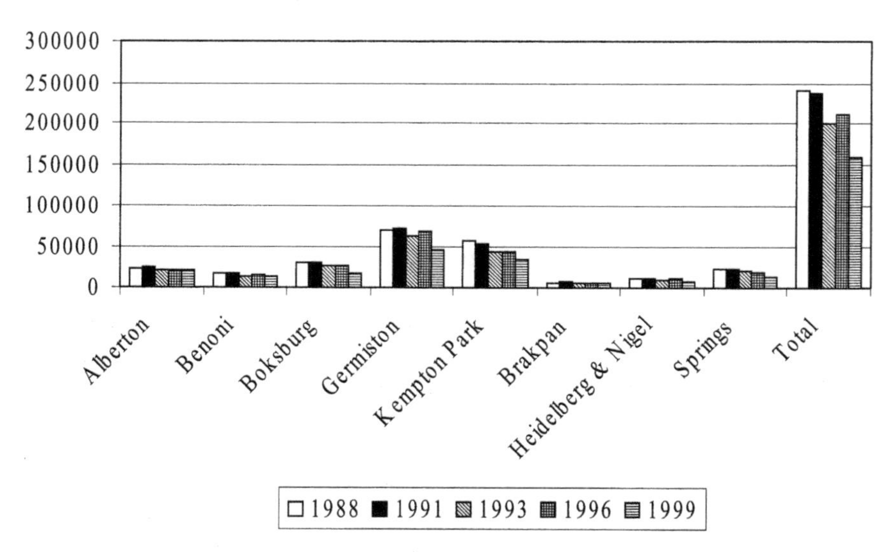

Figure 3. Total manufacturing employment East Rand 1988–1999.
Sources: 1988–1993: Bureau of Market Research, *Spatial Dynamics of the Manufacturing Sector of South Africa, 1988–1993*, UNISA, Research Report 256 (Pretoria, 1998); 1996: Statistics South Africa, *Census of Manufacturing, 1996; Principal Statistics on a Regional Basis: Gauteng* (Pretoria, 2001); 1999: WEFA, 1999.

the 1988–1999 period, with a partial recovery in the 1993–1996 period and an accelerated downturn in the post-1996 period, coinciding with the introduction of GEAR and the full embrace by the South African government of a liberalized trade regime. This graph shows that job losses in manufacturing in the East Rand in this period amount to approximately 80,000 units.

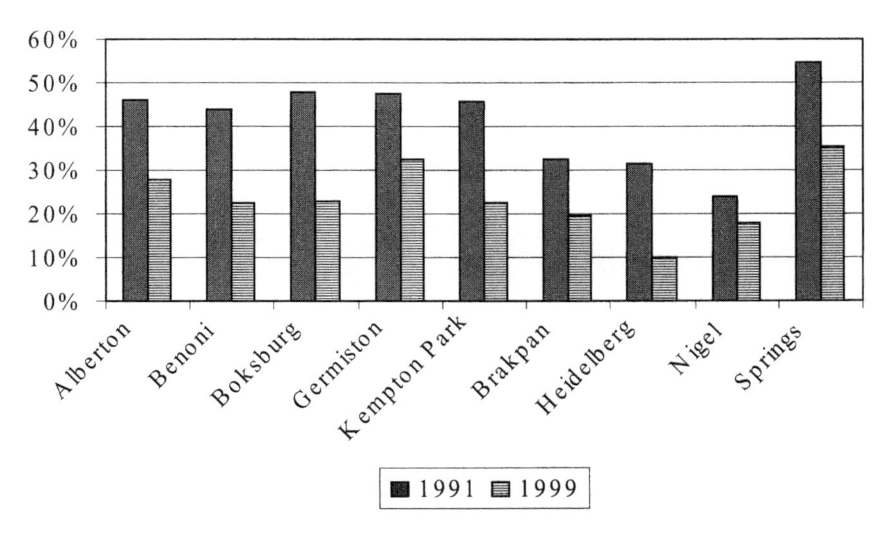

Figure 4. Contribution of manufacturing to GGP, East Rand towns, 1991, 1999.
Source: 1991: Kok, *South Africa's Magnifying Glass*; 1999: WEFA, 1999.

Disaggregated data by town show that the contribution of manufacturing to the GGP of many centres has been reduced in 1999 by as much as half its size in 1991, with losses of 18 and 20 percentage points respectively in the two most important areas of Germiston and Springs. Kempton Park is confirmed as the most rapidly de-industrializing area; however, in this town as well the role of "new-economy" sectors (6.2 per cent of GGP) remains limited in providing a growth alternative (see Figure 4).

Finally, parallel to the decline of the sector in the area, a reduction in the average size of enterprises can be noticed (Figure 5), which is particularly marked in those areas (such as Kempton Park) that previously had the highest concentration of employees in relation to the number of establishments. This can be a reflection of job losses in the sector, but it is also probably related to processes of restructuring that are facilitating the emergence of smaller companies and contractors and subcontractors[36] or even, as in Brakpan, Benoni, and Germiston (where there are solid traditions in this sector) a strengthening of an SME-type industrial texture.

In conclusion, the 1990s have seen a process of decline of the East Rand's manufacturing industry in what has been for the past sixty years the core of the sector in South Africa, as it is apparent from both output and employment statistics. This process has greatly accelerated a trend started in the previous decade, conferring on it a depth and a breadth dramatic in

36. Cf. Rogerson and Rogerson, "Industrial Change in a Developing Metropolis", p. 92.

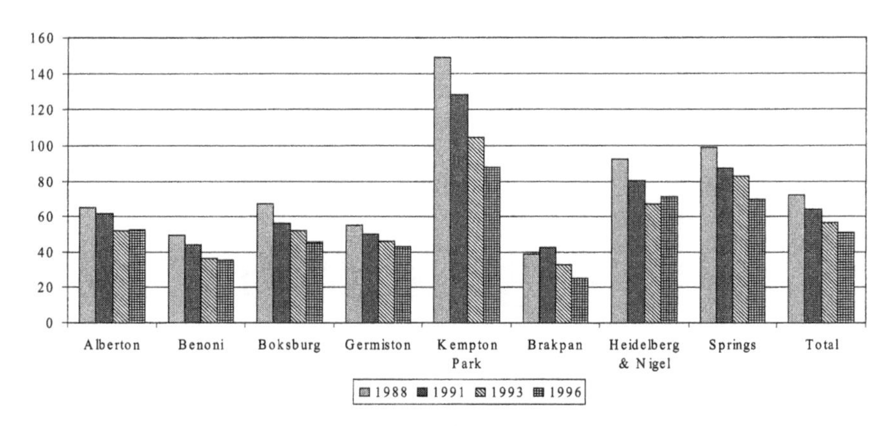

Figure 5. Number of employees per establishment, East Rand, 1988–1996.
Sources: 1988: Bureau of Market Research, *Spatial Dynamics*; 1988, 1991, 1993: Statistics South Africa, *Census of Manufacturing*.

the economic history of the country. On the other hand, while signals of divergent paths and different kinds of de-specialization seemed to emerge in the 1980s, these have not led to the establishment of new sectors capable of driving regional growth in the 1990s. In particular, the "new economy" remains an elusive concept for the area, which seems to be left behind in this respect by the neighbouring Pretoria–Midrand–Johannesburg corridor, while services and public administration, themselves targeted by fiscal constraints, remain a crucial source of employment.

The lack of viable economic alternatives is reflected in worker attitudes and responses to the manufacturing crisis of the area. The next section looks at how workers in the engineering industry have elaborated this socioeconomic transition in terms of subjectivities and organization.

WORKING-CLASS RESPONSES AND ORGANIZATIONAL IMPACTS: THE CASE OF THE ENGINEERING INDUSTRY

The Wits East region of the National Union of Metalworkers of South Africa (NUMSA) includes the locals of Alrode, Germiston, Wadeville, Benoni, Springs, and Nigel. At the beginning of 2000 the region had a membership of approximately 28,600,[37] which represents a 26 per cent decline on the 1996 membership levels.[38] This massive downturn can partly be explained by the already noticed general manufacturing decline

37. Figures provided by locals, April 2000. Franco Barchiesi acknowledges the help of Meshack Robertson (Wits East regional organizer) in gathering the information.
38. National Union of Metalworkers of South Africa [hereafter, NUMSA], *Minutes of the 5th National Congress*, 25–27 September 1996 (n.p., 1996).

after 1996 (and engineering remains the most important industrial sector in the area), but it also reflects difficulties facing union organizing as a result of the dynamics of restructuring in production and employment that accompany those shifts.

Liberalization of trade following South Africa's accession to GATT has led to intensifying competitive pressure on the metal-engineering industry.[39] On the other hand, policies of export promotion facilitated by GEAR and by a declining exchange rate have led to uneven restructuring strategies. In particular, intensified technological innovation, strategies for specialization and differentiation of the product cycle have generally not been accompanied by renewed investment in training and human-resource development.[40] This has facilitated downsizing and retrenchments, which have been particularly intense in larger workplaces that have also provided historical strongholds for the East Rand black unionized working class. According to union organizers, this process has been countered by the rise in small-medium manufacturing, which confirms the data previously provided, often started by managers retrenched by bigger concerns. Rather than starting networks of an "industrial-district" model, however, SMEs in the area tend to enter competitive market relations, enabled by their more specialized and focused approach, which further undermines the market opportunities of larger firms. In this context, market difficulties and the search for competitiveness, rather than the dynamics of outsourcing, seem to be the most relevant dynamics of restructuring.

The crisis of union organizing in the context of large-scale manufacturing is particularly evident in the most important NUMSA locals, as in the case of Springs. Here, a steady membership decline in larger workplaces over the past five years has been counteracted only through renewed organizational efforts in dispersed, small-size, previously unorganized workplaces (generally with less than fifty employees).[41] From this point of view, small companies that have emerged out of the restructuring of bigger ones provide new grounds for recruiting. However, this approach presents obvious disadvantages. First, it stretches the resources of the union, instead of concentrating them into a few major companies, as union strategies on the East Rand have always preferred. Second, the geographical dispersal of small, non-unionized productive sites allows the recruitment of the most vulnerable sections of the workforce, and often the very workers retrenched by large companies, under "atypical" contracts of employment,

39. Z. Rustomjee, "An Industrial Strategy for the Engineering Sector", unpublished report, Cape Town, 1993.
40. A. Kesper, "Small and Medium-Sized Metalworking Companies in the Witwatersrand: Facing the Global Challenge", paper presented at the TIPS 1999 Annual Forum (Johannesburg, 1999).
41. Interview with George Magaseng, NUMSA Springs organizer, 11 November 1999.

usually casual, three to six months contracts, and labour broking. Albeit these usually provide wages, benefits, and working conditions of a lower level than that of unionized workers, the precariousness of employment and job insecurity act as deterrents against unionization. As one union organizer recalls:

> One night I just went to the township. I sat in a house, of course I knew what I was looking for. I bought a beer, and there were people busy doing Marconi's [a communication appliances company, formerly TEMSA] job. Because it's a manual job, very, very easy. They assemble small pieces of rubber and so on, then the company comes and collects, paying them very poorly. They're taking advantage of the social situation of the workers. These people, due to poverty situation, are compelled to accept that kind of conditions.[42]

On the other hand, NUMSA, which generally does not organize casual and temporary employees, recognizes that the overwhelming majority of jobs created in the industry is under these contractual forms. The dispersed production and employment geography imply new difficulties in organizing, and representing the demands of already organized workers. In other words, the union is now facing a three-pronged challenge that raises important questions for its continued existence in what once was its historical core and the breeding ground for a highly organized and conscious working-class vanguard. First, retrenchments and factory closures are facing NUMSA with new worker demands to devise strategies to deal with restructuring. This is an inherently defensive battle for the union, which requires in-depth knowledge and the capacity to elaborate on operational requirements, liquidation procedures, and financial information. Moreover, the existing legislative framework, and in particular the 1995 Labour Relations Act, does not enforce any negotiating role for organized labour in this regard. Second, the fragmentation of production implies an increasing spread of the unions' human and financial resources across expanding areas and a plurality of workplaces. Third, the fragmentation in forms of employment, and the rise of "atypical" forms often imply a diversification of worker needs and a greater emphasis on extra-workplace dynamics of survival, evidenced by inadequate wages and poor working conditions in relation to household expenses. These need to be addressed by the union as part of meaningful organizing strategies, which are, on the other hand, hampered by the vulnerability inherent in these contractual arrangements.

The companies analysed for this paper reflect a spectrum of situations that well represent these interlinked challenges. At the same time, worker perceptions of, and attitudes towards, changes related to de-industrialization articulate this scenario from inside the union's rank-and-file. The first

42. *Ibid.*

company, Kelvinator South Africa, an electric-appliance producer in Alrode, was liquidated and closed at the end of 1999, leaving 1,200 workers unemployed,[43] following expansion plans that were frustrated by limited demand and the requirements of financial investment. The second company, Union Carriage and Wagon (UCW), in Nigel, is a subsidiary of Murray and Roberts that manufactures and repairs railway carriages. Following the expiration of important contracts and the lack of new markets (also due to Spoornet's restructuring and drastic cuts in the number of carriages, consequent to the collapse of rail travel in South Africa) the company has embarked on a series of retrenchments that has reduced the number of workers from 600 to 250 between 1997 and 1999. The third company, Baldwins Steel (Brakpan) is a structural steel trading and cutting firm owned by another giant conglomerate in the sector, Dorbyl. After having been relatively untouched by the first waves of restructuring in the area, rumours of retrenchments started circulating on the shopfloor while this research was in progress. This followed market uncertainties consequent to intensified international competition and the decline of the East Rand's construction industry, in itself a result of the general economic crisis in the area.

The link between employment uncertainty and the loss of rights and power is reflected by worker narratives of the crisis in all these situations. In particular, the experience of casualization, independently from whether it is faced personally, is a decisive factor questioning established and deeply engrained life strategies. This is accompanied by the feeling that not only the union is inadequate in this regard, but that being a union member constitutes a specific target for management's unfettered authority:

> They retrench today and they hire tomorrow. Today they retrench twenty, tomorrow they hire five on contract. Since 1982 I have been retrenched and called back four times. NUMSA has tried many times to talk with them, but at the end of the day they are still retrenching people. [...] Workers are no longer coming to union meetings, maybe they are afraid of being retrenched. Now they have started firing also white supervisors, but otherwise NUMSA members are still those most likely to be retrenched.[44]

At the same time, workers' perceptions of vulnerability are heightened by the permanence of historically unaddressed forms of disadvantage linked to racist managerial styles, unfair discrimination in career prospects, workplace authoritarianism, and lack of recognition of informal skills:

> Whites are moved from this position to that position for reasons that are suitable to them. But we blacks cannot move at all. Talking of myself, I've been stuck in one area for twenty years. Only names change, but the job is always the same. I

43. F. Barchiesi, "Kelvinator: Restructuring, Collapse and Struggle", *South African Labour Bulletin*, 23 (1999) 6, pp. 65–70.
44. Interview 20, (12 September 1999).

made applications for promotion and I've been interviewed, but they always find some reasons to put you aside. I improved many white boys they brought here, and now they are sales managers, directors. When they came here they all came through me, I showed them the job. They were boys, I mean, boys. I'm not undermining them, just reflecting on their age. Today they are senior guys, and I haven't moved an inch, not even an inch from where I was. I'm supposed to be multiskilled here. I don't know what to answer to my children when they ask me what job I am doing, I have to be at the workshop and I have to be at the office. I have to solve problems at the phone. It's a skill, not a skill you can get at technical school, but it's a skill. Instead white boys that have done a three-week course of marketing are immediately promoted to sales manager. I've done that also, but I'm stuck.[45]

The codification of social antagonisms in racialized terms still provides an important cognitive device to understand challenges and support a moral claim for a greater power at the point of production. However, this pattern of discourse finds a limitation precisely in many references to "affirmative action" as failing to provide new shared opportunities and forms of collective identity between black workers and black managers: "Black managers in human resources don't have any power, they just send instructions to the shopfloor. Affirmative action is implemented only on their side of the coin, but not for us workers, this side is not receiving it. You have to be a big shot to be promoted."[46] These limitations of a racialized imagery as a form of emancipatory discourse reveal deep continuities with established ideological patterns on the shopfloor. The identification of "whites" as counterparts, in other words, seems to be specifically functional to reinforcing an image of the radical "otherness" of the managerial authority, rather than in identifying the company as a more democratic space enabled by political and legislative changes. This is, at the same time, reflected in strong references to workers' self-worth and demands for recognition as a more effective empowering strategy:

In my view, instead of training the workers they would prefer to train them in lousy jobs. And at the same time they say they're raising the awareness of the workers on the conditions of the company and the economy to tell them that they have to work more diligently. But they don't train us to do more difficult stuff because they say this would cost company's money. We don't have an opportunity of scrambling our own eggs, of fixing things when they break down.[47]

It would be impossible, on the other hand, to separate workplace discourses of race from this broader perception of devaluation of workers' specific contribution, arising from their daily interaction with a produc-

45. Interview 11, (15 July 1999).
46. Interview 15, (20 July 1999).
47. *Ibid.*

tion process that is shaped by their own inner knowledge of problems and forms of interaction. The denial of these cognitive mechanisms is, in the final analysis, the most damaging aspect of restructuring, since it undermines the forms of worker subjectivity that constitute the basis for worker demands for better wages and working conditions, but also for a more dignified life. It is inside this contestation for worker subjectivity that the existence of racialized forms of authority is manifested through oppositional discourses.

Restructuring trends and the associated job losses are generally received by workers with a sense of uncertainty that articulates a perceived threat to long-established forms of citizenship and social insertion, linked to waged labour and relative employment security. While this stability had facilitated in the past forms of collective consciousness, organization and militancy, the undermining of their very foundations is defining a new sense of powerlessness accompanied by a growing sense of inadequacy of traditional radicalism on workplace issues:

> A: Management is reducing employees' numbers, they say workers must be expandable, by which they mean you must be able to do many jobs. Employees lost are never replaced. This is one of those tricks the company uses to its employees. Maybe the next time you'll come back only not to find me. You never know, these days anything is possible. Today I'm here, tomorrow I'm not, after sixteen years [...].
> Q: Well, they can't fire people just like that [...].
> A: They can't, but they have many means you can lose your job: frustrate you, make you run around, make you feel lost, many things.[48]

On the other hand, the existence of a "government of the black people", as one worker puts it, is not enabling a recodification in racial or nationalist terms of patterns of solidarity and expectations of social promotions. Rather, the fact that a government representing the majority of the population is in power inside a formal alliance with the union movement, while enforcing spending constraints and disciplining socio-economic expectations, contributes to workers' disorientation and lack of direction. In fact, these developments sanction the continuity between workplace-based and community demands that had provided a fundamental contribution to the definition of black working-class identities in the East Rand:

> This government, we don't trust it any more. They say they are going to make changes, but workers don't know nothing about the changes. It's only us who are feeling who are going to be suffering. We say we are going back. We voted for our government, and we thought things would be better, but our government is making us suffer.[49]

48. Interview 12, (16 July 1999).
49. Interview 38, (12 October 1999).

Discourses of government delivery remain, however, in arguments that, while not identifying the government as an ally in immediate socio-economic concerns, try to focus on the reasons of its disappointing performance in the continuing domination by elements linked to the "previous white government". They are accused of mistrusting the democratic government and undermining transformation:

> You complain to the manager and he tells you: "Go to Mandela to give you money and to give you a job". Now, I asked the white guy that comes here for deliveries: "How's the business in your company?" And he says, "I don't know man, we don't know Thabo Mbeki, we don't trust that man". That is why business is like this.[50]

But it is, however, in workers' criticisms of the government's ability, or even willingness, to deal with the broad social impacts of restructuring that the limitations of a racialized-cum-nationalist worker imagery appear most evident. A consequence of the rising proportion of "atypical" employees is that lower wages and benefits increase the burden of reproduction in working-class households. This is particularly evident in the fact that a rising proportion of workers' wages (up to 50 to 60 per cent in the case of workers interviewed) is directed towards the payment of municipal services (mainly rents and fees for housing, electricity, and water). The price of these necessities has generally increased as a result of "cost recovery" policies introduced by municipalities to restore levels of payments eroded by apartheid-era boycotts and as a condition to upgrade infrastructures. This also creates renewed antagonisms between residents and local councillors or ANC leaders identified as enforcing these policies. In this case, worker demands seem to indicate the need for organizational strategies and alliances that are more sensitive to community demands and forms of social protection (in many cases this is witnessed by workers' participation in boycotts of rates and tariffs for municipal services):

> If you are not working the government should send 50 to 100 bucks. You have children, families, and if no-one is working there's lots of problems. The government can do that and it's not. Since when I've been working for [labour broker] I've been short of money for food every week.[51]

The majority of workers interviewed argue that the government has abdicated its fundamental functions in the sphere of job creation, which remains an important source of expectations. However, in many answers there is a surfacing feeling of a decreased centrality of waged employment in personal strategies of citizenship and social insertion. This is reflected in the relatively high number of respondents (fifteen out of fifty) who have a second occupation in the form of informal activities, to which are added

50. Interview 3, (12 July 1999).
51. Interview 20, (12 September 1999).

twenty respondents who argue that they would engage in such activities if they had the necessary access to financial capital and social relations. These results underline a specific feature of the current restructuring phase as increasingly blurring the divides between formal and informal economy. At the same time, the redefinition of life strategies as a consequence of a possible exit from formal waged employment is conducive to workers' re-evaluation of prospects of self-entrepreneurship. While affirmative action remains a significant factor in workplace-based demands in relation to the government, this seems relatively less significant for workers who are planning individual competitive strategies outside the workplace. Here the equalization of conditions for market competition seems to rise to a greater prominence: "Government can bring in education that can help employees to develop themselves. That should be compulsory, so that once they are retrenched workers can form cooperatives. Because jobs are there, even in the townships."[52] While opinions concerning government's role and responsibilities in the current situation are highly diversified, they seem to be unified by autobiographical narratives and diverse life strategies that are increasingly internalizing a decreasing significance of waged labour as a source of worker power and citizenship rights. This common element in a context that sees worker responses becoming increasingly fragmented, raises important questions for the union as the historical locale of collective worker strategies of empowerment. In particular, the possibility of workplace-based militant action seems to be weakened by the economic scale of processes facing individual workplaces. Therefore, views demanding a fighting union "because we are their bosses", are often accompanied by arguments that codify the "fight" increasingly in terms of technical crisis management or deployment of expertise which redefines union allegiances in markedly instrumentalist forms. This is particularly apparent in a context most directly affected by the crisis, such as Kelvinator:

> The union has got a great deal to do, and I don't think they haven't done much upon this issue. If management brings its statements here, do we have qualified chartered accountants that can read financial statements, or qualified lawyers? Unions are like our lawyers. They need to gather information from government on what is happening in the industry. We don't want to find ourselves in a situation where they make a follow-up after actions have been taken. Then they can help us, now they are coming after, after everything is done. They don't take a sense of urgency when they deal with these issues. They know that at the end of the month the debit order money is coming in, but they can't use our money even to save our jobs.[53]

The union is therefore caught in a problematic situation defined by a

52. Interview 41, (20 October 1999).
53. Interview 37, (12 October 1999).

double inadequacy. On one hand, the scale and depth of economic processes at play undermine its role as negotiating industrial change on the basis of deep-seated grassroots militancy. This outcome had represented the organizational crystallization of historical process through which a stabilized urban proletariat on the East Rand had come to define itself as an actor in the political dynamics of citizenship and grassroots power. On the other hand, this transition leaves the union unprepared to deploy services and expertise that are demanded to support the two "exit" options that East Rand workers identify. These refer to, first a "collective" option of community mobilization and alliances aimed at regaining, at least partially, in the sphere of reproduction what has been sacrificed in production through job losses and casualization. Second, an "individualist" response to the crisis prefers options of market-driven and entrepreneurship-based strategies of social promotion, where informality retains a strong appeal.

NUMSA is invested by the rise of a new distribution of economic power in the Gauteng area, which privileges new axes of accumulation around financial and information-based activities to the detriment of established manufacturing areas on the East Rand. In this context the union finds itself in the uncomfortable position of devoting most resources to dealing with occupational and restructuring crisis management, while trying to unionize a highly vulnerable workforce to replace its lost historical strongholds. As a result, and related to the uncertain significance of nationalist politics to this purpose, the definition of political and organizational forms that can express diffuse strategies responding to the crisis of large-scale manufacturing employment in the region remains a largely open question. However, if we examine the workplace experiences of food retail workers, representative of many contingent, low-wage jobs replacing manufacturing in the region, we get a bleak picture, indeed, of further constrained mobilization and increased fragmentation.

WHAT'S IN STORE: RETAIL-SECTOR WORKERS DETACHED

The decline of a unionized manufacturing working class is paralleled by the growth of casualized and vulnerable employment linked to the tertiarization of the East Rand's economy. Research shows that while young women occupy the majority of temporary and part-time jobs, the process has also affected male workers through subcontracting of previously permanent retail employment.[54] In addition, many older male subcontracted merchandizers previously held jobs in East Rand manufacturing firms. Their displacement from that work not only reduced job stability and wages, but also served to disconnect them from collective workplace solidarity:

54. Kenny, "Selling Selves".

> I used to work for a chemical firm in Benoni. We would work together. Next to each other, right next to each other. OK, it was hard work, but we would sing songs all day long. I was nice. We'd sing loud. When the company closed, I found this contract [job]. But sometimes I remember that [singing]. Now we can't do that. [*laughs*] You can't sing songs with customers all around. Sometimes I sing to myself while working, but it doesn't feel the same. Now I just get on with what I have to do for the day.[55]

Metaphorically through song, this worker remembers the camaraderie of work on the factory floor compared to individualized work in the store. While NUMSA members struggle with the erosion of workplace rights, and reformulate solutions based in technicist attempts to stall greater incursions, the life strategies of many East Rand food-retailing workers suggest an even greater detachment from former collective responses centred around broad social citizenship rights. Casual food-retail workers' expectations have been curtailed from hope of workplace training and advancement to weak calls for more hours or at best permanent jobs:

> I wish to get another job for the days that I do not use for [working in the store]. I should think that will make life better because it is tough with especially with us single mothers [...].Things are worse within this life even if you die you need to pay for your death by paying for the grave more than anything else. Death is everywhere and it is possible that one can die even after this meeting, then if you die or one of your family dies where will you get the money for the burial because with the money you get from one day's work it is impossible to save something. If maybe, if I can be permanent I will try to save R50 a month to be able to look to that and other things.[56]

These comments from a forty-year-old female casual till packer who has worked in the same job for six years show that engrained survival strategies target gaining access to more days of work to earn a meagre few Rands. While women have predominated in front-line retailing jobs historically, this worker would have been more likely to have worked in a permanent, full-time position fifteen years ago.[57] Combined with the loss of male full-time manufacturing jobs, the relative importance of casualized employment held by women has increased. This worker's role in maintaining her household and her explicit identification with "single mothers" underlines the terms of her vulnerability. Indeed, her concern with death and the costs of death hint at the unpredictability of contingency costs.

While the South African Commercial, Catering and Allied Workers Union (Saccawu) has attempted to deal with the gendered character of employment through a long-term gender education campaign, it still faces deep challenges to organizing collective responses to gendered insecurity

55. Interview 11, (31 August 2000), Daveyton.
56. Interview 5, (27 May 1999).
57. Kenny, "Selling Selves".

tied to processes of casualization. As the case of NUMSA has shown, these processes have militated against the construction of sustained worker solidarity and have reinforced defensive workplace struggles.

For instance, the casual quoted above evokes a sense of herself as better off than many rather than deriving radical demands for herself and her children from her actual conditions:

> However, it is also better with us because at the end of the week I am able to get money for bread, there are people who sleep and wake up with nothing to eat and some sleep on the streets. It is better with me because I have a house, a temporary job and my kids can be able to eat and go to school because with others are worse.[58]

Casual employment engenders uncertainty and insecurity, on the one hand, but also reminds workers of their closeness to real poverty. If you have money for bread and a house, you are better than many. This employment, then, shifts workers from memories of militant demands for greater participation and full social citizenship that NUMSA members recall in frustration to their present. There is in the narratives of many retail-sector workers a thorough sense of loss of rights and power.

At the same time, this worker was one of few casuals attending union meetings. She cultivated an awareness that the meeting should provide a base of solidarity from which to make demands:

> You know our problem is that we are divided as casuals. You'll find that only five attend the meeting. I always tell them to attend meetings and make them aware of the importance of unity as casuals. What they tell you is that "We have come to work for our kids". As much as that is important, our rights are also important for us to fight for [...]. Things only get fixed if people are united and act as a collective.[59]

Compared to NUMSA rank-and-file members, however, her articulation of what those rights were and of what her and other casuals demands should be, seemed particularly limited. They wanted to be made, if not permanents, than at least "permanent casuals". In other words, their fight was for a marginal degree of security. Asserting a right to (relatively) secure employment articulated claims to a limited social citizenship.

The codification of social antagonisms occurred through racialized views of management prerogative, similar to the engineering workers' experiences, but they also came through division on the shopfloor among workers by employment category. While workers still spoke of white racist management like the engineering workers, much of these comments occurred within discussions about the lack of opportunities for job promotion. Otherness was not only defined in terms of white manage-

58. Interview 5, (27 May 1999).
59. *Ibid.*

ment, or white casuals who were quickly promoted to supervisory positions, but also in terms of their fellow workers, sometimes fellow union members:[60] "It's like they are the permanent staff of the [store], we are the merchandisers. It's like they just separate themselves and if they say, OK we're going to strike, they *tell* us, they don't ask us."[61] The authority and privilege, which casuals and subcontracted merchandizers often portrayed permanent workers having, divided workers, undermining solidarity that East-Rand retail sector workers had in unions organized against racist management and poor conditions and wages under apartheid. This translated into reformulations of rights to limited participation, such as when casuals fought to be able to wear store uniforms worn by permanents – and hence symbolically become recognized as fellow employees – rather than the black-and-white street clothes which marked them as casuals, which surfaced as one of the more emotional demands during 1998 interviews conducted.

While retail sector workers also felt frustrated with the anaemic attempts by the ANC government to better the conditions of "the people", most of their anger was taken out on "sell-out" local councillors who left the township for the posh (former white) suburbs: "It's a very, very big problem, they stay far away. They are no longer with us".[62] One worker vocalized the distance felt between themselves and former comrades, local anti-apartheid activists turned councillors: "How can you drive through once every few weeks in your new E-class [Mercedes Benz], and know what our problems are".[63] The disillusionment with local (black) councillors and quick wealth seen to be obtained by them served to reproduce a sense of township resident oppositional character.

On the other hand, conditioned by greater insecurity of the East Rand's changing labour market and the vulnerability of their insecure part-time jobs, casual retail sector workers belied the increasing fragmentation of black working-class subjectivity. This process of subjectivity formation, we argue, is not about a simple growing economic division between a labour aristocracy and a growing underclass, as Seekings[64] might imply, but about the production of contradictory subjectivities marking the destruction of former solidarities on the East Rand while meanings of race and class become bound together in new formulations significantly reducing workers capacity to project social citizenship rights into a future alternative order. As one young (twenty-two-year-old) casual said of the next generation: "If you haven't worked before, you really are scared to join any organization because you don't want to lose your job. Especially

60. Kenny, "Selling Selves".
61. Interview 10, (31 August 2000), Daveyton.
62. Interview 42, (7 September 2000), Daveyton.
63. Interview 11, (31 August 2000), Daveyton.
64. Seekings, "Is There an Underclass in South Africa?".

these days where there are many [more] retrenchments than getting a job".[65] While manufacturing workers battle to reconstitute new life strategies in a context of declining workplace power, the tertiarization of the East Rand's economy only exacerbates this reality.

CONCLUSION

The black working class of the East Rand has been affected in the past decade by a contradictory process that is not simply questioning the material basis of its existence and reproduction. Most importantly, what is at stake here is the erosion of a whole world view built on specific practices of solidarity and organization that had sustained under apartheid an image of social integration based on worker and citizenship rights in a democratic South Africa deeply linked to waged labour positions. Not only has the prospect of stable, quality manufacturing employment been undermined by socioeconomic dynamics of industrial restructuring, but alternative job prospects, for instance in casual retail jobs, leave little room to reconstruct collective orders asserting rights to full social citizenship.

The contradictory nature of this process is, in fact, particularly expressed by the fact that these forms of uncertainty and disorientation among workers have been ushered in precisely through policies adopted by a new democratic government that had previously driven broad expectations for a fundamental social change. The resulting impact in forms of identity, strategies and organization is particularly apparent in images of the new government. This is portrayed often as still kept hostage by the forces of reaction, but also as an actor increasingly unable to affect in significant ways workers' demand for either employment protection or support in alternative "post-manufacturing" life strategies. The limited appeal of nationalist ideologies can be read as a result of these approaches.

This also explains how a discourse of race as part of a broader inventory of responses remains confined to strategies of workplace-based self-empowerment and defence against racist and authoritarian management styles, without on the other hand a convinced, wholehearted adhesion to affirmative-action programmes or forms of common identification with black managers and supervisors. This pattern, which is inscribed in a strong continuity with practices proper to the "apartheid workplace regime"[66] underlines the relevance of race, paradoxically, in those particular areas where it reinforces the identification of the adversary or the counterpart in the structures of capitalist management. This, at the

65. Interview 24, (7 August 1999), Daveyton.
66. K. von Holdt, "From Resistance to Reconstruction: a Case Study of Trade Unionism in the Workplace and the Community (1980-1996)", unpublished Ph.D. dissertation, University of the Witwatersrand (Johannesburg, 2000).

same time, does not necessarily suggest that "class" identities have been left unchanged by these processes. Rather, the diversification of responses and strategies emerged out of the crisis of large-scale manufacturing indicates that a far more nuanced picture is emerging out of the hollowing out of previous forms of solidarity, socialization, everyday construction of meanings and sense. The demand for social citizenship rights in this context has probably retained a subversive character, heightened by current levels of exclusion, fiscal discipline, and the marketization of basic social necessities. However the style, strategies, and discourse of this "character", and the ways in which working-class identities are reconfigured inside it probably require a detachment from polarized debates over the primacy of "class" and "non-class" *identities* and a closer look at *processes* of oppositional subjectivity formation,[67] whose urgency is barely signalled by this paper.

67. F. Barchiesi, "Restructuring, Flexibility and the Politics of Workplace Subjectivity: A Worker Inquiry in the South African Car Industry", *Rethinking Marxism*, 10 (1998), pp. 105–133; Kenny, "Selling Selves".

IRSH 47 (2002), pp. 65–85 DOI: 10.1017/S0020859002000780

Whose Left? Working-Class Political Allegiances in Post-industrial Britain*

DARREN G. LILLEKER

A romanticized view of class alignment in Britain exists that has been attacked and defended equally in academic works over the last twenty years.[1] Historically, the Labour Party was seen as the defender of working-class interests, though critics within the party and the British socialist movement have often questioned this notion.[2] Such questions have appeared more pertinent with the diminution of the working class due to the de-industrialization of the British economy. In 1983 Andrew Gamble noted that: "The greatest threat to this underlying strength of the British labour movement are the twin trends of declining manufacturing output and rising unemployment".[3] He argued that it was the failure of the Labour Party to arrest these trends and "translate the overwhelming objective strength [...] into organizational strength and political leadership"[4] which had led to the dealignment of the working class away from Labour.

Clearly, however, the Labour Party has never enjoyed the support of the working class in totality and the politics of the party have, on occasions, led sections of the working class to abandon the party.[5] The fact that the British working class has historically had a weak partisan attachment to the Labour Party had been highlighted as evidence of dealignment long before the 1980s. Studies of partisanship decline have illustrated that working-class dealignment has been a long-standing feature of British politics. Franklin argues that this began in the mid-1960s,[6] a thesis reinforced by

* The author would like to thank Janet Foxcroft, Ros Pinder, and Teresa Thorn for their invaluable and unpaid assistance with conducting the pilot studies, and Steve Ludlam and James Stanyer for their helpful comments on an earlier draft.

1. For an outline of the debate on dealignment see G. Evans, "Class Voting: from Premature Obituary to Reasoned Appraisal", in *idem* (ed.), *The End of Class Politics? Class Voting in Comparative Context* (Oxford, 1999), pp. 1–2.
2. For example see R. Miliband, *Parliamentary Socialism: A Study in the Politics of Labour* (London, 1972).
3. A. Gamble, "The Impact of the SDP", in H. Drucker (ed.), *Developments in British Politics* (London, 1983), p. 299.
4. *Ibid*., p. 300.
5. J.E. Cronin, *Labour and Society in Britain 1918–1979* (London, 1984).
6. M.N. Franklin, "Is Class Still the Basis of British Politics?", *Strathclyde Papers on Government and Politics*, 2 (1983), pp. 1–3; M.N. Franklin and A. Mughan, "The Decline of Class Voting in Britain: Problems of Analysis and Interpretation", *American Political Science Review*, 72 (1978), pp. 523–534.

analyses based on the Alford indexes of class voting which show a steady decline after 1966, though some highlight that dealignment only became worthy of attention during the 1980s.[7] Gallie highlighted the link between dealignment and de-industrialization by discussing the decline of class in terms of the diminution of class-consciousness.[8] In arguing that the traditional sources of grievance – salaries and working conditions – are no longer as serious to the majority of working-class employees, he hypothesized that conflict was becoming avoidable through "social integration" in the modern workplace. This minimized the social distance between management and workforce, allowed equal participation in decision-making, and made trade-union activists irrelevant in securing benefits for the workforce.[9] Gallie's conclusion was that the British working class, particularly those in the post-industrial economy, act upon personal, rather than class-conscious motivations and no longer need representation by a party whose agenda is built upon the interests of a nonexistent stereotypical social class. Such arguments allude to the inference that, as the working class became more affluent, parties claiming to represent the working class have had to adopt policies with a broader appeal. However, Goldthorpe *et al.*, in their seminal study of the "affluent worker" (1969), did not propose that social divisions along class lines were in anyway being eroded. The authors observed that: "in the case of manual workers, a shift away from a community-oriented form of social life towards recognition of the conjugal family and its fortunes as concerns of overriding importance".[10] This indicates that, while still working-class, the interests of the family and personal wealth had begun, as early as the 1960s, to inform voting behaviour.

The perception that class and class-consciousness were becoming increasingly irrelevant in political terms led Tony Wright to argue that the term class needed to be exchanged for "people". In his highly plausible account of the role of the working class in British politics, he recognized that, more often than not, the working class has failed "to perform its necessary revolutionary or historic role". This, he argues, should not signal the end of socialism but prompt socialists to search for a new constituency consisting of "those people in search of a more rational, secure and human way of ordering society".[11] While this observation is prescient in terms of the post-1995 adjustment of Britain's "New" Labour party programme, it is certainly not a new phenomenon. As the British working class has

7. D. Robertson, *Class and the British Electorate* (Oxford, 1984), p. 20.

8. D. Gallie, *In Search of a New Working Class: Automation and Social Integration within Capitalist Enterprise* (Cambridge, 1978), p. 295.

9. *Ibid.*, pp. 300, 308–309.

10. J.H. Goldthorpe, D. Lockwood, F. Bechhofer, and J. Platt, *The Affluent Worker in the Class Structure* (London, 1969), p. 163.

11. T. Wright, *Socialisms: Old and New* (London, 1996), p. 104.

historically refused to adopt the role Marxist theorists ascribed to it, it would seem that the working class has been placed on a pedestal undeservedly. Within Britain, in the writings of key theorists and political actors, as Kreiger explains: "a few core male manufacturing industries were allowed to stand symbolically for the whole of a segmented and highly sex-segregated labor force".[12] These industries became symbolic because they allowed "an understanding of a shared lot"[13] which encouraged collectivist behaviour.[14] This gave an impression of unity, cohesion, and collectivity but was actually limited to certain sectors of the economy, specific modes of production, and centred on key trade unions. These factors are largely no longer a feature of the British political scene.

The above brief discussion provides an introduction to the debate surrounding the influence of class-consciousness upon voting behaviour in an historical perspective. This article seeks to revisit and question some of the assumptions of class alignment before discussing the effects of de-industrialization on the position and influence of the working class in Britain at the turn of the twenty-first century. The study will be structured in the following way. Firstly, an overview of the traditional alignment of the working class; secondly, an introduction to Britain as a post-industrial economy, which will necessitate us rethinking various assumptions regarding the nature and composition of the working class. The third section of the paper will attempt to define the socioeconomic profile of the modern British working class and, once a broad definition of the post-industrial working class has been established, the final section can then focus upon the voting behaviour of those who can be classified as working-class. The main aims of this article is to examine whether class can be realistically described as a factor which influences voting in Britain and, if we reach a negative conclusion, develop some sense of what factors do determine voting patterns.

THE WORKING CLASS IN BRITAIN: PARTISANSHIP VERSUS SELF-INTEREST

A traditional, and arguably a rather utopian, view of partisanship would be that the British working class coalesced behind the Labour Party as the parliamentary force which represented their interests.[15] This is highly

12. J. Kreiger, *British Politics in the Global Age: Can Social Democracy Survive?* (Oxford, 1999), p. 42.
13. A. Przeworski, *Capitalism and Social Democracy* (Cambridge, 1985), p. 100.
14. On this point see E.O. Wright, *Classes* (London, 1985), p. 10.
15. This was certainly the view of the key theorists of the party, such as Sydney Webb, Harold Laski, and G.D.H. Cole, and was supported by many on the left of the party who argued for a more "socialist" agenda. Such a stance would be exemplified in the works of Tony Benn and Konni Zilliacus.

questionable. While the Labour Party did emerge "from the bowels of the trade union movement" it was hardly an easy delivery. Only just over 50 per cent of delegates voted to establish the Labour Representation Committee at the 1899 Trade Union Congress[16] and it took a further ten years for the party to attract the majority of large trade unions away from the Liberal Party.[17] It remained even more difficult for the Labour Party to attract a core electorate. As Ralph Miliband argued: "most Labour supporters were not socialists, only anti-Conservatives. And, for those who did not want to vote Conservative, there was no serious alternative to the Labour Party, just as there was no longer any serious alternative to the Conservative Party for those who would not vote Labour".[18] While 1945 represented the highpoint for Labour support, it also marked the watershed. Labour's victory was underpinned by a cross-class consensus of public opinion that demanded better public services and substantial welfare reforms and believed Labour was the party to deliver; class identity arguably held little significance. Therefore we can offer the perspective of the working class as a highly amorphous group, the interests of which were often divided between group identity and personal economic interests.

This hypothesis is substantiated by the phenomena of working-class conservatism. Surveys show that 25 per cent of the core Conservative vote[19] comes from households within the lowest income bracket and, moreover, 22 per cent of Conservative Party voters count themselves as working-class. However, these are not, perhaps, those who are traditionally seen as possessing a working-class consciousness. A survey conducted in 1994 found that the majority of this cohort own their own property, are aspirant, oppose the closed-shop trade-union policy, have no significant view on privatization and also have strong nationalistic tendencies. They are ambivalent to the idea of the strong "nanny" state and desire the ability to accumulate wealth unhindered by high "tax and spend" governments.[20] This is a significant, and arguably expanding, group whose members are currently seen as "middle Englanders" and who lack a strong partisan identity. The first evidence that this cohort existed was presented by Goldthorpe *et al.* in 1969 who argued that there was

16. A. Thorpe, *A History of the British Labour Party* (Basingstoke, 1997), p. 5.
17. A major advance was the affiliation of the Miner's Federation of Great Britain in 1909, giving the party 88 per cent of the members of the Trade Union Congress (TUC). See Thorpe, *A History*, p. 23.
18. Miliband, *Parliamentary Socialism*, p. 119.
19. This figure denotes those who are loyal Conservative voters rather than working-class voters who may vote Conservative in reaction to the Labour Party failing to deliver on promises. The majority of surveys and studies give the figure as 25 per cent, though some argue that the average is as high as 30 or even 33 per cent.
20. P. Whiteley, P. Seyd, and J. Richardson, *True Blues: The Politics of Conservative Party Membership* (Oxford, 1994).

> [...] a considerable shift of working-class sentiment away from Labour [...] [and] likely defectors are individuals who had looked to the advantages which a Labour Government could bring in terms of prices, full employment, social benefits and now feel cheated mainly because it is these direct personal advantages that have been withheld.[21]

Twelve years prior to publication of Goldthorpe *et al.*'s study the Labour leaders had also recognized the need to appeal to a broad range of individualist interests. Hugh Gaitskell, Party Leader 1955–1963, told the 1957 Labour Party annual conference that a further programme of industrial nationalization had little appeal among "the so-called marginal voters, ordinary decent people who do not probably think a great deal about politics". He therefore argued that it would be a grave error for the party to develop a policy based purely on ideological socialist premises, particularly one that: "in our hearts we did not believe we could carry out [...] which in our hearts we believed the electorate would reject".[22] Gaitskell firmly believed that the majority of the working class were not socialists and so would reject Labour if the party offered a socialistic manifesto. This led Butler and Rose to conclude that all Labour intrinsically asked of the electorate was to adopt the view that the party "could administer the mixed economy welfare state better than the Conservatives".[23] The firm proof that the working class would reject a socialist Labour programme was provided at the 1983 General Election, but we can also point to 1970, 1979 and the period 1951–1959 to reinforce the point that the working class often did reject the politics of the Labour Party. In 1983 studies show that over one-third of those who were classified as working-class by the Alford index, 34 per cent and 36 per cent respectively, voted for the Conservative Party and 21 per cent indicated that this was a shift in their voting behaviour. Some analysts argue that this was more in reaction to Labour's leftward trajectory than evidence of a broader pattern of dealignment, and highlight 1983 as providing the necessary proof. Heath is quoted as arguing that: "in 1983 Labour fared badly in all classes alike. [But] It remained relatively stronger in the working class than in the middle class – in other words it remained a class party, but in 1983 it was an unsuccessful class party."[24] Class, despite being described as irrelevant, continues to hold some significance. In 1993 Marshall found that only 6 per cent of respondents refused to assign themselves to a social class, therefore highlighting that some form of class-consciousness existed. However, his survey also discovered that

21. Goldthorpe *et al.*, *The Affluent Worker*, p. 191; see also M. Abrams, "The Lost Labour Voter", *Socialist Commentary*, (February 1969), pp. 4–5.
22. *Labour Party Annual Conference Report* (1957), p. 155.
23. D.E. Butler and R. Rose, *The British General Election of 1959* (London, 1960), p. 17.
24. G. Marshall *et al.*, *Social Class in Modern Britain* (London, 1993), p. 230.

employment sector, housing tenure, and level of benefit dependency also featured as variables which influenced voting behaviour.[25] Evidence presented by more recent polls on voting behaviour suggest that traditional Labour voters are no longer loyalists at electoral polls but have become disillusioned and so voluntarily disenfranchized.

This process of disillusionment with Labour was first noted by Barry Hindess in 1971. He highlighted that:

> [...] the determination of local policy is now very largely in the hands of [...] [the] middle-class. [...] [D]ebate is able to centre more round questions of means and less around those of ends, and [...] for local or national government action to be judged in terms of its promise rather than its practical consequences. [...] The apparent growth of consensus is [...] directly related to the political isolation of a fairly substantial section of the population.[26]

Panitch reinforced these claims, highlighting that Labour had attempted "to develop a policy of national and party interest which will be acceptable to a broad range of sectoral organizations".[27] The concern is which sectors will be prioritized and which will be excluded in the modern British political arena.

It was the middle class that New Labour specifically targeted when adopting a market-oriented approach to electoral campaigning.[28] Philip Gould, senior adviser to the Labour Party campaigns and communications strategists since 1986, described these people as: "Not disadvantaged, not privileged, not quite working-class, not really middle-class – they don't even have a name."[29] Drawing on the Democrats' campaign in the United States, Gould argued the party "need[ed] to reassert their claim to represent the majority of working [people]. The working middle class needs to figure at least as centrally in the party's identity as the traditional blue-collar [manual labourer] imagery".[30] This does not mean, however, that Labour has abandoned, or indeed lost, what is known as "heartland" support. In the 2001 General Election, key constituencies showed a substantial support for Labour, despite also evidencing voter apathy by a reduced turnout. Across the Barnsley wards, the former centre of the Yorkshire mining community and a traditional stronghold of Labour supporters, Labour gained above 60 per cent of the vote. This was mirrored in almost all the industrial heartland constituencies, the Conservative vote often struggled to top 20 per cent and the only gains

25. *Ibid.*, pp. 249–253.
26. B. Hindess, *The Decline of Working-Class Politics* (London, 1971), pp. 143–145.
27. L. Panitch, *Working-Class Politics in Crisis: Essays on Labour and the State* (London, 1986), p. 57.
28. See J. Lees-Marshment, *Political Marketing and British Political Parties: The Party's Just Begun* (Manchester, 2001), pp. 181–210.
29. P. Gould, *The Unfinished Revolution* (London, 1998), p. 17.
30. *Ibid.*, p. 173.

in terms of percentage of votes went to the Liberal Democrats, Labour's main opposition on the centre-left.

The Labour heartland was as easily definable in the 1983 General Election, the low point for Labour voting. Those constituencies which experienced the greatest difficulties under Prime Minister Margaret Thatcher's neoliberal economic reforms were staunch Labour voters. These included the South Yorkshire and Nottinghamshire mining communities, Tyneside, Teeside, Liverpool, the West Midlands, Manchester, and parts of London, and can be classified as the traditional centres of the manufacturing and extraction industries. Beyond these areas Labour struggled to hold seats that were previously regarded as "safe". This led many electoral analysts to argue that class dealignment was well underway.[31] However, this was not simply a case of the working class moving away from social-democratic parties; in Britain they moved away from Labour. Labour's failure to arrest economic depression 1976–1979 and the leftward drift 1980–1983 led the party to lose the support of all but those voters who would not under any circumstances vote Conservative. Crewe's surveys found that the reason for this was that the majority of working-class opinion "coincided more closely with Conservative policy-stances".[32] Crewe found a "spectacular decline in support for the collectivist trinity of public ownership, trade union power and social welfare".[33] Therefore the working-class Conservative voting cohort increased as a result of the Labour Party's failed economic policy and subsequent leftward shift. These voluntarily dealigned or realigned voters were the people who Gould would encourage the party to reorient itself towards at the 1997 General Election. However, should the realignment that occurred in 1983 be accepted as evidence of class dealignment?

Saunders argued that 1983 represented a rejection of the values of the Labour Party and evidenced the emergence of a "culture of consumption" among a substantial section of the working class. This led him to conclude that: "[w]e are moving towards a dominant mode of consumption in which the majority will satisfy most of its consumption requirements through private purchase". Here Saunders was not only discussing the family car, videorecorder, or personal stereo, but also essential welfare services. He also hypothesized that an underclass would emerge: "cast adrift on the waterlogged raft of the welfare state".[34] This gives the impression that Saunders predicted a society of "haves and havenots" would emerge and

31. I. Crewe, "The Labour Party and the Electorate", in D. Kavanagh, *The Politics of the Labour Party* (Oxford, 1982), pp. 20, 23. See also I. Crewe, "The Electorate: Partisan Dealignment Ten Years On", *West European Politics*, 7 (1984), pp. 19–28.

32. E. Shaw, *The Labour Party Since 1979: Crisis and Transformation* (London, 1994), p. 23.

33. Crewe, "The Labour Party", p. 37.

34. P. Saunders, *Social Theory and the Urban Question* (New York, 1986), p. 318.

that the majority of the former would lack any party identification. Kreiger developed this point thus:

> The political-electoral implications of the politics of consumption are [...] as much behavioural as structural, the use to which they can be put in party competition depend upon the policy options that drive them, the vision of politics that frames them, and the contemporary popularity of the party and the leader who enunciate them.[35]

Thus, as was discussed twenty years previously in the affluent-worker thesis, politics has become contextualized within the personal circumstances of the voter. Kreiger used the selling of council houses to emphasize his argument. The council estates, usually situated within labour-intensive industrial urban centres, were the core of Labour's heartland support. However, with the transition from tenant to home-owner, new "anticollectivist" concerns became prominent. The newly empowered homeowners rejected the notion of community and class interest and embraced Thatcherite individualism. This process of gradual dealignment, due to the shifting values of working-class voters, is argued to have started in the late 1960s, as consumerism first became a feature of British society, and caused an erosion of Labour's electoral support.[36] Many argued that this was evidenced most acutely in 1983, and claim that it was only when Labour rejected traditional socialist policies that the party was able to reverse the trend.

Clearly a large section of the working class did reject Labour in 1983, some of whom would not return until 1997, suggesting substantial dealignment. Furthermore the use of marketing techniques, attempting to inject the "general will" into Labour party policy 1995–1997 through a prolonged market-research exercise, gives the impression that Labour lacked a core constituency. However, what overrides these arguments is the notion of competence. Labour, post-1997, has been able to command a large majority of the electorate while the Conservatives appear to have lost a large majority of both their "heartland" voters and the non-aligned electorate. Labour is seen as more capable and, therefore, has currently established itself as the natural party of government. This argument is reinforced by the fact that a large percentage of the modern electorate is either apathetic to all major parties, or at least do not identify with either the Conservatives or Labour, but vote on the strength of a parties image of competence. This is linked to a popularized view that the parties are "too

35. J. Kreiger, "Class, Consumption, and Collectivism: Perspectives on the Labour Party and Electoral Competition in Britain", in F.F. Piven (ed.), *Labour Parties in Post-industrial Societies* (Cambridge, 1991), pp. 47–70, especially p. 58.

36. I. Crewe, "Labour Force Changes, Working-Class Decline, and the Labour Vote: Social and Electoral Trends in Postwar Britain", in Piven, *Labour Parties*, pp. 20–46, especially pp. 21–24.

similar", "lack a clear identity" and, to some, "are not ideologically driven".[37] However, it could also be argued that the working class, due particularly to de-industrialization, has declined in numbers to such an extent that it is now a negligible political force. Therefore all the parties are fighting for the support of an apolitical, middle-England cohort who are motivated purely by economic concerns and who have no ideological affinities.

DE-INDUSTRIALIZATION: THE REORIENTATION OF THE BRITISH WORKER

The working class is traditionally seen as the manual worker, centred within the manufacture or extraction industries. This is clearly no longer the case. As Graham and Spence highlighted, "[t]he decline of industrial manufacturing and the concurrent growth in service-sector-oriented activity have been features of change in most advanced urban economies over the last two decades".[38] Crewe observed this process in 1991 and described the ramifications as "a smaller labour force, a smaller working class, a contraction of trade unionism, mass unemployment, and a much larger 'peripheral' workforce of part-time and temporary workers".[39] Social trends data reinforce these claims. In 1971, 54.7 per cent of the total workforce[40] was classed as manual workers, by 1991 this had fallen to 37.7 per cent.[41] More indicative of the level of reorientation is the fact that in 1995 only 17.6 per cent of the total workforce worked within the manufacturing industry, a figure which included those employed in specialized manufacturing such as pharmaceuticals. Additionally only 1 per cent worked in energy-supply industries, which includes extraction, and 3.9 per cent in the construction sector. This means that the traditional working class industries employed an average of only 22 per cent of the workforce.[42] So where do the British people work in the post-industrial economy? Twenty-four per cent work in the distribution, and hotels and

37. Comments made by those interviewed who responded that they did not intend to vote, or had not voted, in 2001. See *The Guardian* (8 June 2001) and *The Daily Telegraph* (8 June 2001). These responses were also recorded by local newspaper journalists: see, for example, *Leicester Mercury* (5 June 2001), p. 10; *ibid.*, (6 June 2001), pp. 4–5. While those interviewed obviously cannot reflect a representative sample of all nonvoters, they are indicative of the opinions held of the major parties at that time.

38. D. Graham and N. Spence, "Contemporary Deindustrialisation and Tertiarisation in the London Economy", *Urban Studies*, 32 (1995), p. 885.

39. Crewe, "Labour Force Changes", p. 25.

40. This includes full-time and part-time workers, male and female productive units and covers every industry.

41. Census records, Social Trends Dataset: ST30A2; Percentage of Manual Workers 1911–1991.

42. Figures use data for 1995, 1996, and 1997, See Office for National Statistics, Annual Employment Survey Revised: Employment Analysis 1995–1997, Dataset AES95–97.

restaurants categories, within which are included the retail and wholesale trade and the majority of leisure-related services: hotel, restaurant, and licensed bar staff particularly. Eighteen per cent work within the finance sector (43 per cent of this cohort are classed as skilled), though the remaining 57 per cent come under the category of other business-related activities. This category mainly includes clerical staff attached to the finance industry, in particular call-centre workers, the sector referred to by Third-Way intellectual Charles Leadbeater as: "the factories of the modern service economy".[43] The other large category is public administration, employing 25 per cent of the workforce: the majority of these employees are skilled in educative or social-work skills, but 22 per cent are classified as routine administrative staff.

These dramatic changes in the structure of the British economy occurred between 1970 and 1980, and had serious political repercussions. The overall levels of employment had dropped steadily from 1966 due to a contraction in manufacturing, the service industry was able to offer some relief to the employed but became the employer for a greater number of women than men.[44] The decline of manual industry caused a general unease among employees in the heavy industries – fuel extraction and steel manufacture – particularly as working conditions and real-wage levels began to decline. In many industries antagonism between management and workers was characterized as a battle over shopfloor control. The working classes sought guarantees over tenure and wage increases above the level of inflation, but underpinned these with demands for workplace democracy. Those manual workers who felt their personal circumstances were most under threat equally recognized that the Labour party was both ill-equipped and ill-prepared to arrest social change in favour of the working class. Thus the increase of militancy, in the workplace and within the Labour party, was an attempt to gain true working-class power. Those workers who felt that they could adapt to a service economy rejected the politics of the Left and embraced the individualism of Conservative politics. These members of the working class, and their descendants, are the modern era's floating, or nonaligned, voters. Their political allegiances are no longer defined by their employment and though, as we shall see, they face an even more uncertain future as a member of the fragmented working class in an unstable service economy they are, as Cronin observed: "more self-confident and assertive, less inclined to accept the dismally low standards of the past and quite intolerant towards the pretensions and authority of employers, trade union officials and the state".[45]

43. C. Leadbeater, *Living on Thin Air* (London, 2000), p. 61.
44. Cronin, *Labour and Society*, p. 195.
45. *Ibid.*, p. 208.

Social-trends data reinforce this picture of the post-industrial British economy. They indicate that there has been a significant shift away from industrial and manual labour and towards the service sector. Traditionally these "white-collar" or "blue-stocking" occupations were seen as well paid and semiskilled or skilled. Studying data on age, gender, wages and education, we can see this is no longer the case. In terms of age and gender there is little significant difference, apart from the fact that young males, sixteen to thirty years of age, and females, thirty to forty years of age, are preponderant within the "other business-related category" with young females aged eighteen to twenty-five forming a further sizeable cohort. Males within the administration and service sectors earn on average £188.40 per week more than their female counterparts with the greatest disparity – £261.20 – being in the London area.[46] The average wage for 30 per cent of all service sector employees is between £4 and £6 per hour with a further 12 per cent earning the minimum wage. Only 37 per cent of service sector employees earn over £8 per hour.[47] Around 20 per cent of the total employees are part-time, 65 per cent of which are female.[48] Within the latter cohort we find that wages are on average lower and more likely to be set at the minimum level. Furthermore 52 per cent of service sector employees have no qualifications above GCSE and 10.3 per cent have no qualifications at all.[49]

This indicates that the service sector employs a large amount of women, often those who have devoted a significant period of their early adult life to childbearing. They have a low level of educational qualifications and, therefore have low earning capacity and lack basic employment-related skills such as computer literacy. These would have traditionally been the staple employees of the manufacturing industry. Using various social stratification measures we could define these people as working-class, though it is debatable whether they would classify themselves as such. Without carrying out a survey of all call centre operatives, low-grade administrators and other "customer-care" employees, it is impossible to gain a complete picture of the social and economic circumstances of this cohort, though a limited survey did produce some indications.

A pilot study of employees in three call centres, based in Leicester, Preston and Wakefield,[50] revealed that 50 per cent do classify themselves as

46. Office for National Statistics, *Average Weekly Earnings: by Industry and Gender*, Regional Trends Dataset RT35511.

47. Office for National Statistics, *Distribution of Hourly Earnings: by Industry*, (Spring 2000), New Earnings Survey Chart 5.10.

48. Office for National Statistics, *Labour Force Survey*, Regional Trends Dataset RT35503.

49. Department of Education and Skills, Regional Trends Dataset RT35413.

50. Simple questionnaires were designed and passed to a random sample of call-centre employees asking how they saw themselves, why they were in this occupation, and how long they planned to remain doing this type of work.

working-class. And that 47 per cent do so on the strength of their background or, in the case of 16 per cent of respondents all of whom are female, based on the occupation of their partners. Only 24 per cent made a clear link between their occupation and their social class.[51] Despite describing their jobs as "repetitive", "boring" and "scripted" – the latter in terms of the phrasing they use when discussing customer's complaints – 37 per cent see themselves as skilled and a further 47 per cent described themselves as semiskilled. All said they had some qualifications, but few of these thought they were relevant to their current occupation. The majority, 63 per cent, stated they were working because their household needed the money; only 14 per cent responded that they were working for personal spending money. But do their circumstances influence their voting? Forty-three per cent argued that they voted because of class partisanship, arguing that the Labour Party represented "people like them" or talked of "traditional", "family", or "community" ties to the party. The remainder, 57 per cent, all claimed they voted on the strength of "who would do best", "competence" or "who came across as a good leader".

A further indicator that also tells us much about the modern British economy is the lack of job security and increased mobility. This means that 75 per cent of the call-centre employees argued their job was "short-term" and a "stepping stone to a better job". Only 15 per cent saw themselves as restricted to call-centre work, while 10 per cent, obviously all females, were working in order to afford time off to have a baby. These indications are reinforced by nationwide studies. A survey of employment duration published in spring 2000 found that only 10 per cent of women between 20 and 49 years of age remain in a single post for more than one year. Fifty-two per cent of women aged 16 to 19 hold one job for an average of three months while 69 per cent of women aged 50 to 59 held the same job for less than twelve months. This data also shows that only 15 per cent of male employees enjoy job security of three years or more. Over all age ranges we find that 74 per cent of employees change jobs every six months, or have periods of unemployment between jobs. This is exacerbated by the increased role of employment agencies which offer short-term contracts, often on a day-to-day basis. This means that the workforce is fragmented and, due to the high turnover within the low-skilled job market, in a constant state of internal competition.

Of greatest concern, evidence also shows that there is a high level of poverty in Britain. A government survey showed that one-quarter of families spend between one and five years in poverty and that once in poverty it becomes increasingly likely that individuals will remain below the poverty line. The majority of those living in poverty are single-parent

51. The remaining 13 per cent gave no reply to the question "Why do you see yourself as a member of this class?".

families with a female as head of the household. There is unlikely to be anyone in full-time, long-term employment in the household, despite being predominantly within the "prime" working age range. Thirty-two per cent have more than one child and overwhelmingly they have a low level of education.[52] These figures were summarized to infer "those lone parents who moved into work [...] stopped work again within a year, and half drifted in and out of unemployment for five years".[53] These people have little stake in the consumer society and find themselves largely excluded. Callinicos argues that this means they are unlikely to identify with procapitalist parties and so will reject the democratic process.[54]

THE POST-INDUSTRIAL WORKING CLASS: AFTER BOILER SUITS AND PIT HELMETS

There is, then, a working class as defined using traditional socioeconomic indicators: employees who have little or no power within the workplace, whose rights are under attack, who lack job security, who suffer from alienation and who find it difficult to move beyond certain types of employment. These are characteristics shared by the majority of those employed in the labour intensive industries throughout the first three-quarters of the twentieth century. In the post-industrial economy, however, they are also significantly different. While once the domain of the male, it is now the female who is preponderant in labour-intensive, usually office-based, unskilled jobs. Equally, while once labour-intensive industries were the recruiting base for the trade unions, the reduction in union influence, and the end of the closed shop, has shown a steady decline in union membership. Across the manual industries only 29 per cent belong to a trade union; within the nonmanual occupations the membership is 30 per cent. The majority of call centres have an on-site union which most employees join. However, there is dissatisfaction with the ability of large unions, such as USDAW, to exert leverage over corporations.[55]

52. HM Treasury, *Persistent Poverty and Lifetime Inequality*, CASEreport 5; HM Treasury, *Occasional Paper*, 10 (March 1999), pp. 142–143.
53. *The Guardian* (7 September 2000).
54. A. Callinicos, *Against the Third Way* (Cambridge, 2001), p. 51.
55. This was particularly the case at Empire Stores, Wakefield. The employees in the call centre were offered a wage increase of 1.5 per cent on 9 September 2000; this was rejected. The company refused to increase their offer. Although members discussed wildcat strikes, USDAW refused to back them and entered into negotiations with the management that saw meetings delayed and interest reduced. Also, due to the high turnover of staff, 35 per cent of employees who had originally voted "No" had left the company in the interim period. Those employed over the same period signed a contract stating they would not demand a wage increase within a 12-month period from the start of employment. The result was that when the management demanded a fresh ballot 22 September 2001, by which time a fresh pay review should have been underway, members who could not vote against were in the majority. Though most did not attend the

We should ask then what political issues motivate the post-industrial working class. The results of opinion polls can provide a picture of what issues are important to the electorate. Matching this with socioeconomic data can offer some indications of what determines current voting patterns in Britain. Crewe noted that, as unemployment increased under the Thatcher government, Labour should have been the natural beneficiary. Unemployment was of key concern to public opinion, as shown by MORI polls conducted between November 1982 and the General Election of June 1987. This data informs us that an average of 80 per cent of respondents placed unemployment as the highest priority. However, a combination of "apathy and fatalism" among the unemployed and those in insecure employment, coupled with a "profound scepticism that a Labour government would do much better in the short term", meant that Labour "lost the political argument".[56]

A similar case can be found on other issues of key public concern. In 1979 reducing the power of the trade unions was an issue that had wide support. As Labour was the "organ of the trade unions", public opinion was clearly weighted against the party. However, the shockwaves of the "winter of discontent" 1978–1979, when the nation was brought to a virtual standstill due to industrial unrest, were short-lived. Unemployment became the key issue but as the overall level fell it was soon equalled by another Labour tenet: the National Health Service (NHS). The only reason this was kept from the agenda in the prelude to the 1992 General Election was because the electorate also prioritized the economy. While Labour retained the image of offering a high taxation and high spending policy; in contrast the Conservatives were seen as prudent and responsible. It was only the economic recession following Britain's forced exit from the European Exchange Rate Mechanism on 16 September 1992, subsequently dubbed "Black Wednesday", that shattered this perception.[57] By 1996 the NHS became the public's top priority followed closely by education, Europe, law and order, unemployment, and the economy. Owing to the stability of the economy this issue received little attention and it was the aforementioned social-policy aspects that were prioritized by the Labour Party in the 1997 election campaign. These have remained key policy areas

meeting, those who voted against were a minority of the total employees so the pay increase of 1.5 per cent was passed without conflict. This information was gained informally through members of staff and union members. Empire Stores refused to pass any comment beyond the fact that a group of union members had held up the pay-review process which meant that no increase was awarded to employees for a year; this was publicized in the company newsletter to staff, undermining USDAW's position.

56. Crewe, "Labour Force Changes", p. 30.

57. H. Thompson, "Economic Policy under Thatcher and Major", in S. Ludlam and M.J. Smith, *Contemporary British Conservatism* (Basingstoke, 1996), pp. 180–183.

for the party and have been addressed while maintaining an image of economic competence.

The prioritization of collectivist concerns, particularly welfare and education, indicates that the politics of consumption are not as dominant now as they were ten years ago. However, polls also indicate that personal self-interest plays a significant role in voting. In June 2001, mirroring the voting patterns of the election 4 days later, a national opinion poll found that 44 per cent believed they would be "better off" under Labour, only 23 per cent responded Conservative while indicatively 26 per cent, close to the average figure who did not vote in the election, said neither party. In the same poll, 50 per cent of respondents stated that "none of the parties really represents me".[58] This shows that a significant section of the electorate were ambivalent about either of the major parties, sceptical regarding the importance of voting, and appeared to have rejected politics in favour of, as one non-voter argued, "getting on with my own life".[59] An ICM poll found that 45 per cent of respondents believed there was little difference between the Conservatives and Labour, while 57 per cent argued that the outcome of the election would not affect their daily lives.[60] Though there are several factors which are argued to have led to a low turnout in 2001,[61] one aspect is the fact that a significant section within the British electorate no longer feel any strong partisan tie to any political party. Furthermore, and more importantly, this section saw the election result as a foregone conclusion and neither saw a need to vote or cared about the consequences.

REALIGNMENT: MYTHS AND REALITIES

Voter apathy may indicate a significant dealignment of the electorate in general and particularly of the traditional working-class Labour voter who, it seems, has almost disappeared from the political landscape. However, to substantiate this conclusion we must revisit our definition of the modern working class. This group is almost impossible to classify in socioeconomic, political, or cultural terms. They are from various backgrounds, have vastly differing political allegiances and represent a cross-section of race and gender. They are also far less likely to hold the same job, or work for the same company, for much more than twelve months. This means that there is extreme fragmentation, that working people can no longer be mobilized as a coherent group and that they have a

58. NOP poll published for *The Sunday Times* (3 June 2001).
59. Quoted in the *Leicester Mercury* (2 June 2001).
60. *The Observer* (3 June 2001).
61. See P. Whiteley *et al.*, "Turnout", *Parliamentary Affairs*, 54 (2001), pp. 775–788.

very different view of community than their predecessors had during the 1960s.

Equally the working class are no longer a group in stasis. As Crewe observed, they enjoy: "greater social mobility [...] [and] internal migration".[62] No longer will the sons of miners automatically be drawn to follow in their father's footsteps. The meritocracy of Thatcherism has liberated the post-industrial working-class generation: they can now break their own shackles and some have moved into the "professional classes". Furthermore, they are no longer tied to the community and have to be geographically mobile within Britain. This has led to a drift away from the industrial heartlands and the close-knit communities where Labour enjoyed a substantial majority. This encourages a break from filial partisanship and the adoption of the ideas of a new community. All this was predicted to dealign the supporters of the Labour Party unless the party developed new strategies that would enable them to retrieve working-class support as well as drawing support from other classes.[63] This Labour seems to have done, updating many of the party's values in response to developments in both domestic and international politics and economics and in line with public opinion.[64] To some extent this has led to re-alignment, but also for some to reject politics completely.

The 2001 General Election saw Labour's majority retained. The Conservative Party made only two gains from Labour after attempting to run a populist electoral campaign. However, the real winner on 7 June 2001 was argued to be apathy. There are various reasons for this: that the election was a foregone conclusion, that there was little significant difference between the main parties, and that there was a lack of identification with the parties.[65] These factors, however, underline the fact that significant voter dealignment has taken place in the wake of de-industrialization. To some extent the two factors are linked: the breakdown of the working-class community that often worked and socialized together is one strong factor. More important though are the fragmentation of the working class in response to the post-Fordist production methods, and the growth of a large service sector. This has meant that the working class can no longer be mobilized as a coherent political actor, even within the regions where manufacturing is still the major source of employment. The significant alteration of the patterns of working means there are increased numbers of part-time workers, agency-employed

62. Crewe, "Labour Force Changes", p. 26.

63. *Ibid.*, pp. 36–46. Interviews with former Conservative MPs and losing Conservative candidates at the 2001 General Election draw similar conclusions about the Conservatives; this is also expressed in A. Seldon and P. Snowdon, *A New Conservative Century* (London, 2001).

64. J. Lees-Marshment and D. Lilleker, "Political Marketing and Traditional Values: 'Old Labour' for 'New Times'?", *Contemporary Politics*, 7 (2001), pp. 205–216.

65. Whiteley *et al.*, "Turnout", pp. 775–788.

workers, short-term contractors, and a high turnover of staff throughout the unskilled and semiskilled employment sectors, all of which emphasize fragmentation. Finally, there is an increased level of understanding of politics and economics, a factor which is worth some consideration.

The increased awareness of the effects of inflation, deflation, and recession on the ordinary person's budget is clearly a product of the Thatcher years. As Prime Minister 1979–1990, Margaret Thatcher recognized the importance of making the individual understand the economics of government and enforced upon the public "New-Right" ideas. While the ideology was not accepted universally, the introduction of this level of knowledge has made the electorate think carefully when choosing who should manage the economy. Party election broadcasts throughout the 1980s dwelt on the economic competence of both parties, with Labour suffering from having a weak record in economic policy. Black Wednesday, and the criticisms of the Major government by Labour leader John Smith and rising star Gordon Brown, restored public confidence in Labour. It is this confidence that now allows them to appear as the natural party of government; that is, until they make a mistake. Therefore, increasing insecurity and reliance on a strong economy means the electorate are increasingly forced to calculate which party will be the most economically competent. Overwhelmingly in both 1997 and 2001, Labour were able to assert this image. It appears then that the voter has realigned in favour of competence and stability, or using the terminology of the economist "utility and probability". Heath, Jowell, and Curtis (2001) argue that the electorate subconsciously "weights the utility of a given policy by the probability of its being implemented and sums this across the different policies".[66] The voters' calculations reflect their social status: housing tenure, union membership etc., but are dominated more by an equation that calculates which party will improve their personal economic circumstances, not by any sense of class loyalty. Party ideology, name, or persona may have little significance to the individual with an insecure job, a mortgage, an overdraft, and a family to support.

Does this mean that there are no longer any such phenomena as political alignment and partisanship? Using MORI polls on party identification as a measure, it would appear that there is currently a strong sense of identification with, on average, 40 per cent of respondents 1996–2001 reporting that they thought of themselves as "Labour voters". However, looking at polls going back to 1990 we see that in that year 42 per cent claimed to be Labour supporters but that this figure waned to 32 per cent by the 1992 General Election. By March 1993 the figure increased steadily

66. A.F. Heath, R.M. Jowell, and J.K. Curtis, *The Rise of New Labour: Party Policies and Voter Choices* (Oxford, 2001), p. 159.

to 38 per cent and maintained this level until it steadily increased 1996–1997 in time for the 1997 General Election. Troughs in support after 1997 coincided with the refinery blockade in protest against tax on fuel and the outbreak of foot-and-mouth disease, though Labour's lowest point was 34 per cent while the Conservatives could not muster more than 27 per cent. The main beneficiary during these troughs was the "none of these" or "no-party" response which increased from an average of 10 per cent from 1993 to 1997 to 16 per cent in May 2001.[67] This tells us that party identification is highly volatile and more dependent upon perceptions of competence than loyalty or class-consciousness.

But what of the other sections of society: those who are unemployed, who retain class loyalties and a contiguous partisanship to the Left. It would seem that some have rejected the Labour model and have elected to support other left-wing political groupings. Both the Socialist Alliance, the major left-wing electoral alternative to Labour, and the Socialist Worker's Party (SWP), a Marxist revolutionary party, claim to enjoy a substantial level of working-class support. The SWP has been prominent in many anticapitalist demonstrations as well as supporting the pay claims of various public-sector workers. This has gained them some trade-union sponsorship. However, SWP activists are predominantly intellectuals, often within the education sector, while their volunteers tend to be unemployed. Furthermore, the SWP refuse to take part in elections and therefore their support is difficult to measure.[68]

Electorally, the Left appears to be in disarray. Dave Nellist, former Labour Member of Parliament, and local councillor representing the Socialist Alliance in Coventry, gained only 2,638 votes, though this was 7 per cent of those who voted. Elsewhere, left-wing luminary and former leader of the National Union of Mineworkers (NUM), Arthur Scargill, gained only 912 votes, 2.4 per cent of the turnout, in the former NUM heartland of Hartlepool, and the average result for a Socialist candidate was 1,500 votes or 5 per cent of the turnout. We could conclude that a 5 per cent swing to non-Labour left-wing political parties is significant, and that many of those who did not vote may also have voted for these parties but refused to do so in the belief that they had little chance of winning. However, there is little evidence to substantiate these claims. In many constituencies the Left appeared extremely fragmented, with Socialist Alliance, Communist Party, Socialist Alternative, and Socialist Labour

67. Archives of MORI polls can be obtained from the Nuffield College, Oxford website: http://www.nuff.ox.ac.uk/library/statistics.shtml

68. Two interviews with SWP workers were carried out: they gave an interesting picture of their membership but were unable to provide any figures. Their annual event, the Marxism Conference, held at the University of London campus, attracts around 7,000–8,000 delegates from a cross-section of society. In a survey of socioeconomic status, carried out at the 2001 event, students were massively over-represented however.

candidates fighting each other for a very small proportion of the electorate. In Aberavon, the Socialist Alliance candidate found himself last, beaten by a Mr Tutton standing as a "rate payer" and the "joke" candidate representing the "New Millennium Bean" party. Even in Scotland, where the Scottish Socialist Party is established and nationally known, the picture is identical. Only right-wing neofascist National Front and British National Party (BNP) candidates made advances against the stranglehold of the major three parties. But the BNP gains of 16 per cent of the turnout in two constituencies in Oldham, in the heart of the former industrial area of Greater Manchester, was a reflection of long-standing conflicts between the White and Asian-English communities which had become inflamed in the months prior to the 2001 election.

CONCLUSIONS

Class partisanship has never been a clear-cut, definable phenomena in Britain. Voters make their choices based upon a range of factors, but personal interest has often been a more serious consideration than class-consciousness. As de-industrialization altered the shape of British society, Labour appeared initially unable to offer a credible response and personal economic circumstances, and the perception that the Conservatives offered the working class a better standard of living, predominated. Thus, filial ties to the Labour Party were weakened. Since 1997, it appears that the majority of the working class do vote Labour, but respondents to opinion polls seldom argue that they do so because they are obliged to out of a sense of class loyalty. It is arguably the case that without surveying every individual voter who holds working-class credentials it is impossible to quantify how the working class votes, or whether any partisan identity remains among those who can be classified as working-class. This is perhaps the central conclusion of this paper. The post-industrial working class is fragmented: it lacks a clear political or class identity and is dominated by self-interest rather than class-consciousness. Therefore, each individual will have a personal reason for voting and class-consciousness holds little significance. As Wright argued "people" have replaced "class" as the integer of politics, and concerns can be identified more with race and gender than by socioeconomic classifications. Though some group activism is engaged in, this represents postmodern social movements: voting is influenced more by personal aspirations and beliefs than group identity. But how far is this different to the working class of previous decades?

Various periods within the nineteenth and twentieth centuries witnessed the working-class acting in unison, a feature of the centralized production methods of mining and the steel industry. However, despite this image of unity and class solidarity, the members often fought for personal gains.

Working-class solidarity may have been the battle-cry of the strike leader but many individual workers sought pay increases and job security on a personal basis as well as in the name of the community. The inequalities that led classes, or sections of a class, to mobilize still exist; it is the mobilization structures and the loci of working-class activities that have been eroded. This has not occurred, as Goldthorpe argued, because "class inequalities of condition and opportunity progressively diminish",[69] but because the inequalities in the modern world are not faced by any one single class. They cut across classes, and are now the terrain of groups who can be more accurately defined in terms of race, gender, age, education, skills, and experience. These factors also shape the individual's consciousness to a far greater extent than notions of social status. Using socioeconomic stratification measures, a large working class still exists. They work in alienating conditions and face obstacles in moving above that socioeconomic status, though this group can no longer be characterized as white male manual workers who think of themselves as working-class. The post-Fordist, post-industrial working class is a far more disparate animal.

The most marked changes are: the reduction in the power of the working class and the decline in class identity; a change in the composition of those employed in the lowest paid, labour-intensive occupational sectors; the fragmentation of trade-union membership; and a degree of acquiescence or political apathy among all but a militant minority. All of this is reinforced by increased affluence in a consumerist society. The culture of acquisition distracts the worker from the alienating conditions of production by providing an end product for their labours: the car, television, DVD player etc. have become of greater symbolic value than class unity or party politics. Labour's failure to provide economic benefits led those classified as affluent workers to vote Conservative in increasing numbers in order to protect their standard of living; thus, Labour have had to become a party of the centre ground, representing the aspirant while claiming to also protect the deprived.

It is those who we can characterize as the "deprived", or in New-Labour terms the "socially excluded", that represent the most interesting section of the British electorate. This section of society feels keenly the need for political representation and workplace activism. However, in reality these individuals have largely become marginalized and consequently are apathetic to the political process. In many ways it seems these people share a collective memory of mass unemployment and its effects upon local communities. As Bagguley argues "in some localities there were powerful organizational and cultural resources for the unemployed to draw upon". But as the larger trade unions had their powers curbed and

69. P. Mair, S. Lipset, M. Hout, and J. Goldthorpe, "Critical Commentary: Four Perspectives on the End of Class Politics", in Evans, *The End of Class*, p. 320.

saw their membership decline, while communist parties and workers' cooperative societies became unable to sustain themselves financially, such institutions disappeared. This resulted in "a shift in political response amongst the unemployed from protest to acquiescence".[70] The left-wing organizations failed to attract the unemployed or those in unstable employment because they lacked credibility and could muster no more than 2,638 votes at elections; thus perhaps socialism is dead after all. Apathy appears to have been the real beneficiary of dealigned working-class voters, a factor that could indicate complete dealignment without any form of realignment. Calls for tactical voting,[71] the similarity between the major parties, and the growth of personality politics have all been highlighted as reasons why the electorate was "turned off" in 2001. However, the lack of credible working-class representation, the position put forward by the Socialist Alliance, could also be a legitimate hypothesis. Among the respondents who claimed all the parties were similar were a subgroup who argued that none spoke "their language", that all the parties "represented business not people", and that "balancing the budget meant more than doing what the people wanted". This is disaffection and dealignment of a serious nature. These respondents not only did not vote for their traditional party but rejected the democratic process completely. Some did opt to vote for marginal parties: in the most obvious case it was the neofascist British National Party that benefited. Others it seems stayed at home and watched the election as a foregone conclusion. As one worker put it, "it didn't matter how you voted, you knew a bloody politician would get in".

70. P. Bagguley, *From Protest to Acquiescence: Political Movements of the Unemployed* (London, 1991), p. 203.

71. The tactic whereby Labour voters will vote Liberal Democrat if the combined Labour and Liberal Democrat vote would defeat the incumbent Conservative was first used in 1997 when Liberal Democrats urged their supporters to vote Labour in order to remove the Conservatives from office. In 2001 tactical voting was mainly promoted by Liberal Democrats in marginal constituencies where the anti-Conservative vote was divided between Labour and the Liberal Democrats, but was also suggested, more surreptitiously, by Labour canvassers in key marginal constituencies, though the tactic was condemned by the Labour leadership.

IRSH 47 (2002), pp. 87–111 DOI: 10.1017/S0020859002000792

Betterment without Airs: Social, Cultural, and Political Consequences of De-industrialization in the Ruhr

Stefan Goch

At one time, the region of the Ruhr[1] was one of the most important areas for coal, iron, and steel production in Europe. This is no longer the case. The once abundant production of coal and steel found in this region is steadily dwindling, and what remains of the industry can fairly be considered antiquated.[2] On the whole, the region has already undergone economic structural change, although some problems connected with it still need to be resolved. A few abandoned industrial areas need to be redeveloped and not all economic structures in the region are trend-setting; there are deficits in the infrastructure, such as in the transportation system; and the level of unemployment is clearly above the average of the Federal Republic of Germany (FRG) and of the *Land* North Rhine-Westphalia (NRW). In light of the degree to which industrial jobs have been lost, the region has survived structural change better than other old industrial regions, albeit with an obvious variation in the rate of success within the region.

Iron and steel regions like that of the Ruhr also once exhibited distinct

1. The Ruhr region is understood here to be the area of the Kommunalverbandes Ruhrgebiet [hereafter, KVR: Communal Association of the Ruhr]. This includes the district cities of Bochum, Bottrop, Dortmund, Duisburg, Essen, Gelsenkirchen, Hagen, Hamm, Herne, Mülheim an der Ruhr, Oberhausen and the districts Ennepe-Ruhr, Recklinghausen, Unna and Wesel. In this region of 52 independent communities with an area of 4,433 square kilometres approximately 5.3 million people currently live. For a history of this regional institution in the otherwise administratively rather fractured region, see Andreas Benedict, *80 Jahre im Dienste des Ruhrgebiets: Siedlungsverband Ruhrkohlenbezirk (SVR) und Kommunalverband Ruhrgebiet (KVR) im historischen Überblick 1920–2000* (Essen, 2000).

2. See my evaluation of structural change in the Ruhr as a success story, with several exceptions naturally: Stefan Goch, "Strukturwandel im Ruhrgebiet: Eine Erfolgsgeschichte?", *Mitteilungsblatt des Instituts zur Erforschung der europäischen Arbeiterbewegung*, 22 (1999), pp. 159–190; appearing earlier, *idem*, "Politik zur ökonomischen, sozialen und ökologischen Bewältigung des Strukturwandels im Ruhrgebiet: Ein Überblick", in Rainer Bovermann *et al.* (eds), *Das Ruhrgebiet – ein starkes Stück Nordrhein-Westfalen: Politik in der Region 1946–1996* (Essen, 1996), pp. 380–426; and Stefan Goch, "Strukturpolitik als Lernprozeß", in Karsten Rudolph *et al.* (eds), *Reform an Rhein und Ruhr: Nordrhein-Westfalens Weg ins 21. Jahrhundert* (Bonn, 2000), pp. 26–35. My most recent and extensive work on this topic is: Stefan Goch, *Eine Region im Kampf mit dem Strukturwandel: Strukturpolitik und Bewältigung von Strukturwandel im Ruhrgebiet* (Essen, 2001).

social and political-cultural characteristics: a labour force with an exceptionally high degree of relative homogeneity, middle and upper classes that were complementarily small, a close connection between the areas of production and reproduction, an authoritarian factory structure that extended even into leisure activities, male dominance, a modest degree of employment among women that represented nearly the opposite of large rural families, poor educational opportunities in an insufficiently urbanized environment, a sharp distinction by the masses of workers from "the bigwigs upstairs" including the white-collar employees, and a relatively intensive degree of state intervention based on the importance attributed traditionally to mining and later also to the new heavy industries.

What impact did the economic structural change have on social and political-cultural structures in the region, on the attitudes and behaviour of people in an area that had been previously influenced overwhelmingly by the coal, iron, and steel industry? And did an (endogenous) potential exist among regional actors and in the regional political culture that would enable the region and its inhabitants to experience a relatively peaceful and successful structural change with only a small amount of social friction – instead of decline, was this a slow (re-)ascent, albeit not a soaring flight?

Whereas the economic dimensions of structural change were constantly discussed, certain other dimensions only became evident with time, needed more time to be even recognized, and are now being rather hesitantly addressed in social-history research. These were the social and cultural, particularly political-cultural, dimensions that arose with de-industrialization, the change and diversification of the economic structure, the emergence of service industries, the production of knowledge, and the accompanying pluralization of the working world and life in general. This explains why to date there are no long-term studies on the social structure of the Ruhr[3] that extend to the present day, just as there are, for example, none on the history of education in the region – where opportunities to attend advanced institutions of learning only became available to the public at large during the 1960s – or studies on individual professions and occupational groups. Against the backdrop of the special political influence that social democracy has had on the Ruhr for decades, important research findings on the region's political culture have been presented that

3. One exception is Klaus Tenfelde, "Soziale Schichtung: Klassenbildung und Konfliktlagen im Ruhrgebiet", in Wolfgang Köllmann *et al.* (eds), *Das Ruhrgebiet im Industriezeitalter: Geschichte und Entwicklung*, 2 vols (Düsseldorf, 1990), vol. 1, pp. 121–217. Also, Klaus Tenfelde, "Gesellschaft im Wohlfahrtsstaat – Schichten, Klassen und Konflikte", in Karl Teppe *et al.* (eds), *50 Jahre Nordrhein-Westfalen: Land im Wandel* (Münster, 1997), pp. 23–42; Klaus Tenfelde, "Das Ruhrgebiet und Nordrhein-Westfalen: Das Land und die Industrieregion im Strukturwandel der Nachkriegszeit", in Jan-Pieter Barbian *et al.* (eds), *Die Entdeckung des Ruhrgebiets: Das Ruhrgebiet in Nordrhein-Westfalen 1946–1996* (Essen, 1997), pp. 28–38.

begin to examine social change.[4] Although the initial studies in the contemporary history of the Federal Republic as a whole were in political history, research has now begun to turn more attention to its social history.[5]

Because the scope of such research is still rather limited, it is only possible at this point to present the important developmental trends in the social and political culture of the Ruhr that have occurred as a result of structural change. What has become clear is that the Ruhr – which was once a region dominated by the coal, iron, and steel industry and now, after roughly forty years of structural change, a "completely normal" region featuring a range of industries and services – still has its particularities, that the people in the region will long be affected by their historical experiences, and that the experiences of change and of adaptation to it will continue to influence the region and its people.

THE DIMENSIONS OF ECONOMIC STRUCTURAL CHANGE IN THE RUHR REGION

As the heartland of heavy industry in West Germany, North Rhine-Westphalia generated 40 per cent of the industrial production in the Federal Republic in 1951, even though production levels had not yet reached those prior to the Second World War because of extensive destruction, the lack of permits, or the dismantling of factories. Ninety per cent of the coal mined and 80 per cent of the iron and steel produced in the Federal Republic came from NRW. Whereas about 35 per cent of the labour force in West Germany as a whole were employed in crafts and industry in 1950, the figure equalled about 50 per cent in the Ruhr region. With regard to its social structure, the Ruhr was "the" proletarian region of the Federal Republic, since 66 per cent of its labour force were workers as opposed to the national average of 50 per cent (white-collar employees: 22 to 23 per cent).[6]

4. For a survey of the political development, see Bovermann *et al.*, *Das Ruhrgebiet*; especially on the history of economic development, see Köllmann *et al.*, *Das Ruhrgebiet im Industriezeitalter*.
5. See this research report: Stefan Goch, "Deutschlands Erfolgsweg? Forschungsbericht zu neueren Darstellungen der Entwicklung der Bundesrepublik Deutschland", *Archiv für Sozialgeschichte*, 41 (2001), pp. 633–662.
6. Werner Plumpe, "Das 'Arbeitshaus' des neuen Staates? Die wirtschaftliche und wirtschaftspolitische Bedeutung Nordrhein-Westfalens für die Bundesrepublik zwischen 1946 und 1955", in Landeszentrale für politische Bildung Nordrhein-Westfalen (ed.), *Der schwierige Weg zur Demokratie: Die Bundesrepublik vor 40 Jahren* (Düsseldorf, 1990), p. 253; Anselm Faust, "Das Schwungrad des Wiederaufbaus: Die Wirtschaft an Rhein und Ruhr", in Nordrhein-Westfälisches Hauptstaatsarchiv (ed.), *Nordrhein-Westfalen: Kernland der Bundesrepublik* (Siegburg, 1989), pp. 95f. A general account is found in Walther Däbritz, "Das Ruhrgebiet: Geschichtliche Tatsachen und Gegenwartsprobleme", in Institut für Raumordnung (ed.), *Ordnung und Planung im Ruhr-Raum: Tatsachen und Aufgaben* (Dortmund, 1951), pp. 11–21.

When the first short-time shifts occurred in Ruhr mining on 22 February 1958, there were 136 mines in operation that employed 488,941 people. Forty years later, in 1998, only 13 mines existed, providing about 60,000 jobs.[7] In the iron industry of North Rhine-Westphalia, the number of jobs, most of which were located in the Ruhr, sank from 219,000 in 1958 to 154,000 in 1987 and, following another round of drastic job cuts, dropped to 85,000 in 1994. Currently the figure is 60,000.[8] The loss of jobs in the core operations of the coal and steel industry was accompanied by a simultaneous loss in dependent branches of industry. In NRW, producing industries lost 1.5 million jobs between 1961 and 1987, and since then another 500,000 jobs have disappeared.[9] Despite this, the Ruhr generally kept pace with NRW and FRG trends in the rate of registered unemployment after the crisis of the coal, iron, and steel industry began. However, the actual level of unemployment was always higher. Economic crises hit harder and lasted longer in the coal-mining region. Therefore, the labour-exchange districts of the Ruhr always topped the unemployment statistics, although their figures deviated considerably from one another once West Germany's "economic miracle" finally ended around 1974.[10]

The Ruhr not only suffered from the shrinking of a major sector of industry, but also from the fact that the entire structure of production, as had developed over time, was being effected by structural change. Already in the 1950s, production growth lagged behind that of the Federal Republic as a whole. This can be attributed to the rebuilding of the traditional industrial structure of the Ruhr and its relative weak growth during the reconstruction period after the Second World War, whereas other regions

7. Joachim Huske, *Die Steinkohlenzechen im Ruhrrevier: Daten und Fakten von den Anfängen bis 1997* (Bochum, 1998), 2nd edn, pp. 34ff.; and current information of the RAG.

8. Ministerium für Wirtschaft, Mittelstand und Technologie des Landes Nordrhein-Westfalen [hereafter, MWMT], *Bericht der Kommission Montanregionen des Landes Nordrhein-Westfalen* (Düsseldorf, 1989), pp. 238f., 246ff.; *NRW-Lexikon: Politik, Gesellschaft, Wirtschaft, Recht, Kultur* (Opladen, 1996), pp. 23, 55, 255, 261.

9. MWMT, *Bericht der Kommission Montanregionen*, pp. 238f., 246ff.; Wolfgang Köllmann *et al.*, "Bevölkerungsgeschichte", in Köllmann, *Das Ruhrgebiet im Industriezeitalter*, vol. 1, p. 191; Rolf G. Heinze *et al.*, "Entwicklungen und Perspektiven industrieller Produktion in Nordrhein-Westfalen", in Rolf G. Heinze *et al.*, *Strukturwandel und Strukturpolitik in Nordrhein-Westfalen: Entwicklungstends und Forschungsperspektiven* (Opladen, 1992), p. 40; Dietmar Petzina, "Zwischen Neuordnung und Krise: Zur Entwicklung der Eisen- und Stahlindustrie im Ruhrgebiet seit dem Zweiten Weltkrieg", in Ottfried Dascher *et al.* (eds), *Die Eisen- und Stahlindustrie im Dortmunder Raum: Wirtschaftliche Entwicklung, soziale Strukturen und technologischer Wandel im 19. und 20. Jahrhundert* (Dortmund, 1992), p. 540; Dietmar Petzina, "Wirtschaft und Arbeit im Ruhrgebiet 1945 bis 1985", in Köllmann, *Das Ruhrgebiet im Industriezeitalter*, vol. 1, p. 539. See Karl Lauschke, *Schwarze Fahnen an der Ruhr: Die Politik der IG Bergbau und Energie während der Kohlekrise 1958–1968* (Marburg, 1984), p. 2; *NRW-Lexikon*, pp. 23, 55, 255, 261.

10. See Andreas Gallas, "Arbeitsmarktpolitik im Ruhrgebiet", in Bovermann *et al.*, *Das Ruhrgebiet*, pp. 428f.

Table 1. *Breakdown by economic sector in % of those employed and unemployment rates.*

	Agriculture and forestry			Producing sector			Service sector			Unemployment rate		
	KVR	NRW	FRG	KVR	NRW	FRG	KVR	NRW	FRG	KVR	NRW	FRG West
1950	4.5	11.7	23.3	63.4	55.1	43.3	32.1	33.2	33.4		4.8	10.3
1961	2.4	6.4	13.6	61.3	56.4	47.6	36.3	37.2	38.8		0.4	0.5
1970	1.5	4.3	9.1	58.4	55.7	49.4	40	40.1	41.5	0.6	0.5	0.5
1980	1.4	2.5	5.3	51.7	48.4	45.3	47	49.2	49.4	5.3	4.4	3.5
1990	1.2	2.2	3.6	44.4	42.5	40.6	54.4	55.3	55.8	10.8	8.4	6.6
2000	1.2	1.7	2.5	33.3	33.5	33.5	65.4	64.9	64.0	12.2	9.5	8.1

Compiled according to the statistics on the cities and districts of the KVR and Statistical Yearbooks of NRW and FRG. Starting in 1991, the FRG is as given in the territorial survey from 3 October 1990.
Sources: Charge of KVR territory 1975.

were experiencing a catch-up effect or surge of development at the time. The weak rate of growth was caused in turn by factors such as substitution processes and the diminishing demand for raw materials and production goods. The branches of industry responsible for the underdevelopment of the Ruhr in comparison with the average FRG (and the average NRW) development were also those that were either growing or maintaining their employment levels in other regions. Overall, the other branches in the region grew at a rate below the FRG level because of their connections to old industry. The differences in development between regions within the Federal Republic, particularly between the Ruhr and other regions were the fundamental result of parallel trends in development. The decline of the secondary sector merely hit the Ruhr, with its coal, iron, and steel industry and its other producing sectors, much harder.[11]

Structural change in the Ruhr was supported through an active structural and regional policy implemented at the various political levels (community, regional actors, NRW, federal, EU) but particularly at the NRW level. Whereas in 1970 58 per cent of those employed (1,285,700) were still working in industrial production, 20 years later this figure was only 44 per cent (963,500), while the share of those employed in the service sector rose from 40 per cent (881,100) to 54 per cent (1,180,600). Just in the 1980s alone, a total of 210,000 new jobs were created in the service sector.[12] The sectoral structure of the region currently corresponds closely with that of the Federal Republic as a whole. Still, there are several cases where the Ruhr lags behind in the development of various economic sectors and branches, especially in the area of production-oriented and highly specialized (consulting) services.[13] With its relatively high rate of

11. MWMT, *Bericht der Kommission Montanregionen*, p. 254. See the contributions in Willi Lamberts (ed.), *Nordrhein-Westfalen in der Krise: Krise in Nordrhein-Westfalen* (Berlin, 1985), pp. 7–37; Dietmar Petzina, "The Ruhr Area: Historical Development", in Joachim Jens Hesse (ed.), *Die Erneuerung alter Industrieregionen: Ökonomischer Strukturwandel und Regionalpolitik im internationalen Vergleich* (Baden-Baden, 1988), pp. 496ff.; Petzina, "Wirtschaft und Arbeit", pp. 544, 564f.; Rolf G. Heinze *et al.*, "Industrial Clusters and the Governance of Change: Lessons from North Rhine-Westphalia (NRW)", in Hans-Joachim Braczyk *et al.* (eds), *Regional Innovation Systems: The Role of Governance in a Globalized World* (London, 1998), pp. 263ff.; Dieter Läpple, "Zwischen gestern und übermorgen: Das Ruhrgebiet – eine Industrieregion im Umbruch", in Rolf Kreibich *et al.* (eds), *Bauplatz Zukunft: Dispute über die Entwicklung von Industrieregionen* (Essen, 1994), pp. 37ff.

12. KVR, Initiativkreis Ruhrgebiet (eds), *The Ruhr: The Driving Force of Germany – An Investors' Guide* (Essen, 1992), pp. 25f.; Jürgen Aring *et al.*, *Krisenregion Ruhrgebiet? Alltag, Strukturwandel und Planung* (Oldenburg, 1989), pp. 67f. Concerning these trends, see also MWMT (ed.), *Strukturwandel in Nordrhein-Westfalen: Entwicklung und Perspektiven des Dienstleistungssektors* (Düsseldorf, 1988), pp. 29 and 29–39 on the type of services.

13. Empirical reference: KVR (ed.), *Kleine und mittlere Betriebe im Ruhrgebiet: Bestand, Struktur und Entwicklung im Vergleich zu anderen westdeutschen Verdichtungsräumen zwischen den Jahren 1980 und 1993* (Essen, 1996), pp. 97–119. See Klaus Brake, *Dienstleistungen und regionale Entwicklung: Eine empirische Untersuchung* (Oldenburg, 1993), pp. 11, 87f.

unemployment, the Ruhr has become a "normal" area of agglomeration with regard to its economic structure – a place almost like any other. The Ruhr is no longer a monostructural region for the coal, iron, and steel industry; instead, it has become a highly diversified, and thereby less crisis-prone, economic region with coal mining and steel production. New, important, and (according to all current evaluations) promising economic activities have been established there. Various networks of new production lines, products, and processes have arisen around the "old" industries of coal, iron and steel, chemicals, and energy. Throughout the process of structural change over the decades, the actors in the Ruhr have been repeatedly successful in mobilizing means used to cushion the resulting blows of economic change to the social structure. As a result, structural change has taken place with relatively little disruption, and no-one belonging to the core work force of Ruhr mining and the iron and steel industry has "landed on the street".

The most critical factor contributing to the success of the economic restructuring policy in and for the Ruhr region was an ability developed early in the process among all relevant actors to cooperate despite diverging interests, and especially to remain undeterred by the boundaries of institutional fragmentation in the political system. Whereas, on the one hand, large sums of public funds were appropriated for social cushions, and on the other the losses suffered by private business and the resulting damage in the region were subsidized by the government, local communities and the NRW government in particular overcame their limited avenues for action by mediating and organizing cooperation, by treating it almost as an immaterial resource. The political actors were benefited by the fact that the coal, iron, and steel industries had a long history of cooperation and tripartisanship, a history that included both the experience of failed cooperation in the Weimar Republic and of renewed cooperation in the era following the fall of National Socialism. In the unique situation of the early postwar period, codetermination[14] was introduced as a special form of industrial relations to the coal, iron, and steel industry, which continued to develop into a specific culture of participation at factory, entrepreneurial, and regional levels. Various forms of cooperative or corporatist policy were the source of major procedural

14. Gabriele Müller-List, *Montanmitbestimmung, Das Gesetz über die Mitbestimmung der Arbeitnehmer in den Aufsichtsräten und Vorständen der Unternehmen des Bergbaus und der Eisen und Stahl erzeugenden Industrie vom 21. Mai 1951* (Düsseldorf, 1984); *idem, Neubeginn bei Eisen und Stahl im Ruhrgebiet, Die Beziehungen zwischen Arbeitgebern und Arbeitnehmern in der nordrhein-westfälischen Eisen- und Stahlindustrie 1945–1948* (Düsseldorf, 1990); Norbert Ranft, *Vom Objekt zum Subjekt, Montanmitbestimmung, Sozialklima und Strukturwandel im Bergbau seit 1945* (Cologne, 1988); Gloria Müller, *Strukturwandel und Arbeitnehmerrechte, Die wirtschaftliche Mitbestimmung in der Eisen- und Stahlindustrie 1945–1975* (Essen, 1991).

innovation in structural policy efforts and involved numerous regional actors in coping with structural change. Not only did this achieve social peace, but to a limited degree diverging interests were articulated and considered, and common solutions to problems were worked out.[15] Despite the economic structural crisis, and with the help of social cushions for many, it was possible within this fabric of cooperation to weave together at least intergenerational structural change with processes of upward mobility.

ADAPTATION TO DEMOGRAPHIC DEVELOPMENT

Together with the economic structural change and particularly the disappearance of the structures inherent in the coal, iron, and steel industry, the old social configurations also faded. At first this meant adapting to the general demographic trends associated with the transition to a shrinking and ageing society, which were most evident in the disappearance of old family structures. Such major developmental trends included the increase of female employment, a drop in the marriage rate, decreasing numbers of children, and an increase in the divorce rate. In place of the poor prospects facing families dependent on the coal, iron, and steel industry, especially women, and families with large numbers of children, came some hope of prosperity with the advent of smaller families and the emergence of new forms of cohabitation and living alone. As early as the 1960s, the demographic constellation of the Ruhr matched that of the average big city with regard to population.[16] Independent of regional influences, the number of children sank in concurrence with other general developmental trends, such as decreasing church membership, increased educational training, and the development of consumer society. As was common in big cities and metropolitan areas, a continuing diversity in private lifestyles followed on the heels of the demographic development, the general improvement of living standards also for employees, and the social diversification.[17] The pluralization of lifestyles also in the Ruhr region, has become quite extensive, as is seen, for example, with regard to establishing a family:

> It is no longer clear whether one marries, when one marries, whether one lives with someone and does not marry, marries and does not live with that person, whether one conceives or raises a child in or out of wedlock, with the person

15. Summarized in Goch, *Eine Region*, pp. 476–498.
16. Tenfelde, "Soziale Schichtung", pp. 154–167, 179; *idem*, "Das Ruhrgebiet", pp. 29ff. Also, *idem*, *Die "neue Mitte" im Ruhrgebiet: Sozialstruktur und Vergesellschaftung in der Nachkriegszeit*, lecture for the Gesellschaft der Freunde der Ruhr-Universität Bochum e.V., 14 June 2000.
17. See for example the insightful essay by Ulrich Beck *et al.*, *Eigenes Leben: Ausflüge in die unbekannte Gesellschaft, in der wir leben* (Munich, 1995).

> with whom one lives or with the person whom one loves but who lives with someone else, before or after having a career or in the midst of one.[18]

One residual characteristic of the region is the low percentage of homeowners compared with both the averages of North Rhine-Westphalia and the Federal Republic.

The decrease in the number of children per family and the vanishing of semi-open family structures,[19] starting in the 1920s, meant that families could pay greater attention to the welfare of their children. The improvement of living standards and several measures of the extended welfare state enabled more people to begin to plan their lives and to take advantage of the educational opportunities being offered. In turn, more people became upwardly mobile or at least could choose an occupation different from that of their parents.

THE RISE OF THE NEW MIDDLE CLASSES IN THE RUHR

Economic structural change and the changes in production processes linked to it were foremost responsible for the obvious changes that occurred in society, particularly in the social structures. While the percentage of workers in the labour force stagnated and then dwindled, the percentage of white-collar employees increased.[20] Overall, in this formerly proletarian region, we see an expansion of the social groups that are rather imprecisely labelled the middle classes.

Originally, the size of bourgeoisie in the Ruhr was rather insubstantial. This region of coal, iron, and steel was dominated by heavy industry and its industrialists. What few middle-class groups existed were primarily involved in crafts, trade, or the poorly developed service sector that was dependent on industry or the working class. Furthermore, the demand for people in professions was rather limited. In the coal, iron, and steel industry, there was but a small middle-management group comprised of foremen and overseers. Until the phase of catch-up urbanization started in the 1920s, there were also very few civil servants in the region. Following a verdict by the German emperor, no military forces were stationed in the

18. Ulrich Beck, *Risikogesellschaft: Auf dem Weg in eine andere Moderne* (Frankfurt am Main, 1986), pp. 163f. Translated into English for this article.

19. Franz-Josef Brüggemeier *et al.*, "Schlafgänger, Schnapskasinos und schwerindustrielle Kolonie: Aspekte der Arbeiterwohnungsfrage im Ruhrgebiet vor dem Ersten Weltkrieg", in Jürgen Reulecke *et al.* (eds), *Fabrik, Familie, Feierabend: Beiträge zur Sozialgeschichte des Alltags im Industriezeitalter* (Wuppertal, 1978), pp. 139–172; Lutz Niethammer *et al.*, "Wie wohnten Arbeiter im Kaiserreich?", *Archiv für Sozialgeschichte*, 16 (1976), pp. 61–134; Stephen H.F. Hickey, *Workers in Imperial Germany: The Miners of the Ruhr* (Oxford, 1985), pp. 48ff.

20. Werner Plumpe, "Das Ende der Koloniezeit: Gedanken zur Sozial- und Wirtschaftsgeschichte des Ruhrgebietes in den 50er und frühen 60er Jahren", in Barbian *et al.*, *Die Entdeckung des Ruhrgebiets*, pp. 153f.

Ruhr, which could have been incited by the working masses. Universities were also not planned for the working class, thus making academics and scholars a rarity in the region.[21]

With economic structural change emerged a large salaried class. The employment structure changed in the wake of the regional restructuring, specifically the overall modernization of production processes, the increasing influence of the service sector as a whole, and the obvious expansion of government involvement in the 1960s and 1970s. In addition to the trend toward greater expansion of the public sector evident across the entire FRG, the Ruhr sought to catch up with the rest of the country, for example in communal administration, welfare institutions, and the entire educational system. Since the Ruhr is primarily administered "from outside", the region still lacks today other major administrative institutions, the jobs that these would provide, and consequently the labour force with the necessary qualifications and influences. On the whole, however, the number of white-collar employees grew rapidly in the old working-class region. As early as 1970, the percentage of workers among the total employed population dropped below the 50 per cent mark. The share of professionals in the population reached a level typical for the rest of NRW, and in connection with the expansion of the educational system, the personnel of educational institutions constituted an important percentage of the growing middle classes.[22]

More women entered the workforce, and many but not all of them found white-collar jobs especially in the service sector. As a result, the below-average percentage of employed women slowly began to rise. With the advent of structural change, and to a degree in the early postwar period, jobs for women opened up, for example, in light industries, in the newly built plants for electronics, temporarily in the textile industry, and especially in the service sector. Often women first began to work in order to afford the amenities offered by a growing supply of consumer goods. At the same time, women were "discovered" as a reservoir of labour, particularly in the service sector. Employment offered women another type of access to life outside the realm of the family, which constituted nothing less than a cultural break with the patriarchal society of heavy

21. As a case study on change in the urban bourgeoisie, see Karin Schambach, *Stadtbürgertum und industrieller Umbruch: Dortmund 1780–1870* (Munich, 1996). Also, e.g. Tenfelde, *Die "neue Mitte"*. On the neglect of education in the region, see Kurt H. Biedenkopf, "25 Jahre Ruhr-Universität: erfüllte und nichterfüllte Reformerwartungen", in Burkhard Dietz *et al.* (eds), *Universität und Politik: Festschrift zum 25-jährigen Bestehen der Ruhr-Universität Bochum* (Bochum, 1990), pp. 295f.; Rolf-Dieter Volmerig, "Hochschulen im Ruhrgebiet: Entwicklung – Funktion – Transfer", in Heiner Dürr *et al.* (eds), *Erneuerung des Ruhrgebiets: Regionales Erbe und Gestaltung für die Zukunft* (Paderborn, 1993), p. 94. See Ulrich von Alemann *et al.*, *Nordrhein-Westfalen: Ein Land entdeckt sich neu* (Stuttgart, 2000), p. 200.

22. Tenfelde, "Soziale Schichtung", p. 176. Tenfelde, *Die "neue Mitte"*, examined the number of medical doctors and of teachers in relation to the population of the Ruhr.

industrial workers.[23] Starting in the late 1950s, the technical breakthroughs in household appliances and new eating habits introduced by the consumer society changed housework and made it possible for many more women to work, a development with far-reaching, as yet insufficiently studied consequences for both family life and society.[24]

Because these "new" employees very often originated from the working class, social distance in the industrial plants between workers and their supervisors did not develop to the degree it had in earlier times. As the old, authoritarian managers and white-collar workers of the coal, iron, and steel industry left the labour force, the working class as a whole became more skilled, and the previously small group of salaried employees grew correspondingly; the labour force became more homogeneous and the authoritarian style of management was replaced with more cooperative behaviour.[25] While being rocked by major structural change economically, the region experienced less social distancing during the metamorphosis of its social structure because people in the region quickly learned that blue-collar workers and white-collar employees could only be successful in defending their interests in an jeopardized industrial region if they worked together. Many mining employees who were no longer members of a separate union turned to the nonpartisan industry-based union, just as did a similarly large number of employees in the iron and steel industry.[26] This also contributed to the further diminishing of distancing. Since consensus-oriented forms of structural policy were implemented to handle structural change in the region, a trend emerged among white-collar employees and

23. Ingrid N. Sommerkorn, "Die erwerbstätige Mutter in der Bundesrepublik: Einstellungs- und Problemveränderungen", in Rosemarie Nave-Herz (ed.), *Wandel und Kontinuität der Familie in der Bundesrepublik Deutschland* (Stuttgart, 1988), pp. 115–144; Robert G. Moeller, *Geschützte Mütter: Frauen und Familien in der westdeutschen Nachkriegspolitik* (Munich, 1997). For a long-term trend, Tenfelde, "Soziale Schichtung", p. 147.

24. Overall, however, the amount of housework has not actually diminished because standards have been raised, a point made by Wolfgang König, *Geschichte der Konsumgesellschaft* (Stuttgart, 1999), p. 244. See also Michael Wildt, *Vom kleinen Wohlstand: Eine Konsumgeschichte der fünfziger Jahre* (Munich, 1996), pp. 232f.

25. See also Helmuth Trischler, "Partielle Modernisierung: Die betrieblichen Sozialbeziehungen im Ruhrbergbau zwischen Grubenmilitarismus und Human Relations", in Matthias Frese *et al.* (eds), *Politische Zäsuren und gesellschaftlicher Wandel im 20. Jahrhundert: Regionale und vergleichende Perspektiven* (Paderborn, 1996), pp. 168ff.

26. Emil Schrumpf, "Gewerkschaftsbildung und -politik im Bergbau (unter besonderer Berücksichtigung des Ruhrbergbaus", (unpublished Ph.D. thesis, University of Bochum, 1958), pp. 33ff. See Lauschke, *Schwarze Fahnen*, p. 143; figures taken from Klaus Armingeon, *Die Entwicklung des westdeutschen Gewerkschaften 1950–1985* (Frankfurt am Main etc., 1988), pp. 170–174. See Hans-Eckbert Treu, "Stabilität und Wandel in der organisatorischen Entwicklung der Gewerkschaften: Eine Studie über die organisatorische Entwicklung der Industriegewerkschaft Bergbau und Energie", (unpublished Ph.D. thesis, University of Erlangen, 1979), pp. 53, 74. On the influence of salaried employees in mining, which after 1945 was at first still rather limited, see Helmuth Trischler, *Steiger im deutschen Bergbau: Zur Sozialgeschichte der technischen Angestellten 1815–1945* (Munich, 1988).

workers alike to perceive themselves as a unified workforce, regardless of status, in order to be able to play a sufficiently powerful role in the tripartisanship typical for the coal, iron, and steel industry, to avoid being divided and conquered. Many individuals moved upward economically but did not soar socially; instead they continued to associate themselves with the great majority of salaried employees.

UPWARD MOBILITY THROUGH EDUCATION

The main avenue to social change in the changing industry was at first the differentiation taking place in each plant, in which a growing white-collar workforce emerged. When the long-neglected educational system of the Ruhr was expanded in the 1960s, a new generation was given the opportunity to rise through the "floodgates" of education to the middle class within a generation. However, the children of "real" workers benefited from this relatively less than did the children of those workers who had advanced to salaried positions but remained loyal to the industrial working class.

The shortcomings of the educational infrastructure were spotted quickly, and reform was initiated as part of the policy designed to cope with structural change. Thus, a long-term, extremely successful facet of regional policy turned out to be the expansion and development of the educational system in the region. International comparisons had made it clear in the 1960s that higher levels of participation in education and training were imperative. At the same time, emphasis was placed on increasing the educational levels of those classes and regions that had previously been so inadequately served, and there was much debate about equal opportunity in education. In the Ruhr, the argument of structural change was used to support this effort: by creating greater educational capacities, a more highly skilled and better qualified labour force would emerge over the long run, which in turn would make the region more adaptable to the process of structural change. In addition, the expansion of the educational system and of scientific capacities (particularly in the area of technological development) was seen as a factor both to stimulate economic growth and to enhance competitiveness.[27]

Consequently, the Ruhr received its own universities, particularly in the central Hellweg zone, in Bochum (founded in 1961, built 1964–1984, classes offered as of 1965) and in Dortmund (founded 1962, at first as a

27. Peter Hüttenberger, "Hochschul- und Wissenschaftspolitik", in Hans Boldt (ed.), *Nordrhein-Westfalen und der Bund* (Cologne, 1989), pp. 203f., 207ff.; Volmerig, "Hochschulen im Ruhrgebiet", p. 88; Bernd A. Rusinek, "Hochschulen", in *NRW-Lexikon*, pp. 130f.; Alemann *et al.*, *Nordrhein-Westfalen*, pp. 200f.; NRW according to Burkhard Dietz, "Hochschulpolitik in Nordrhein-Westfalen und die Gründung der Ruhr-Universität Bochum", in Dietz *et al.*, *Universität und Politik*, pp. 56–67.

technical university following a conflict with Bochum over location, opened 1968). As other comprehensive universities were established, the government sought also to create these as more occupationally-oriented educational institutions meant to integrate the tasks of several types of institutions of higher education including colleges, universities, and technological and pedagogical institutes. Between 1972 and 1974, comprehensive universities were established in Essen, Duisburg, and Hagen (as a correspondence university). In addition, the universities and other institutions of advanced training were to base their coursework on a strong scientific-methodological foundation, geared especially toward the needs of the job market. Such institutions were established in Bochum and Dortmund, for example.[28] Not until 1992 did the northern Emscher region, long neglected with respect to an academic infrastructure, receive its own tertiary educational institution in the form of the technical college (*Fachhochschule*) in Gelsenkirchen.[29] Currently, North Rhine-Westphalia, including the Ruhr region, constitutes one of the most concentrated areas of institutions of higher learning. About 160,000 students are enrolled at the universities in the Ruhr, approximately 500,000 in all of NRW.[30]

In conjunction with the founding of new universities and similar institutions, secondary schooling in the Ruhr, as in all of Germany, was expanded, although in the Ruhr it was first necessary to also make up for the huge deficiency in pupils. Still in 1965, when there was an average of sixty-two inhabitants for every *Gymnasium* pupil in all of NRW, there were ninety-three inhabitants per pupil in Gelsenkirchen, ninety-one in the Recklinghausen district, and ninety-one in Wanne-Eickel. The cities in the Hellweg area, however, came closer to the NRW average. By the

28. Volmerig, "Hochschulen im Ruhrgebiet", pp. 87–107; Hüttenberger, "Hochschul- und Wissenschaftspolitik", pp. 210ff.; Werner Mayer, *Bildungspotential für den wirtschaftlichen und sozialen Wandel: Die Entstehung des Hochschultyps "Fachhochschule" in Nordrhein-Westfalen 1965–1971* (Essen 1997); Franz-Josef Jelich, "Von der Industriegesellschaft zur Wissensgesellschaft: Bildung und Wissenschaft in Nordrhein-Westfalen", in Rudolph *et al.*, *Reform an Rhein*, pp. 45ff. as was recommended by the *Wissenschaftsrat*, the Council of Sciences and Humanities, see p. 48; Dietz, "Hochschulpolitik in Nordrhein-Westfalen", pp. 69–101; Burkhard Dietz, "Eine Hochschule für das Revier: Die Gründung der Ruhr-Universität Bochum", in Nordrhein-Westfälisches Hauptstaatsarchiv Düsseldorf (ed.), *Nordrhein-Westfalen. Ein Land in seiner Geschichte. Aspekte und Konturen 1946–1996* (Münster, 1996), pp. 400–405. See Eberhard Wadischat, "Die Hochschulpolitik des Landes Nordrhein-Westfalen in den Jahren von 1948 bis 1968", (unpublished Ph.D. thesis, University of Düsseldorf, 1993); Rainer Stierand, *Hochschulgründungen in Nordrhein-Westfalen: Prozeßanalyse einer "wirklichen" staatlichen Planung* (Dortmund, 1983); Wolfgang Böttcher *et al.*, "Bildung fürs Proletariat", in Peter Grafe *et al.* (eds), *Der Lokomotive in voller Fahrt die Räder wechseln: Geschichte und Geschichten aus Nordrhein-Westfalen* (Berlin etc., 1988), pp. 141ff.

29. Volmerig, "Hochschulen im Ruhrgebiet", p. 91; Günter Strüder *et al.* (eds), *Etappen des Hochschulstandortes Recklinghausen* (Recklinghausen, 1995).

30. Alemann *et al.*, *Nordrhein-Westfalen*, p. 200; Volmerig, "Hochschulen im Ruhrgebiet", p. 106; Rusinek, "Hochschulen", p. 133.

middle to late 1980s, the region had achieved a density of secondary schools comparable to that of other major municipal areas and major cities and had reached a number of completed school diplomas comparable to the NRW average, although the northern Ruhr region continues still today to deviate clearly from this.[31]

The expansion of the education system has served to eradicate most of the deficiencies in education and training that once existed in the Ruhr. The Ruhr universities have succeeded in developing the educational potential of the region. The qualification patterns of the Ruhr population, particularly of people at an employable age, are similar to those of other highly populated metropolitan areas. Students comprise 2.98 per cent of the Ruhr population, whereas this figure is greater than the average number of students in the FRG population as a whole. Another group that has emerged here consists of university employees, who, together with their families, number several tens of thousands living in the Ruhr region. As a social group, people associated with the universities have an influence on the lifestyle and political culture that should not be underestimated. Some places even create a "campus scene" with their own places of communication, etc. It is, however, difficult to measure how greatly the students have influenced the region. In 1968, when in several cities throughout the Federal Republic students stormed the streets, offered what in the long run turned out to be some thought-provoking impulses, and exhibited alternative, convention-flouting forms of behaviour, the universities in the Ruhr were still being established and the student movements were correspondingly weak.[32] The various youth cultures popularized by secondary school pupils and university students evolved only later in the major metropolitan areas of the Ruhr and never possessed the same intensity as elsewhere.[33] Even outside the scope of student and youth movements, students in the Ruhr region appear to be "down-to-

31. Between 1968 and 1978 alone, twenty-four new *Realschulen* and twenty-one new *Gymnasiums* were established in the Ruhr region. The majority of the new comprehensive schools in NRW were located in the Ruhr (1976: fifteen comprehensive schools). Petzina, "Wirtschaft und Arbeit", pp. 532, 556. Statistics taken from Reiner Eismann *et al.*, "Sozio-ökonomische Daten zum IBA-Planungsraum", in Rolf Kreibich *et al.* (eds), *Bauplatz Zukunft*, pp. 265ff., 277f. See Tenfelde, "Das Ruhrgebiet", pp. 34f.; *idem*, "Soziale Schichtung", p. 180.

32. For example, see Norbert Kozicki, *Aufbruch im Revier: 1968 und die Folgen* (Essen, 1993); Daniel Rieser, "Die Studentenbewegung an der Ruhr-Universität Bochum vom Wintersemester 1965/66 bis zum Sommersemester 1971", (unpublished Ph.D. thesis, University of Bochum, 1973); Daniel Rieser, "Ein 'APO-Opa' erzählt [...]: Die Bochumer Studentenbewegung", in Wilfried Breyvogel *et al.* (eds), *Land der Hoffnung – Land der Krise: Jugendkulturen im Ruhrgebiet 1900–1987* (Berlin [etc.], 1987), pp. 218–225; Wilfried Breyvogel, "Die '68er' im Ruhrgebiet", in Barbian *et al.*, *Die Entdeckung des Ruhrgebiets*, pp. 329–338.

33. Werner Helsper, "Vom verspäteten Aufbruch zum forcierten Ausbruch: Jugendliche Gegenkultur im Ruhrgebiet", in Breyvogel *et al.*, *Land der Hoffnung*, pp. 226–239.

earth" individuals, who have not let their prospects of later becoming upwardly mobile go to their heads. The Ruhr universities are predominantly "commuter universities", that is, the students live in urban communities scattered throughout the Ruhr, drive to the university campuses for classes, but remain integrated in the daily life of their home towns and faced with the realities existing there.

With the coming of improved educational opportunities, a new, subtly diversified middle class evolved as part of the de-industrialization process within a society that until then had been shaped almost exclusively by coal, iron, and steel workers and their way of life. This new middle class created a new "bourgeoisie through training". As the "first-generation upwardly mobile" (and even in the second generation), the members of this new class still remained in many ways entrenched in their original milieu and linked to the region and the particularities characteristic to the way of life so heavily influenced by of the working class of the Ruhr; this was facilitated by the fact that structural change was being handled primarily with cooperative and consensus-oriented means and measures of social cushioning. The social history of the "first-generation upwardly mobile" has not been comprehensively examined. There are no studies on the history of the various occupational groups, and no research has been done on the degree to which the widely diversified salaried workforce is splitting up into subgroups, each tending to nurture its own "culture", or on the degree to which various "social milieus"[34] are evolving that share a set of common values and mentalities in addition to the same social status and position. The changes in West German society chipped away at and glossed over the differences in the way of life and behavioural norms specific to class, social group, or stratum. Just as this affected the working-class society of the Ruhr,[35] so too was the bourgeois demeanour altered. The rapid rise in the number of salaried employees, the entry of many women into the workforce in (usually lower-level) white-collar jobs, and finally the loss of the exclusivity associated with a salaried position relativized the self-esteem of salaried employees and eroded bourgeois self-confidence; in other words, this helped bring about a "debourgeoisization", just as the process of upward mobility contributed to the "deproletarianization" of the working class.[36]

34. Sinus-Institut, *Die Sinus-Milieus und ihre Anwendung* (Heidelberg, 1998); Michael Vester *et al.*, *Soziale Milieus im gesellschaftlichen Strukturwandel: Zwischen Integration und Ausgrenzung* (Cologne, 1993).

35. With respect to the working class, for example, see Josef Mooser, *Arbeiterleben in Deutschland 1900–1970* (Frankfurt am Main, 1984).

36. For example, see Josef Mooser, "Arbeiter, Angestellte und Frauen in der 'nivellierten Mittelstandsgesellschaft': Thesen", in Axel Schildt *et al.* (eds), *Modernisierung im Wiederaufbau: Die westdeutsche Gesellschaft der 50er Jahre* (Berlin [etc.], 1993), pp. 370f.

SELF-ASSURANCE AND THE CULTURE OF MEMORY IN THE RUHR REGION

Since many people belonging to the middle class in the Ruhr region see their own personal histories as a part of the history of structural change, they also seek self-assurance in the history of the region as a region of change. Such a specific culture of memory, as is evident in the kindling of interest in regional history and industrial culture, befits a middle class that evolved from the working class of the Ruhr. Within the framework of an increasing interest that started in the late 1960s in the topic of regional studies and specifically in the history of the Ruhr region itself, work began on regional self-image and thereby also on regional awareness. Since the mid-1970s, there has been an outburst of research and consequently of literature on the Ruhr.[37] Even though the number of scholarly works on the history of the Ruhr is still somewhat limited, these have a significant impact through popularized and currently nostalgic ("there's no place like home") publications, whereby the function of history is referred to "as a genuine element of every spatial and psychic 'location' of people".[38]

Since the 1970s, the Ruhr has discovered the value of the material and architectural traditions of its industrial history, quite in contrast to its previously fast-paced attitude and general irreverence for tradition in this regard. Following the founding of the Museum technischer Kulturdenkmale (Museum of Technological Heritage) in 1975 in Hagen, the industrial museums of the Rhineland and of Westphalia began in 1979 to preserve characteristic industrial monuments and to present these in their original environment and function. The struggle to save factory settlements and historical buildings are also linked to these projects. Still today, architectural witnesses to the history of the Ruhr are being preserved at great expense as meaningful elements of identification among the people of the region and as an expression of regional political culture. In cooperation with the International Bauausstellung Emscherpark (1989–1999), restored industrial monuments found in many locations throughout the Emscher region were not turned into museums, but given new purposes including that of housing technology centres. As usually quite visible landmarks, these monuments embody and symbolize the region's past and present and

37. See Klaus Tenfelde, "Neue Mitte, neues Selbstbewußtsein", in Gerd Willamowski *et al.* (eds), *Ruhrstadt: Die andere Metropole* (Essen, 2000), pp.18ff.; Stefan Goch, "Stadtgeschichtsforschung im Ruhrgebiet: Ein Forschungs- und Literaturbericht", *Archiv für Sozialgeschichte*, 34 (1994), pp. 441–475; Karl Teppe, "Regionalismus und Regionalgeschichte: Zum Verhältnis von kulturpolitischen Interessen und regionalgeschichtlichen Konzeptionen am Beispiel Westfalen", *Informationen zur Raumentwicklung*, (1993), pp. 729–737.

38. Detlef Briesen *et al.*, *Regionalbewußtsein in Montanregionen im 19. und 20. Jahrhundert: Saarland, Siegerland, Ruhrgebiet* (Bochum, 1994), p. 2 (quotation translated into English for this article).

indeed the change itself as a structural element of regional political culture.[39]

Since the new middle classes in the Ruhr did not possess any bourgeois cultural models or a traditional urbanity, they created specific cultural forms that are oriented particularly toward their experiences in mastering structural change. While these new and growing middle classes are busy evolving their own behavioural norms, attitudes, and ways of life, older influences and associations from both the small original bourgeois realm and the working-class milieu are disappearing in the diffuse heterogeneity of the new middle classes. Included in the barely definable middle classes of the Ruhr are the conventional urban bourgeoisie, the old and new self-employed (as the equivalent to the old economic bourgeoisie) who remain rather few in number relative to other comparable regions, the academic professionals or those in correspondingly trained professions (as the educated social groups), the functional elite in local business, politics, and administration, and the educated groups from a wide diversity of occupations that are relatively new to the region. In this way, a social configuration has arisen out of the middle of society, one that hardly existed when the society of the Ruhr was dominated by the working class, mine owners, and magnates. Large numbers of the middle class share the experiences of upward mobility and of the search for individual alternatives to the milieu of their social background. Above all, they have in common the generation-specific experiences of the expansion of educational opportunity, of popular culture since the 1960s and the new social movements, and a critical perspective on change, based on insight into the Janus-faced aspect of modernity.[40] In the Ruhr, which earlier was such a non-bourgeois region, it is the shared experience of upward mobility that links the middle classes best. This "first generation" to move into the middle classes has remained extremely sedentary and tied to the region; these people associate with pride their own experience in moving upwards with structural change and thereby cultivate the heritage of their industrial culture and a regional culture of memory.[41] Not only the brief history of the new middle classes and their ties to their social origins, but also the similarities in the lives of those making up the diversified middle classes, which are primarily salaried middle classes, prevents the degree of individualization from becoming all too great. Therefore, an employee

39. Andrea Höber *et al.* (eds), *IndustrieKultur: Mythos und Moderne im Ruhrgebiet* (Essen, 1999); Henry Beierlorzer *et al.* (eds), *SiedlungsKultur: Neue und alte Gartenstädte im Ruhrgebiet* (Braunschweig [etc.], 1999); Manfred Sack, *70 km Hoffnung: Die IBA Emscher Park* (Frankfurt am Main, 1999).
40. See Tenfelde, *Die "neue Mitte"*, pp. 16f.; Ulrich Heinemann, "Die neue soziale Mitte: Was sie prägt und wie man mit ihr Politik macht", in Rudolph *et al.*, *Reform an Rhein*, pp. 171f.
41. Heinemann, "Die neue soziale Mitte", p. 175.

mentality can also continue to exist among the salaried middle classes even after upward mobility has been achieved.

IN THE SHADOW OF SUCCESSFUL STRUCTURAL CHANGE

Structural change and the entire development of so-called modern industrial society have not only led to processes of upward mobility; there have also been losers in the development of adapting the Ruhr region to the average structures of the Federal Republic. Economic migrants, especially from southeastern Europe, comprise in many cases a new underclass. Those hit particularly hard by unemployment are relatively unskilled workers from the producing industries, foreigners or those individuals who have migrated, and young people under the age of twenty-five. In the shadows of the modernized industrial and service economy and the salaried middle classes have evolved, especially in the north, "islands", quarters, city neighbourhoods, or even streets in which poverty and a culture of poverty have spread among the losers of modernization. This is where a potential of people gather, through a selective process of migration, who no longer have the means at their disposal to avoid the downward spiral of poverty. In particular, this is where we find one-parent families, minors, and migrants. With the aid of social services and a still existing capacity for self-help, it has been possible to prevent the development of slums,[43] although distinct differences between the various city neighbourhoods are clearly identifiable in an analysis of social spaces.[44] These groups of losers created by structural change, those marginalized by the job market, and others pushed to the periphery of urban society neither possess sufficient capabilities to organize themselves and articulate their interests, a lever of influence or veto power, nor are they able to come together as a group due to the extent of their heterogeneity. Therefore, they are not a great source of conflict and remain instead hidden in the shadows of society.

CHANGE IN REGIONAL POLITICAL CULTURE

Whereas underprivileged groups are able to exercise little influence on regional politics, the new middle classes also only shape politics to a limited degree; that is, they remain entrenched in the old, established

42. Hermann Bömer, *Ruhrgebietspolitik in der Krise: Kontroverse Konzepte aus Wirtschaft, Wissenschaft und Verbänden* (Dortmund, 2000), pp. 135f. Studies are rare, but one example is on Duisburg-Bruckhausen by Gertrud Tobias *et al.* (eds), *Von der Hand in den Mund: Armut und Armutsbewältigung in einer westdeutschen Großstadt* (Essen, 1992).

43. Klaus Peter Strohmeier *et al.*, "Sozialraum Ruhrgebiet: stadträumliche Differenzierungen von Lebenslagen, Armut und informelle Solidarpotentiale", in Bovermann *et al.*, *Das Ruhrgebiet*, pp. 451–475.

political culture of the region. After World War II, the workers of heavy industry in the region made a lasting mark on the political culture. Whereas the development of the region following the liberation from National Socialism, as for most of its history, was primarily shaped by decisions made elsewhere, there emerged in the factories and in the local and communal governments of the cities and city districts of the Ruhr in the months immediately after the war ended a regional model of politics that has come to be known as *basisnahe Stellvertretung* (grassroots representation). This model incorporated old Social Democratic free-trade union traditions of participation politics and class compromise; the model was also influenced by the conditions present in the Ruhr region with its influential heavy industry and its corporatist structures. In this model, a Social Democratic elite was selected from among the functionaries of trade unions, communal politics, and the political party and assigned a major role in mediating between the lives of the workers and the economy, between politics and the entire society, without the workers having to be continually active themselves. The demise of older structures of solidarity made the model of politics based on acting representatives the only accepted concept of collective lobbying. Strengthened institutionally by the codetermination law passed for the coal, iron, and steel industry in the early postwar period, trade unionists and Social Democrats now articulated the emancipatory aims of the people of the Ruhr and their claims to justice and social security. Social democracy in the Ruhr and its trade-unionist and political functionaries and mandates came to embody the collective experiences of "ordinary people" working in the factories and living in the region's industrial communities. As their lobbyists, these representatives developed in the region a special "culture of the man in the street" that can be called the "reshaping of a sociopolitical milieu centred around trade unions, large factories, and communal institutions".[44]

44. Especially for the political model of grassroots representation, see Michael Zimmermann, "Basisnahe Stellvertretung: Zur sozialdemokratischen Dominanz im Ruhrgebiet", *Revierkultur*, 2 (1987), 2, pp. 46–53; *idem*, "'Geh zu Hermann, der macht dat schon': Bergarbeiterinteressenvertretung im nördlichen Ruhrgebiet", in Lutz Niethammer (ed.), *"Hinterher merkt man, daß es richtig war, daß es schief gegangen ist": Nachkriegserfahrungen im Ruhrgebiet* (Berlin, 1983), pp. 277–310; Alexander von Plato, "Nachkriegssieger: Sozialdemokratische Betriebsräte im Ruhrgebiet: Eine lebensgeschichtliche Untersuchung", in *ibid.*, pp. 311–359; *idem "Der Verlierer geht nicht leer aus": Betriebsräte geben zu Protokoll* (Berlin, 1984); Bernd Faulenbach, "Mitbestimmung und politische Kultur im Ruhrgebiet", in Helmut Martens *et al.* (eds), *Mitbestimmung und Demokratisierung: Stand und Perspektiven der Forschung* (Wiesbaden, 1989), pp. 216–228. For the quotation translated here into English, Karl Rohe, "Regionale (politische) Kultur: Ein sinnvolles Konzept für die Wahl- und Parteienforschung?", in Dieter Oberndörfer *et al.* (eds), *Parteien und regionale politische Traditionen in der Bundesrepublik Deutschland* (Berlin, 1991), p. 33. See Bernd Faulenbach, "Die Herausbildung eines neuen sozialdemokratischen Milieus nach dem Zweiten Weltkrieg", in Peter Friedemann *et al.* (eds), *Struktureller Wandel und kulturelles Leben: Politische Kultur in Bochum 1860–1990* (Essen, 1992), pp. 456f. on the emergence of a political milieu or a specific political style.

Because the model of politics was geared toward the comprehensive cooperation of regional actors, it was possible to reconcile the anachronistic administrative and political fragmentation of regional institutions (*Länder* and federal government, communities, regions, communal associations, organizational boundaries, etc.).

The coal-mining crisis since 1958 and the job cutbacks in the coal, iron, and steel industry of the Ruhr strengthened the grassroots model of politics further because labour representatives and local politicians were the ones administering the social plans, meaning the diverse social measures to cushion the population from the consequences of structural change in the industry. Therefore, with the help of public subsidies, it was possible to carry out the job cutbacks in a manner that was, for the most part, socially just.[45] The hopes of the workers in the Ruhr region for a comfortable life and protection from the consequences of the crisis in the coal, iron, and steel industry were fulfilled by the efforts of Social Democrats, the trade unions and their labour representatives. Overall, the demise of the coal, iron, and steel industry actually strengthened a political model based on cooperation and compensation: the conflicting interests of employers and employees and their organizations were dwarfed by the pressure of the economic crisis and by their common interest in cushioning the decline of the coal, iron, and steel industry. Therefore, it became relatively simple to agree on social cushions in the plants, mines, and factories. By creating in 1968 the united coal enterprise in the Ruhr, the Ruhrkohle AG, trade-union representatives were able to put a social net in place that prevented any Ruhr miner from falling into the deep crevices of economic insecurity. In the iron and steel industry, the employee councils and unions were also fairly successful in working out a socially acceptable plan for coping with structural change, although the negotiations on these measures was much more conflictual. Overall, a regional model of cooperation between management and labour, with the help of government, was at least able to guarantee social cushions against the repercussions structural change, which in other regions took place much more abruptly and brutally for those affected. In the Ruhr, a special regional culture of cooperation and consensus-building eventually developed out of structural change and was then strengthened. By fulfilling its demands for social compensation and cushions against the repercussions of structural change, the Social Democratic Party became the dominant political party. At the same time, the crisis produced a feeling of belonging

45. For more on the increased influence of the employee councils during the mine shutdowns, see also Lauschke, *Schwarze Fahnen*, p. 139. On the corresponding workers' consciousness, see Josef Esser *et al.*, *Krisenregulierung: Zur politischen Durchsetzung ökonomischer Zwänge* (Frankfurt am Main, 1983), pp. 208–221.

together, of camaraderie, and corporatist structures of consensus-seeking became the trademark of political behaviour in the Ruhr.[46]

The corporatist model of politics "rubbed off" on all of North Rhine-Westphalia. Against the backdrop of the successful social cushioning during the crisis created by structural change and in light of the corporatist mode of politics that integrates particularly the unions into the formation of policy, NRW is considered among the *Länder* to be the "social conscience" of the federal government.[47] North Rhine-Westphalia earned this reputation in good part through the workers and their movements, particularly in the Ruhr region. A basic social consensus unites the industry-based union, some ranks of management, the social-Catholic wing of the workers associated in part with the Christian Democratic Union (CDU), and the SPD.[48] The concepts on issues of social justice existing in the regional political culture were also influenced by a defensive mistrust of the "bigwigs upstairs", an employee-oriented corporatism, a fundamental predisposition toward solidarity and justice, a pronounced pragmatism, and personalized communication.[49] In its role as the "social

46. See Bernd Faulenbach, "Merkmale und Entwicklungslinien der politischen Kultur des Ruhrgebiets", in Bovermann *et al.*, *Das Ruhrgebiet*, pp. 373f.

47. This position follows a long tradition, also within the social-Catholic wing of the CDU. Minister President Karl Arnold (CDU) said in his inaugural speech on 21 September 1950, as criticism of the federal government led by Chancellor Konrad Adenauer and the liberal economic policy adopted by Bonn: "Das Land Nordrhein-Westfalen will und wird das soziale Gewissen der Bundesrepublik sein" ["North Rhine-Westphalia wants to be and will be the social conscience of the Federal Republic"]. Cited in Ursula Rombeck-Jaschinski, *Nordrhein-Westfalen, die Ruhr und Europa: Föderalismus und Europapolitik 1945–1955* (Essen, 1990), p. 85. See Rolf G. Heinze *et al.*, "Gewerkschaften und Modernisierung der Wirtschaft: Langsamer Niedergang oder Flucht nach vorn", in Dieter Schulte (ed.), *Industriepolitik im Spagat* (Cologne, 1995), p. 75 on the participation of the unions in structural policy in NRW (as opposed to other *Länder*). In Petzina, "Wirtschaft und Arbeit", p. 567, reference is made to the "vielfach bestätigte Fähigkeit zum sozialen Interessenausgleich zwischen Unternehmen und Gewerkschaften" ["frequently proven ability to achieve a social settlement between the companies and the unions"]. See Stefan Goch, "'Der Ruhrgebietler': Überlegungen zur Entstehung und Entwicklung regionalen Bewußtseins im Ruhrgebiet", *Westfälische Forschungen*, 47 (1997), pp. 613ff.

48. See Dietmar Petzina, "Das 'soziale Gewissen' des Bundes: Nordrhein-Westfalen, Die Montan-Mitbestimmung und die neue Sozialpolitik", in Landeszentrale für politische Bildung Nordrhein-Westfalen, *Der schwierige Weg*, pp. 265–278.

49. Karl Rohe, "Vom sozialdemokratischen Armenhaus zur Wagenburg der SPD: Politischer Strukturwandel in einer Industrieregion nach dem Zweiten Weltkrieg", *Geschichte und Gesellschaft*, 13 (1987), p. 531, speaks of the "Lebensweisen und Mentalitäten, den Sentiments und Ressentiments, dem Stolz und der Selbstachtung der kleinen Leute" ["ways of life and mentalities, the sentiments and resentments, the pride and self-respect of the ordinary people"], which social democracy reflected, although little ideological content is attributed to these. It is also forgotten that a part of the Ruhr culture still retains a dichotomous view of the world, transmitted through a grassroots elite, a view that distinguishes between the "man in the street" and the "bigwigs upstairs". Lutz Niethammer, "'Normalisierung' im Westen: Erinnerungsspuren in die 50er Jahre", in Gerhard Brunn (ed.), *Neuland: Nordrhein-Westfalen und seine Anfänge*

conscience", the region reflects an older influence through the nearly homogenous working and living conditions among the workers in the coal, iron, and steel industry, which in a social sense distinguished the Ruhr from other regions decades ago and was expressed in the self-image of the region with all of its working-class pride and its inferiority complexes. A political tradition that transcends all ideological camps and social strata is, in this context, the rather limited trust in the ability of free enterprise to direct the economy, although highly organized forms of control, particularly tripartisan ones, are viewed more positively.[50]

The corporatist influence has been passed onto the middle classes, which have become in many ways the co-supporters of processes of transformation, adaptation, and modernization. Social responsibility and at least an effort at pursuing a politics of cooperation and social partnership between labour and management comprise the central aspect of all attempts to cope with structural change, regardless of whatever alterations have been made in the strategies of structural policy. The continuing experience in coping with crisis has fused the region together and has enabled the development of a repeatedly proven ability to achieve social settlements.[52] In all their efforts to provide a social cushion and to extend the timeframe of structural change, the various actors overall have – contrary to widely held beliefs – not fought structural change but attempted to shape and direct it. For the future wellbeing of the region, its most important capacities of development may well lie in its achieved diversity even economically, the variety of its structural policy projects and initiatives, the widespread participation of regional actors in coping with change, the incentive for consensus in the tripartisan model of politics, and the orientation toward self-stipulated social and ecological norms. These capacities will help the region to face whatever insecurity the future holds because they offer it various options and avenues of development. No longer will the region be dependent, for better or for worse, on a mono-industrial structure and a single avenue of development, as it was in earlier times.

As the region has prospered, the regional Social Democratic Party been transformed by social change. Not only have its voters improved their economic status, so have its members, functionaries, and elected officeholders. The party has become less of a people's party and more of a party of all people, meaning that it has attempted to integrate large

1945/46 (Essen, 1986), p. 206, states that the "economic miracle" of postwar West Germany and the stabilization of the standard of living among the workers of the Ruhr created "keine Illusion einer klassenlosen Gesellschaft" ["no illusions of a classless society"].

50. Karl Rohe, "Politische Traditionen in Rheinland, in Westfalen und Lippe", in Landeszentrale für politische Bildung Nordrhein-Westfalen (ed.), *Nordrhein-Westfalen: Eine politische Landeskunde* (Cologne, 1984), p. 29.

51. Petzina, "Wirtschaft und Arbeit", p. 567. See also Tenfelde, "Gesellschaft im Wohlfahrtsstaat", p. 38.

segments of the gainfully employed population.[53] The political model, which has for so long been centred around the regional SPD, is now showing clear signs of age as change has progressed. It is becoming increasingly difficult to integrate the interests of a society that is continually diversifying as the economic and social structures are being transformed. The election results show that a growing amount of effort is needed in order to maintain the balancing act between various groups in the diversified population and that the party is finding itself more and more in strategic "Catch-22s" between the various interests and social groups.[54] Furthermore, the political elite have, in many cases, lost touch with their constituency and tended to "raise themselves above the crowd", unlike a large number of their voters. They also have failed politically and morally in many places. The communal elections of September 1999 represented a major turning point for the party: the SPD lost significantly – albeit under extremely difficult conditions caused by national politics – and the CDU won significantly, albeit with a very low voter turnout. The SPD lost its dominant position nearly everywhere in the region. The election results signal that the old political model centred around the Social Democrats and the unions has structurally come to an end. Although patterns of action geared toward consensus and cooperation are still effective, the continuing process of societal differentiation forces the actors involved to repeatedly adapt these to new problems that arise in organizing consensus in the region.

CONCLUSION: IS THE RUHR A NEW MIDDLE-CLASS SOCIETY?

Finally we must ask ourselves whether, with the emergence of the diversified new middle classes, a new social configuration with possibly a new political culture has arisen in the region that is shaping or will shape the Ruhr. Helmut Schelsky saw a "levelled middle-class society"

52. In this sense, the title of this article has been inspired by Bodo Hombach, "Aufsteigen ohne Abzuheben: Der Wandel der Mitgliedschaft der SPD in NRW", in Lutz Niethammer *et al.* (eds), *"Die Menschen machen ihre Geschichte nicht aus freien Stücken, aber sie machen sie selbst": Einladung zu einer Geschichte des Volkes in NRW* (Berlin, 1984), pp. 226–234.

53. The political model of grassroots representation was also referred to as a "class-transcending lobby", "corruption" or "we-are-all-in-the-same-boat partnership" and "corporatist model of communication and action"; Ulrich Borsdorf (ed.), *Feuer und Flamme: 200 Jahre Ruhrgebiet: Katalog zur Ausstellung im Gasometer Oberhausen* (Essen, 1994), p. 18. Structural conservatism and a subsidy mentality are also attributed to the established structures. Examples of such "Catch-22s" are in Ulrich von Alemann *et al.*, "Parteien im Prozeß der Modernisierung: Auf der Suche nach einem realistischen Bild der Partei", in Ernst-Martin Walsken *et al.* (eds), *Mitgliederpartei im Wandel: Veränderungen am Beispiel der NRW-SPD* (Münster [etc.], 1998), p. 2.

approaching,[54] one emerging from a combination of factors: the coming of increasing prosperity, the social processes of upward mobility, the social diversification following the elimination of parts of the old German elite by National Socialism and war, as well as the destruction of societal hierarchies also by the Nazis and the war. The last national parliamentary election campaign in Federal Republic was directly aimed at addressing a "New Middle"[55] in the electorate, which was understood to be heterogeneous social groups consisting of highly qualified employees, managers, small and medium-sized businessmen, engineers, new entrepreneurs, and scholars and scientists.[56]

Empirically, the interpretation of the "New Middle" and that of the "levelled middle-class society" overlook the considerable degree of social inequality that continues to exist overall and the differentiation taking place within the middle social strata of the populace. Although salaried employees and civil servants comprise a numerical majority of those gainfully employed, a number which clearly exceeds that of workers even in the Ruhr, this "majority" is very heterogeneous and can hardly be jointly addressed as a "New Middle". Existing structures of inequality are also being underestimated. Contrary to the assumption that the "elevator effect" would improve living standards generally and make widely accessible those consumer goods, services, leisure activities, status symbols, etc. once quite socially exclusive, and contrary to the realization that old class differences and social status distinctions and thus the political-cultural identities linked to them have been worn away or have vanished in favour of greater social diversity, social inequalities remain.[57] In other words, the coming of social diversification and pluralization and the evident improvement of living standards overall have not meant the

54. Helmut Schelsky, "Die Bedeutung des Schichtungsbegriffes für die Analyse der gegenwärtigen deutschen Gesellschaft", in Helmut Schelsky, *Auf der Suche nach Wirklichkeit: Gesammelte Aufsätze* (Düsseldorf etc., 1965), pp. 331ff. (from 1954). See also Paul Nolte, *Die Ordnung der deutschen Gesellschaft: Selbstentwurf und Selbstbeschreibung im 20. Jahrhundert* (Munich, 2000), pp. 352ff.

55. Heinemann, "Die neue soziale Mitte", pp. 168f. See Roland Tichy, *Ab in die Neue Mitte: Die Chancen der Globalisierung für eine deutsche Zukunftsgesellschaft* (Hamburg, 1998).

56. However, it was speculated here that definite concepts of a natural and harmonious position, so to speak, at the centre of society are widely held precisely among the middle classes. See Nolte, *Die Ordnung der deutschen Gesellschaft*.

57. Rainer Geißler, "Kein Abschied von Klasse und Schicht: Ideologische Gefahren der deutschen Sozialstrukturanalyse", *Kölner Zeitschrift für Soziologie und Sozialpsychologie*, 48 (1996), pp. 319–338. From a historical perspective, Hans-Ulrich Wehler, *Deutsches Bürgertum nach 1945: Exitus oder Phönix aus der Asche?* (Bochum, 2001), p. 20. Important for the argument on the wearing away of differences at the same time as the "elevator effect" is occurring is the work of Ulrich Beck, "Jenseits von Stand und Klasse?", in Reinhard Kreckel (ed.), *Soziale Ungleichheiten* (Göttingen, 1983), pp. 35–74, and especially Beck, *Risikogesellschaft*. See Peter A. Berger, *Entstrukturierte Klassengesellschaft? Klassenbildung und Strukturen sozialer Ungleichheit im historischen Wandel* (Opladen, 1986).

eradication of an unequal distribution of opportunity available to realize one's goals and ambitions in life. The claim that everyone has benefited from the general prosperity also overlooks the class-specific differences present in the upwardly mobile movement.[58] Recently, it has been determined that the ranks of the elite have become enormously stable, meaning more specifically that social mobility is abating.[59]

Based on the development of the middle classes in the Ruhr region, it can hardly be determined whether in 1945 the German bourgeoisie experienced its demise or its revival.[60] Despite all the continuity in the recruitment from the ranks of the bourgeoisie, the middle classes that were produced primarily by advanced education and training were indeed new and very diversified in the Ruhr. These new middle classes are still in the process of finding their own self-confidence and identity. The first and second generation of the upwardly mobile are just beginning to create their own traditions. During the process of catch-up modernization everywhere in the Ruhr, a white-collar labour force featuring special regional influences has evidently come into being that has remained relatively humble and "down-to-earth" despite the significant upwardly mobile processes and a considerably successful handling of structural change. The reasons for this lie in a regional political culture that is geared strongly toward consensus and cooperation. Therefore, social or sociocultural distance may well be relatively weaker in the Ruhr than in comparable regions and a "social conscience" may be more popular here than is in keeping with these neoliberal times. Indeed, part of the self-confidence of this region, once so dominated by heavy industry, may well be the memory of its developmental process, a memory held with personal pride by the people of the Ruhr.

58. Geißler, "Kein Abschied", p. 327.

59. Wehler, *Deutsches Bürgertum nach 1945*, summarized on p. 20; Michael Hartmann, *Topmanager: Die Rekrutierung einer Elite* (Frankfurt am Main, 1996); Dieter Ziegler (ed.), *Großbürgertum und Unternehmer: Die deutsche Wirtschaftselite im 20. Jahrhundert* (Göttingen, 2000).

60. Wehler, *Deutsches Bürgertum nach 1945*.

IRSH 47 (2002), pp. 113–136 DOI: 10.1017/S0020859002000809

The International Association of Machinists, Pratt & Whitney, and the Struggle for a Blue-Collar Future in Connecticut

Robert Forrant

INTRODUCTION

Riding down Main Street in East Hartford, Connecticut toward the six smokestacks dominating the front of Pratt & Whitney's mammoth aircraft engine factory, one cannot help noticing numerous artifacts associated with rapid industrial decline: empty and trash-strewn lots, boarded-up storefronts, and vacated triple-deckers, once homes for Pratt & Whitney workers. A short drive away on the other side of the Connecticut River one can observe the dichotomies between East Hartford and downtown Hartford with its glittering insurance companies, banks, and the headquarters – known around Hartford as the "Gold Building" – of Pratt's parent, the United Technologies Corporation (UTC). The various social clubs, bars, and purveyors of fast food, ice cream, and fresh baked pies, that have served thousands of lunches and early suppers to members of the International Association of Machinists (IAM) are at risk.

Our mini-tour makes apparent the economic uncertainty and painful "pulling apart" of the social fabric in Connecticut's and the rest of the once-industrial northeast United States' older cities caused in large measure by the disappearance of well-paying manufacturing jobs. With over one million such jobs lost during the most recent US recession, including hundreds of machining jobs at Pratt & Whitney, workers there rightly fear for their futures. The Union Hall for East Hartford's IAM Local 1746 sits directly opposite the main gates of the plant. Inside, local president Mike Stone observed "Well paying, secure jobs which both provided a career for thousands of hard-working people and their families, and supported hundreds of retail and service establishments across the state – jobs workers in the past were able to pass along to their children – continue to disappear." This is why, he said "with 4,500 members in the four Pratt & Whitney locals, job security needs to be the focus of everything we do".[1]

The members of Local 1746 and the three other Pratt & Whitney union

1. Interview with Mike Stone by author, March 2001; *Hartford Courant* (20 June 1993), p. B4.

locals scattered across Connecticut were not supposed to be worrying quite so intently about their futures. After highly contentious 1993 negotiations, the Connecticut legislature and the union gave tax concessions, wage cuts, and weakened seniority language to Pratt/UTC in return for the corporation's commitment to rebuild employment in the state. But, thereafter, Pratt workers clashed several times with UTC over its failure to live up to the bargain. Events culminated at the end of 2001 in the first strike against the company since the 1960s.[2]

At the December 2001 strike deadline, Pratt & Whitney's final contract offer contained a 10 per cent pay increase and a $1,000 signing bonus. However, the proposed agreement permitted management to move 500 East Hartford jobs out-of-state, with only a nebulous commitment to bring in new work. After absorbing thousands of lost jobs in the 1980s and 1990s – Local 1746 had over 9,000 members in 1983 and barely 2,500 on the strike's eve – at 12.01 a.m. on 3 December 2001 unionists established their boisterous picket lines. Despite the threatening economic climate unionists stood out, opposed to further job erosion.[3]

Before the strike vote, Gary Allen, the IAM's national aerospace coordinator, told several thousand cheering workers: "This is your defining moment as a union. You've got to send a message." And East Hartford local president Mike Stone added: "We can either die on the vine or fight to grow jobs in the state of Connecticut. Nothing is won without sacrifice. It is our time to sacrifice." On the picket line several hours later, 15-year Pratt worker Greg Adorno shared similar sentiments noting "What's the point of giving somebody a 10 per cent raise if they're not going to be here to benefit from it?" For James Parent, the directing business agent for IAM District 91 and its chief negotiator, the issues were clear: "We were at a point at the end of negotiations where we were close. It's not an issue of money. It's an issue of whether the jobs are going to be

2. For discussions of plant closings and community dislocation see Robert Forrant, "'Neither a Sleepy Village nor a Coarse Factory Town': Skill in the Greater Springfield Massachusetts Industrial Economy 1800–1990", *Journal of Industrial History*, 4 (2001), pp. 24–47; JoAnn Wypijewski, "GE Brings Bad Things to Life", *The Nation* (12 February 2001), pp. 18–23; Jefferson Cowie, *Capital Moves: RCA's 70-Year Quest For Cheap Labor* (Ithaca, NY, 2000); William A. Adler, *Mollie's Job: A Story of Life and Work on the Global Assembly Line* (New York, 2000); Kathryn M. Dudley, *The End of the Line: Lost Jobs, New Lives in Postindustrial America* (Chicago, IL, 1994). For community studies of de-industrialization, Gordon Clark, *Unions and Communities Under Siege: American Communities and the Crisis of Organized Labor* (New York, 1989); June C. Nash, *From Tank Town to High Tech: The Clash of Community and Industrial Cycles* (Albany, NY, 1989); Roger Keil, *Los Angeles: Globalization, Urbanization and Social Struggles* (New York, 1998); Doreen Massey and Richard Meegan, *The Anatomy of Job Loss: The How, Why and Where of Employment Decline* (London, 1982).

3. Daniel Altman, "Nation's Unemployment Rate Rises to 5.8%", *New York Times* (5 January 2002), p. B1; Reed Abelson, "AT Plans to Lay Off 5,000 Workers", *ibid.*; Sue Kirchhoff, "US jobless rate reaches 5.8%", *Boston Globe* (5 January 2002), p. C1; David Leonhardt, "The Rust Belt With a Drawl", *New York Times* (13 November 2001), p. C1.

here. What good is a good package if you don't have a job?"[4] The IAM's fight for job security in the face of de-industrialization and capital flight is an important part of the larger story about the globalizing economy's impact on industrial workers and their communities.

THE CONNECTICUT ECONOMY RESTRUCTURES: ANY ROOM FOR BLUE-COLLAR WORKERS?

Overview

Less than fifty years ago, the United States accounted for close to half of global manufacturing output. After 1945, war-induced prosperity and increasing productivity coupled with the benefits of Keynesian fiscal and monetary policies contributed to rising living standards for many workers. Gross national product expanded dramatically, from $213 billion in 1945 to more than $500 billion in 1960 and $1 trillion in 1970. Connecticut's capital city, Hartford, sat at the center of the 200-mile-long Connecticut River valley running between Bridgeport, Connecticut and Springfield, Vermont. For much of the nineteenth and twentieth centuries the valley's firms and its machinists and metalworkers related to the rest of the country and the world as an innovative and powerful manufacturing center.[5] The region's diverse manufacturing base was secured early in the nineteenth century when Springfield, Massachusetts (twenty-five miles north of Hartford) became the site for an important federal armory. The armory had functioned as the hub of a flourishing industrial district, with Springfield and Hartford enjoying a comparative technological advantage over many other regions of the country due to the diffusion of manufacturing techniques such as the utilization of gages, fixtures, jigs, and dies and the availability of large numbers of skilled metalworkers.[6] Early in the twentieth century, Massachusetts, Connecticut, and Vermont

4. Barbara Nagy, "Union Votes to Strike at Pratt", *Hartford Courant* (3 December 2001), p. 1; John Moran and Barbara Nagy, "Job Security the Issue for Pratt Strikers", *Hartford Courant* (4 December 2001), p. 1. For a look at what another union is attempting to do with a giant US corporation see Douglas Meyer, "Building Union Power in the Global Economy: A Case Study of the Coordinated Bargaining Committee of General Electric Unions", *Labor Studies Journal*, 26 (2001), pp. 60–71.

5. James A. Henretta, David Brody, and Lynn Dumenil, *America: A Concise History* (New York, 1999), ch. 29, pp. 779–805, 780. I rely in this section on material from Suzanne Konzelmann and Robert Forrant, "Creative Work Systems in Destructive Markets", in Brendan Burchell, Simon Deakin, Jonathan Michie, and Jill Rubery (eds) *Business Organization and Productive Systems* (London, forthcoming 2002).

6. Nathan Rosenberg (ed.), *The American System of Manufactures: The Report of the Committee on the Machinery of the United States 1855 and the Special Reports of George Wallis and Joseph Whitworth* (Edinburgh, 1969). For pre-Civil-War industrialization in New England see François Weil, "Capitalism and Industrialization in New England, 1815–1845", *Journal of American History*, 84 (1998), pp. 1334–1354. See also Felicia Deyrup's *Arms*

ranked second, fourth, and ninth respectively in the US for machine-tool sales. A plentiful pool of skilled machinists and engineers, a well-practiced reciprocal relationship among machine-tool builders and their customers, and the presence of hundreds of tool-and-die shops enhanced the valley's industrial competitiveness.[7]

Declining unions – declining standards of living

This premier position was eroded during the 1970s and the 1980s as Japan, continental Europe, and developing Asian nations emerged to challenge US pre-eminence in autos, steel, major household appliances, and consumer electronics. Job loss intensified during the 1973–1975 recession and spiked between 1979 and 1983 when over 2 million jobs (almost 16 per cent of the national total) in several highly unionized durable goods sectors were lost as corporations shifted large segments of their manufacturing activities overseas. Among the Fortune 500's largest manufacturers employment fell to 12.4 million from 15.9 million between 1980 and 1990. General Motors, Ford, Boeing, GE, and UTC collectively eliminated 230,000 jobs from 1990 to 1995.

Globalization increased the international labor pool and made capital and work more mobile. Firms globalized corporate assets and expanded their direct foreign investment in factories, office buildings, office equipment, and machine tools. Whereas in 1965 this investment amounted to less than $50 billion, it reached $124 billion in 1975, surpassed $213 billion in 1980 and climbed to $610.1 billion in 1994. Even in those industries like jet engines where US-based producers had been successful at maintaining market share in international competition, enterprise success did not necessarily serve to insulate workers from the effects of corporate restructuring and job loss.[8]

Makers of the Connecticut Valley (Northampton, MA, 1948). For Springfield's industrial growth and decline Robert Forrant, "Roots of Connecticut River Valley Deindustrialization: The Springfield American Bosch Plant 1940–1975", *Historical Journal of Massachusetts*, (Winter 2003, forthcoming).

7. The *Fourteenth United States Census* (1920) reported that 25 per cent of the nation's machine tools were shipped from Massachusetts, Connecticut, and Rhode Island, and approximately 20 per cent of the country's machine tool firms employing more than 100 workers were found along the Connecticut River; Deyrup, *Arms Makers*, p. 66; Frisch, *Town into City*, p. 15.

8. By 1996 about three-quarters of all employed Americans worked in service industries, up from two-thirds in 1979. For a discussion of these trends see Stephen Herzenberg, J. Alic, J. and H. Wial, *New Rules for a New Economy: Employment and Opportunity in Postindustrial America* (Ithaca, NY, 1998); Kim Moody, *Workers in a Lean World: Unions in the International Economy* (New York, 1997); Barry Bluestone and Bennet Harrison, *Lean and Mean: The Changing Landscape of Corporate Power in the Age of Flexibility* (New York, 1994); Robert Forrant, "Between a Rock and a Hard Place: US Industrial Unions and the Lean, Mean Global Economy: Unions on the Shop Floor as the Next Century Approaches", *Cambridge Journal of Economics*, 24 (2000), pp. 751–769.

Unionized workers felt the full negative force of this corporate and labor market restructuring. Overall, one in three American workers belonged to a union in the mid-1950s compared to one in seven in 1999. The percentage of unionized manufacturing jobs declined from almost 50 per cent in 1970 to approximately 10 per cent in the mid-1990s. Yet over this 25-year period very little concerted, collective action on the part of trade unions to oppose this massive job loss took place. As organized labor's ranks thinned and manufacturing declined, many communities scrambled to save what jobs they could by offering corporations financial inducement to stay or move into their town. While seeking such "tribute", companies routinely threatened work removal to quash organizing campaigns. And during most rounds of collective bargaining in the 1980s and 1990s corporations demanded and often received wage and benefits concessions from workers.[9]

A consequence of the disappearance of well-paying manufacturing jobs has been wage depression, declining household wealth, and increasing income inequality. For nearly 20 per cent of American households, debts exceed assets, meaning that net worth is zero or negative. Between 1987 and 1996 average employee compensation in the US grew just 1.1 per cent, compared with 4 per cent between 1977 and 1986. For most workers, real wages are below their 1973 levels. In aggregate terms, labor's share of the national income dropped from 66.2 per cent in 1970 to 59 per cent in 1995. In 1998 the International Labour Organization summarized these trends: "Recently, while many trade unions have been pressing for reduced work time, guarantees of employment security and measures to combat unemployment, some employers have been seeking to modify many of the hard-won social protection measures in an effort to make labour markets less rigid."[10]

On the surface, current developments in manufacturing seem inconsistent with US macro-economic and stock-market conditions during the 1990s because they coincide with one of the longest macro-economic

9. For union membership see L. Belsey, "Labor's Place in the New Economy", *Christian Science Monitor* (27 March 2000), p. 1. For a discussion of the global aspects of capital flight, see William Greider, *One World Ready or Not: The Manic Logic of Global Capitalism* (New York, 1997), esp. chs 5 and 7; International Labour Organization [hereafter, ILO], *The Impact of Flexible Labour Market Arrangements in the Machinery, Electrical and Electronic Industries* (Geneva, 1997); William Lazonick and Mary O'Sullivan (eds), *Corporate Governance and Sustainable Prosperity* (New York, 2002); J. Tagliabue, "Buona Notte, Guten Tag: Europe's New Workdays", *New York Times* (20 October 1997), p. D1; L. Uchitelle, "Global Good Times Meet the Global Glut", *New York Times* (16 November 1997), p. D1; Teresa Hayter and David Harvey (eds), *The Factory and the City: The Story of the Cowley Automobile Works in Oxford* (London, 1993); Andre Lipietz, *Mirages and Miracles: The Crisis of Global Fordism* (London, 1987).

10. ILO, *The Impact of Flexible Labour*, p. 1; Frank Hansen, "Compensation in the New Economy", *Compensation and Benefits Review*, 30 (1998), pp. 7–15.

expansions in US postwar history, with unemployment and inflation at record low levels. In 1999, unemployment was 4.2 per cent while inflation was 2.2 per cent. They also coincide with the longest US stock market boom in history, with yields on corporate stock significantly above their depressed 1970s levels. Since 1990, productivity has risen 7 per cent, due to enormous gains in certain sectors. By the mid 1990s, corporate profit rates were back to the level they had reached at the peak of the post World-War-II boom; in 1997, corporate profits rose to 11.8 per cent of revenues, up from 11.5 per cent in 1996, representing their highest level since 1959, when the Commerce Department first began tracking this data.[11]

General Electric: "model behavior"?

Pratt & Whitney and General Electric (GE) have been the global market leaders in supplying engines to power aircraft of all types since the end of the Second World War. In jet-engine manufacturing (as in machine tools and steel), the employment picture was gloomy for most of the 1990s. Both the blue-collar and the white-collar workforces have shrunk by about 35 per cent since 1988. While much of the downsizing in the early part of the decade could be attributed to declining defense orders, the recovery of the aircraft market by the mid-1990s did little to restore employment levels in the jet-engine sector. Employment in the industry remains stuck at a level fully one-third below 1990 employment levels while inflation-adjusted average hourly earnings remained flat throughout. To understand how de-industrialization occurred in many older manufacturing cities in the US the corporate behavior of GE is worth considering, especially since it is Pratt's most important competitor.[12]

GE's search for cheaper production facilities places continuous pressure on Pratt to follow suit. Starting in the late 1950s, GE moved to parallel production, the practice of building several production facilities capable of handling the same work. By so doing, it could extract union concessions and reduce the threat of strikes under the possible threat of work removal. More recently GE has implemented shopfloor programs designed to boost productivity and improve quality. In the late 1980s, GE began to implement continuous improvement strategies called the "GE Workout" in its aircraft engine plants. This program was designed to accomplish four

11. United States Department of Commerce, Bureau of Labor Statistics (2000); Mary O'Sullivan, "Shareholder Value, Financial Theory and Economic Performance", paper presented at the 52nd Annual Meeting of the Industrial Relations Research Association, Boston, 2000; Hansen, "Compensation in the New Economy".

12. This analysis borrows heavily from the work of Beth Almeida. See in particular "Good Jobs Flying Away: The US Jet Engine Industry", in Lazonick and O'Sullivan, *Corporate Governance and Sustainable Prosperity*, pp. 104–140.

things: establish trust on the factory floor between workers and managers; empower employees to make production improvement suggestions; eliminate unnecessary work; and establish a new shopfloor paradigm of boundaryless work. At the same time, GE sought to change the labor agreement to eliminate job classifications and broaden the tasks workers were expected to perform. Employees were told to welcome the freedom that boundaryless work offered and "to take advantage of it by using their minds creatively to figure out how to improve the company's operations". GE's Evendale, Ohio, aircraft-engine facility was the first to respond. When workers there refused to ratify contract changes, the company shifted work to other facilities. Forty per cent of all parts made at Evendale were removed and 3,900 workers lost their jobs.[13] GE then turned to its workforce in Lynn, seeking the same contract concessions, only to be similarly rebuffed. Eventually the Lynn local agreed to contract modifications and the introduction of GE's multiskilling program.[14]

Parallel production and continuous improvement have been richly rewarding for GE: in 1998 the company registered $1.7 billion in operating profits on $10 billion in sales, translating into an operating margin of 17 per cent. Late in 1999, GE flexed its global muscles once more to move well beyond parallel domestic plants, for in a move that will further the deindustrialization of the northeast United States the company launched its "Globalization and Supplier Migration" strategy. Its components suppliers were ordered to achieve 10 to 14 per cent annual cost reductions, savings that could be realized only by shifting work to countries with lower cost structures. GE stated: "Migrate or be out of business; not a matter of if, just when. We expect you to move and move quickly." A carrot was offered: "We sincerely want you to participate and will help, but if you don't we will move on without you." The benefits for a move to Mexico, according to GE, included average daily wage rates of $6.00, friendly unions, and the promise of long-term low labor costs.

According to IAM economist Beth Almeida, what is taking place "should serve as a warning to those who would maintain that the US will

13. Robert Slater, *The GE Way Handbook* (New York, 2000), p. 50; Konzelmann and Forrant, "Creative Work Systems". Employment at Evendale was close to 20,000 in 1988; at the end of 1994 only 8,000 workers remained.

14. For example, former GE engineer Oswald Jones cites GE manager Charles Pieper, who supervised several plant reorganizations in Europe, as he describes how workers relate to participation programs: "I have never see a group of people who are not interested. Never. Never. Never. Whether you are Chinese, Hungarian, Japanese, Swedish, people love to go and make their workplace better". While Pieper was president of GE Lighting Europe, passionately committed workers saw factories drop from 24 to 12 and employment from 24,000 to 13,000. Jones concludes "It is hardly surprising that workers regard GE managerial initiatives to make the workplace better with considerable skepticism." Oswald Jones, "Changing the Balance? Taylorism, TQM, and Work Organisation", *New Technology, Work and Employment*, 12 (1997), pp. 13–24, 20–22.

always win out in the high-tech manufacturing race. The idea that only poor-quality jobs in low-tech industries are being lost to competitor nations is refuted by the experience of aerospace workers".[15] In the context of these disturbing global trends, what happens at Pratt will have wide ramifications, for should the company flee Connecticut or squeeze its hundreds of suppliers in the same way that GE is, it will mark the nadir for large-firm metalworking unions in the entire Connecticut River Valley, once one of world's pre-eminent industrial regions.[16]

De-industrialization and economic restructuring in Connecticut

In Connecticut 4 out of 10 manufacturing jobs were lost between 1980 and 2000, with drastic cuts at Pratt & Whitney contributing to the blood-letting. (See Table 1 for the employment structure of the Connecticut economy.) In 1999 there were 18,700 fewer jobs in primary metals (–66.6 per cent), 37,300 fewer jobs in industrial machinery (–54.2 per cent), and 48,500 fewer jobs in transportation equipment (–53 per cent) than in 1967.[17] Connecticut netted roughly 113,000 new jobs from 1985 to 2000. But employment gains were by-and-large in low-paying services and retail trade – health care, copy centers, temporary help agencies and entertainment. (See Tables 2 and 3 for state employment data.) Finance, insurance, and real estate (FIRE) only added 10,000 jobs over the 15-year period, this in a state that claims it is the insurance capital of the United States. From the third quarter of 1999 to the third quarter of 2000, manufacturing lost 3,700 jobs and services and retail trade added 14,000 jobs in Connecticut. But with the exception of FIRE – average weekly wage $1,359 – average wages in the growth sectors trailed manufacturing wages. In 2000, the average weekly manufacturing wage was $1,117 compared to $717 for services and $427 for retail trade. It should be noted that the average wage for Connecticut aerospace workers was about 15 per cent higher than the statewide average manufacturing wage.[18]

15. Aaron Bernstein, "Welch's March to the South", *Business Week* (6 December 1999), p. 74; J. Millman, "GE boosts Mexican Output as Labor Talks in US Near", *The Wall Street Journal* (5 January 2000), p. 8; Almeida, "Good Jobs Flying Away", p. 106.
16. R. Mokhiber and R. Weissman, "GE: Every Plant on a Barge", see: www.corporatepredators.org. See also Greider, *One World Ready or Not*; Forrant, "Between a Rock"; Kapstein, "Workers and the World Economy"; ILO, *The Impact of Flexible Labour.*
17. Wage data comes from the Connecticut Department of Labor web site, www.ct.dol.ct/us/lmi/20299ct.htm; 1999 is the last year reported.
18. *Connecticut Economic Digest* (April 2001), p. 7; *ibid.*, (August 2001), p. 5; *ibid.*, (September 2001), p. 2. Across Connecticut, the fastest growing occupations include eating and drinking establishments, cleaning and lawn care services, catalog and mail-order houses, and household audio and visual equipment sales. None of these occupations makes any use of the precision manufacturing skills held by Pratt & Whitney workers and none of these occupations pays a remotely similar wage.

Table 1. *Connecticut manufacturing establishments and employment, 1962–1997.*

Year	Establishments	All employees	Production workers
1962	5,697	419,400	294,000
1967	5,829	477,700	329,900
1972	5,836	399,300	258,200
1977	6,485	412,100	255,300
1982	6,693	424,400	245,000
1987	6,747	388,900	216,500
1992	6,282	320,800	171,000
1997	5,911	263,000	–

Source: United States Department of Commerce Manufacturing Census conducted every five years.

Table 2. *Structure of Connecticut economy by employment categories.*

	1985	1999	Job change	% change
Total employment	1,558,100	1,671,500	113,400	7
Manufacturing	408,000	269,200	–138,800	–34
Transportation and public utilities	68,300	78,200	9,900	15
Services	349,600	526,600	177,000	50
Finance, insurance, real estate	130,400	140,700	10,300	8
Trade (wholesale/ retail)	346,000	359,500	13,500	4
Construction	65,400	60,900	–4,500	–7
Government	188,800	235,600	46,800	25
Mining	1,600	800	–800	–50

Source: Connecticut Department of Labor; www.ctdol.state.ct.us/lmi.

Table 3. *Connecticut employment by percentages 1985 and 1999.*

	1985	1999
Manufacturing	26.2	16.1
Transportation and public utilities	4.3	4.6
Services	22.4	31.5
Finance, insurance, real estate	8.3	8.4
Wholesale and retail trade	22.2	21.5
Construction	4.1	3.6
Government	12.1	14.0
Mining	1.0	1.0

Source: Connecticut Department of Labor; www.ctdol.state.ct.us/lmi.

In their research on de-industrialization, Doreen Massey and Richard Meegan make the point the parties to the process – labor and capital – do not suffer the same outcomes. This is the case in the US, for corporate profits had returned to peak post-World-War-II levels by the mid-1990s, yet in Connecticut – home to the corporate headquarters of several leading global corporations – median real family income had fallen 14 per cent from 1990 to 2000.[19] By the mid-1990s, when adjusted for inflation, US workers' median income was 5 per cent lower than in the late 1970s and household wealth was more concentrated than ever before. The top 5 per cent of households (those making $133,000 or more) controlled 21.4 per cent of all income while the bottom 60 per cent controlled 27.6 per cent. This represents a reversal of the 20 years after the Second World War, when as the country's industrial base expanded there had been a steady decline in family income inequality.[20]

In addition, while many central cities in the US added residents and jobs in the 1990s, there was a 15 per cent drop in population and no net employment gains in Connecticut's capital city, Hartford, over the 10-year period. This stagnation was "reflected to a lesser degree in all of Connecticut's large cities with the exception of Stamford in Fairfield County", resulting in a "widening economic and racial segregation in Connecticut, which is the richest state in the country".[21] Among 144 metropolitan areas examined by the federal government, Hartford finished 110th in high-tech employment growth. David Harvey and Erik Swyngedouw documented a similar phenomenon in their discussion of massive layoffs at a Rover assembly plant in Cowley, an industrial suburb of Oxford. There, restructuring

> [...] meant not only the loss of many of those secure jobs which secured community affluence for many, but a transition in the qualities of the jobs that remained (through speed-up, deskilling, and the like) so that the difference

19. In 1997 corporate profits were 11.8 per cent of revenues, representing their highest level since 1959, when the Commerce Department first began tracking this data. Massey and Meegan, *The Anatomy of Job Loss*, p. vii; Andrew Sum, *The Story of Household Incomes in the 1990s* (Boston, MA, 2001). The report can be located at www.massinc.org/publications/reports.
20. Chuck Collins, B. Leondar-Wright, and Holly Sklar, *Shifting Fortunes: The Perils of the Growing American Wealth Gap* (Boston, MA, 1999); Hansen, "Compensation in the New Economy"; David Weinberg, "A Brief Look at Postwar US Income Inequality", *Current Population Reports* (Washington DC, 1996), pp. 60–91.
21. David M. Herszenhorn, "Behind Census Numbers In a Declining Hartford", *New York Times* (22 March 2001), p. A22; Janny Scott, "Connecticut Population Shifts Toward New York," *New York Times* (20 March 2001), p. 1. MassInc reports that for seven of the nine northeast states, "median real incomes were below those of 1989, with Connecticut, Massachusetts, New Hampshire, and New York faring the worst in the region". Connecticut median household income in constant 1999 dollars fell to $49,267, from $56,916 in 1989, the largest drop among the ten northeast states (www.massinc.org).

between the marginalized and the employed became less rather than more marked.[22]

For Pratt workers the downward trends produced a good deal of economic insecurity. Turret lathe operator and IAM Executive Board member, Ted Durkin, noted that while there are some jobs available paying decent wages they require considerable training. "I'm 45 and lots of other workers are older. Not too many folks will want to start all over again and go back to school." The jobs that are available absent education are at the Home Depot or at small-job shops, but for a lot less money. Machinist and union shop committee member, John Cloutier, added that years ago "you could get your foot in the door here [Pratt], project into the future, and see yourself with a steady job for thirty or more years; but no more". He wondered "How do you sign for a mortgage, buy a car, save for your kid's college when your employment future is so insecure?"[23]

UNITED TECHNOLOGIES CORPORATION: GOOD JOBS FLYING AWAY?

UTC, Pratt & Whitney, and the Connecticut economy

Pratt & Whitney is a major business segment of UTC and employs roughly 12,000 people in Connecticut, and 30,000 worldwide. With nearly 2,000 locations in 220 countries, in 2001 UTC ranked 57th among US corporations and 125th in the world. UTC's global workforce totaled 150,000 in 2000, down 25 per cent from 1990. As a result of the transfer of capital commitments abroad, 54 per cent of all employees are outside the US. UTC's other major business segments are: Flight Systems, which includes Hamilton Sundstrand and Sikorsky, producer of such things as engine controls, environmental control systems, aircraft propellers, and helicopters; Carrier Air Conditioner, the world's largest manufacturer of heating, ventilating, and air-conditioning systems; and Otis Elevator, the world's leader in the manufacture of elevators, escalators, and automated people movers.[24]

22. David Harvey and Erik Swyngedouw, "Industrial Restructuring, Community Disempowerment and Grass-Roots Resistance", in Hayter and Harvey, *The Factory and The City*, pp. 11–25, 16; United States Department of Housing and Urban Development, *The State of the Cities 2000* (Washington DC, 2000).

23. Author interviews at the Pratt & Whitney Local 1746 Union Hall in December 2000 and January and March 2001.

24. UTC, *Annual Report 2000* (n.p., n.d.). The states are Arkansas, California, Connecticut, Georgia, Maine, Michigan, Minnesota, Oklahoma, and Texas. European and Asian joint ventures are in Dublin, Ireland, Tapei, Taiwan, Kiev, Ukraine, and Singapore. Hamilton Sundstrand, also in Connecticut, employs 17,000 people worldwide, with about 4,000 in Connecticut. Jet-engine manufacturing, overhaul, and repair operations are located in eight states and Puerto Rico, and there are international overhaul and repair operations in Canada,

Pratt & Whitney and its global competitor, General Electric, are world leaders in the manufacture of jet engines. A truly indigenous New England industry, 128 New England firms and 34,000 people built complex parts, components, subassemblies, and control systems for engines during 1999; the majority of these firms were subcontractors to Lynn, Massachusetts-based General Electric and/or Pratt & Whitney. This represented 28 per cent of total US aircraft engine manufacturing employment.[25]

Originally a machine tool builder, the Pratt & Whitney Company was incorporated in Hartford in 1855. It began to focus on aircraft engines in 1929 and dynamic growth in the decades after the Second World War made Pratt & Whitney the most important industrial employer in Connecticut. For fifty years, thousands of well-paid machinists at Pratt & Whitney built engines, created massive amounts of wealth for investors, and fueled the growth of hundreds of small- and medium-sized metalworking and precision manufacturing firms and retail and wholesale establishments across Connecticut and western Massachusetts. During the 1950s and 1960s Pratt & Whitney established the wherewithal to produce globally; Pratt's manufacturing and engineering projects take place in nine states and several European and Asian countries. This has made it possible for Pratt to whipsaw unions, communities, and entire nations to exact concessions for jobs.[26] As though playing a giant board game, Pratt constantly shifted work between Connecticut, Florida, and Maine, while at the same time participating in its numerous overseas manufacturing ventures. For the IAM in Connecticut – and for other industrial unions in the US where corporations availed themselves of an extended geography of production – these maneuvers served to weaken contractual seniority and job classification language and significantly reduced the threat of strikes.[27]

Highly profitable in the late 1990s, UTC's investors and top managers were handsomely rewarded. In 2001, *Forbes* placed UTC on its prestigious "platinum list" of 400 US corporations, noting that when compared to its aerospace and defense industry peers, "UTC had the second-best five-year average for return on capital (21 per cent) and virtually tied for first place

China, UK, France, Germany, Ireland, Italy, Malaysia, the Netherlands, Russia, and Singapore.

25. I am indebted here to research being done by Beth Almeida, an economist with the International Association of Machinists in Washington DC. For the impact of General Electric's abandonment of Pittsfield, Massachusetts, see Max. H. Kirsch, *In the Wake of the Giant: Multinational Restructuring and Uneven Development in a New England Community* (Albany, NY, 1998). Kirsch notes that GE expanded during the 1970s, adding 30,000 jobs abroad while decreasing domestic employment by 25,000, see *ibid.*, p.13.

26. Robert Forrant, "Too Many Bends in the River: The Decline of the Connecticut River Valley Machine Tool Industry", *Journal of Industrial History*, 5 (2002, forthcoming).

27. Kapstein, "Workers and the World Economy"; Almeida, "Good Jobs Flying Away"; Jones, "Changing the Balance?"; Bryn Jones, *Forging the Factory of the Future: Cybernation and Societal Institutions* (Cambridge, 1997).

in the five-year average for earnings per share growth (21.9 per cent)".[28] Its revenues of $26.6 billion in 2000 were well above 1996's $19.9 billion, and earnings per common share of $3.55 in 2000, compared favorably to $1.74 in 1996. Pratt's 2000 operating profit of $1.2 billion accounted for 35 per cent of UTC's $3.4 billion total. The corporation's 2000 *Year in Review* proclaimed: "Investors do prize consistency, and UTC is committed to this above all. UTC's total share-owner return has compounded at an average 30 per cent annually since 1994, well above market indices." Added the *Review*, "our $1.8 billion in available cash flow also provides the engine of growth for acquisitions". Indeed, 35 acquisitions costing $7.6 billion were completed in 1999–2000. But while profits escalated, workers rolled out the door; during 1999 alone UTC terminated 15,000 employees from its global workforce – 41 firings a day for the calendar year – with Pratt & Whitney worldwide absorbing 5,200 of the terminations. In the next section I discuss how Pratt/UTC achieved this profitability.[29]

1993 concessionary bargaining

Faced with the challenge of sharp defense spending cuts at the end of the Vietnam War, UTC diversified through the purchase of several companies, including Sikorsky Helicopter, Carrier Air Conditioning, Otis Elevators, and American Bosch. This, coupled with the late 1980s boom in the commercial airline industry, produced strong years for Pratt & Whitney. However, consolidation in the commercial airline sector and defense spending reductions after the destruction of the Berlin Wall caused the bottom to fall out of the jet-engine market and in the first quarter of 1991 Pratt's earnings dropped 75 per cent. A new chief executive, Robert Daniell, arrived to slash manufacturing costs.[30] For Daniell, the solution was to squeeze $1 billion from costs; to achieve this 6,700 hourly and salaried jobs at Pratt's US facilities were to be eliminated. Losses continued across the corporation and in 1993 and Daniell introduced a more drastic 2-year restructuring program. UTC-wide, 14,000 jobs were to be eliminated – 7 per cent of the global workforce – and 100 facilities were to be closed. Even before these proposed cuts, the membership of the Pratt local in East Hartford had fallen under 6,000, from over 9,000 in 1983.[31]

28. Howard Banks, "No More Yo-Yo", *Forbes* (11 January 1999), pp. 130–131; Claudia H. Deutsch, "Private Sector: Even His Soufflés Can't Relax", *New York Times* (19 November 2000), section 3, p. 2.

29. UTC, *Year in Review* (n.p., n.d.), pp. 1, 8.

30. In the first quarter of 1991, earnings at Pratt dropped 75 per cent – less than half the predicted earnings. With UTC relying on Pratt for two-thirds of its operating income this was a particularly hard hit; Jonathan P. Hicks, "United Technologies Bumpy Ride", *New York Times* (1 May 1991), p. D1.

31. George Judson, "Pratt & Whitney Threatening to Shut Two Connecticut Plants", *New York Times* (15 April 1993), p. A1.

In 1993 George David – formerly head of Otis Elevators – became UTC Chief Operating Officer under Daniell, and Karl Krapek became President of Pratt & Whitney. As 1993 began, the trio called for the termination of 10,000 Pratt employees worldwide.[32] And in early spring they presented an ultimatum to the IAM and the state legislature: quickly generate $30 million each in cost concessions or Pratt, "crown jewel of UTC and a pillar of Connecticut's economy for seventy years" would cease manufacturing in the state. Absent the concessions, 2,300 jobs were to be cut immediately, with the rest of the jobs phased out over several years.[33] The parties understood that the future of jet-engine manufacturing in Connecticut was at stake. Bill Cibes, the state's budget director, commented "If you let 2,300 jobs leave Connecticut, that means the state is not competitive to retain the rest."[34] "Pratt & Whitney is part of the business heritage of Connecticut", then Governor, Lowell Weicker, stated, "It's done well by Connecticut and its people. It belongs here. You've got to give up something in the tough times. We all do."[35]

David and Krapek commanded the marathon bargaining sessions while deftly courting legislative delegations from Georgia and Maine – the sites of smaller Pratt & Whitney plants – which offered the two men lucrative financial incentives for added jobs in their states. Hourly manufacturing costs in Connecticut, Krapek argued, were $6–$8 per worker higher compared to other states; getting these costs in line must be accomplished for Pratt to continue making aircraft engines in its birthplace.[36] State officials believed that Pratt's cost figures were exaggerated, but they struggled to meet them, believing that Krapek's threat of a total shutdown was all too real. Unionists approached the talks with dim hopes, with many workers believing that the East Hartford plant's demise was imminent, regardless of the negotiations.

Ultimately, the legislature crafted incentives that included a research and development tax credit, loan guarantees for job training, and grants to train workers in Japanese-style lean production, and utility rate reductions. They also enacted policies that granted all Connecticut employers savings in workers' compensation insurance. For its part, the union agreed to a wage freeze, new productivity targets, and modifications to numerous work rules in exchange for vague company commitments to keep a minimum number of jobs in the state, limit their subcontracting, and halt

32. Robert Weisman, "Real Struggle for Pratt's Future Played Out in Private", *Hartford Courant* (26 December 1993), p. A1.
33. Robert Weisman, "How Pratt Flexed its Muscle, and State, Union Relented", *Hartford Courant* (27 December 1993), p. A1.
34. Weisman, "Real Struggle".
35. Weisman, "How Pratt Flexed".
36. Kirk Johnson, "By Pratt & Whitney's Math, Connecticut Costs Too Much", *New York Times* (23 April 1993), p. A1; Judson, "Pratt & Whitney Threatening".

the movement of jobs to Maine and Georgia. After approving the concessions by a four-to-three margin, many machinists – even those voting for the concessions – expressed suspicions about Pratt's true intentions. But, in the words of one member, the feeling was that it was "better to preserve jobs and live to fight another day". Within a year UTC saw a financial payoff, in the form of a 20 per cent earnings increase on just a 1 per cent increase in sales; not surprisingly, workers were less fortunate.[37]

The aftermath: Thanks – but not really

After the concessions bargaining, a letter distributed to Pratt & Whitney workers by Pratt boss, Karl Krapek, noted that "by agreeing to the plan, the workers had expressed faith in the future of our company". The company, he intoned, will undertake "significant redesign of our manufacturing, engineering and administrative processes" and keep work in the state. The *Hartford Courant* on Sunday 27 June 1993 contained a full-page advertisement in which management issued a very public thank you for granting them cost relief to the state's taxpayers and the union. Pratt credited the legislature for measures that now "make business more competitive" in Connecticut, praised the IAM for "convincing us to keep jobs in Connecticut" and applauded workers for their trust. "The spotlight now shines on Pratt & Whitney to deliver on our promises", the ad trumpeted, and it concluded with an optimistic proclamation: "SOME DAY OUR BUSINESS WILL PICK UP AGAIN. THANKS TO YOU, IT WILL PICK UP IN CONNECTICUT".[38] Yet the movement of work abroad intensified and the membership of IAM District 91 – which contained all of Connecticut's union locals representing UTC production and maintenance workers – fell from approximately 13,000 in 1993 to less than 10,000 by 1999. In 2000, UTC announced its intention to trim an additional 14,500 jobs corporation-wide over three years, with many cuts slated for Connecticut.[39]

Worker responses – "We don't use logic with UTC"

In March 2001 Warren Occhialini, Ted Durkin, John Cloutier, and Mike Stone – Pratt workers and active union members – discussed 1993's watershed events. They concurred that despite the corporation's insistence that they wanted an open style of industrial relations and an atmosphere of

37. Author interviews, 2001.
38. *Hartford Courant* (20 June 1993), p. B4; Thomas Lueck, "Jet-Engine Workers Accept Harsh Reality", *New York Times* (25 June 1993), p. B6.
39. Lueck, "Jet-Engine Workers"; Tim Smart, "Global Mission", *Business Week* (1 May 1995), pp. 132–135.

trust, events since 1993 made this impossible. For despite the agreement and expansion promises, thousands more workers lost their jobs. "In the end the Pratt workforce is always smaller, despite assurances that this will not take place", noted Cloutier. Occhialini observed that the Local always loses jobs in the end because UTC believes that it can do whatever it wants. Cloutier noted that in 1998, even after a signed agreement was reached between the union and the company to send 80,000 hours of work from East Hartford to North Berwick, Maine, with 100,000 hours of the Maine plant's work shifting to East Hartford. Work went to Maine, but the reverse trek never occurred.[40]

In describing blue-collar attrition, Cloutier concluded that "two generations of workers are not on the shopfloor". Seventy-five per cent of Connecticut Pratt & Whitney workers are over 45 and the average seniority in the plants is 22.1 years. With layoffs and restructuring, there are virtually no machinists and machine operators in their twenties and thirties and no hiring is taking place. Cloutier noted that "serious, long-term education and training to upgrade the skills of shop floor workers does not take place. This would indicate there is a future here". Durkin commented that Pratt has done such a poor job training people that they often rehire retirees at inflated salaries to train workers in shopfloor skills lost through early retirement and layoffs. Shaking his head, Durkin remarked: "We don't use logic with them when we discuss this kind of thing." Said Cloutier,

> [...] the workforce is so lean that there is almost no way for new work to come into the shop because the existing workforce can not handle it. People are already working tremendous amounts of overtime because the plant is run so much on the margin in terms of needed workers.[41]

For Cloutier and Durkin the restructuring has had little to do with workers being unable to perform the jobs. Since 1998 unionists have willingly participated in numerous efforts to reprocess how work is done to lower production costs and ostensibly save jobs. Yet, in a remarkably cynical maneuver, when job-redesign projects are concluded the work often "gets pulled out of the factory and shipped to an overseas business partner or a local job shop", Cloutier stated. Reacting in 1999 to proposed cuts at Pratt & Whitney's North Haven, Middletown, and East Hartford

40. According to Cloutier, a 1994 management survey of employee morale at Pratt was reported on in *Business Week* in 1995. While 78 per cent of employees reported pride in their work, fewer than half the workers felt any loyalty to the company; author interviews, 2001. The work-shifting agreement is found in the 1998 collective bargaining agreement between District Lodge 91 and Pratt & Whitney and reads in part: "approximately 21 part numbers associated with LPT Blades will be moving from Maine to Connecticut. This work represents approximately 100,000 hours of work annually" (p. 129).

41. Randy Barber and Robert Scott, *Jobs on the Wing: Trading Away the Future of the US Aerospace Industry* (Washington DC, 1995); Smart, "Global Mission".

factories, IAM District 91 directing business representative James Parent expressed unionists' frustrations: "They don't realize that when they talk about a worker, it's not just one worker. They are talking about a whole family whose future is up in the air. They are talking about the tax base of North Haven, and all the surrounding communities where workers live." And in a January 2001 interview, Parent reiterated his concern for keeping jobs in Connecticut and wondered where work that could generate a stable tax base was going to come from. "Why not grow jobs in Connecticut", asked Parent "instead of walking away from a workforce that averages 22+ years seniority?"[42]

In their description of Rover's investment diversions, capital flight, and work relocation, Harvey and Swyngedouw posit that "innumerable companies have cashed in on local productive capacity for decades" only to determine that this capacity "is no longer useful to them, leaving behind thousands of lost jobs, a desolated local economy, and citizens, local governments as well as other community-based institutions (varying from trade unions to the churches) in confusion and disarray". It appeared likely to Parent that Pratt & Whitney and UTC were set to cash-out in Connecticut.[43]

THE TEN THOUSAND JOBS QUESTION

Flip burgers?

In December 1998 IAM District 91 reached agreement on a 3-year contract with Pratt. At the time the company indicated that about 1,000 additional jobs might be eliminated over the next three years due to what it termed "production scheduling problems". But unionists were assured that no rerun of the drastic cuts that took place in 1993 was anticipated. Company officials emphasized that Pratt & Whitney was committed to Connecticut. Increased orders for very lucrative engine repairs and services were expected to boost jobs. But eight months later, without ever talking to the union, Krapek publicly announced that Pratt was going to relocate its engine repair and service work to Oklahoma and Texas and shutter a factory in Connecticut.

For the IAM, the unilateral declaration violated an important clause in

42. Author interviews, 2001.

43. Harvey and Swyngedouw, "Industrial Restructuring", p. 20. Beth Almeida, "Linking Institutions of Governance and Industrial Outcomes: The Case of Global Aircraft Engine Manufacturing", paper for the 52nd Annual Meeting of the Industrial Relations Research Association, Boston, 2000; author interview with James Parent. In 1998 Pratt took a majority interest in Singapore Airlines' engine shop, Hamilton acquired Ratier-Figeac in France, and Carrier commenced a joint venture with the Japanese manufacturer Toshiba. In 1999, Otis formed LG Otis Elevator Company in Korea with LG Electronics, Inc. UTC holds an 80 per cent equity interest in the new company (UTC Form 10-K, 1998, 1999).

the 1998 labor agreement – Letter 22 Workplace Guarantees and Subcontracting – which bound Pratt to discuss with it any plans to remove work and to give the union an opportunity to match the cost savings that might accrue to the company from the move. The letter read in part:

> The Company will make every effort to preserve the work presently and normally manufactured by employees covered by Article 2 of this Agreement. Therefore, it is not the intent of the Company to use subcontractors for the purpose of reducing or transferring work that is presently and normally manufactured by employees in the bargaining unit nor place such work in Maine or Georgia [...].[44]

As news of the North Haven closing spread, Gary Daly, age forty-eight with twenty years of service at Pratt, typified worker reactions. The company is "making record profits, and all they want is cheap labor, to bust the union", he noted. "We've got mortgages and families and are trying to send our kids to school. What are we going to do, flip burgers?" John Amato, who had worked at Pratt for just five years added, "I'm twenty-five and by the time I'm forty, there's going to be nothing left in Connecticut. They are going for cheap labor, that's all they want."[45]

Federal courts intervene: contractual obligations violated

Faced with the possible loss of their most important source of new work, on 16 September 1999 the IAM challenged the restructuring plan in federal court. Pratt's proposed cuts, argued the union, violated the 1998 labor agreement which obligated management to make reasonable efforts to keep work historically performed in Connecticut in the state at least until the contract expired in 2001. Stunning UTC, the United States District Court issued an injunction blocking the company's move until the case was heard. On 18 February 2000, citing specific clauses in the collective bargaining agreement, Judge Janet Hall ruled that, "Pratt made, in fact, no effort to preserve the parts repair work presently and normally manufactured by bargaining unit employees."

44. *Agreement Between Aeronautical Industrial District Lodge 91, IAMAW, AFL-CIO and Affiliated Locals and Pratt & Whitney* (n.p., 1998), p. 126; Barbara Nagy, "Pratt Braces For Upheaval", *Hartford Courant* (13 August 1999), p. 1; Dan Haar and Stacy Wong, "Shift: Connecticut's Gain Comes With Pain", *ibid.* The announced restructuring prompted an immediate 4.7 per cent increase ($3.19) in United Technologies stock price. It was predicted that the combination of layoffs and job transfers could save the company $100 million to $150 million a year, starting in 2001. Matthew Lubanko, "Plan Wins Friends on Wall Street", *Hartford Courant* (13 August 1999), p. D1.

45. Robin Stansbury and Matthew Kauffman, "Local Businesses React", *Hartford Courant* (13 August 1999), p. D1; Patricia Seremet, "Shock Turns to Anger", *ibid.*

IAM members were jubilant when Judge Hall's determined that

> Pratt's object was profit maximization, with no effort made to preserve the work in question. Its decision was driven by a desire solely to lower costs, in order to be more competitive and gain more business, all of which is rational and reasonable from a business perspective, absent Pratt's contractual obligation to the Union.

Pratt appealed the ruling in the United States Court of Appeals for the Second Circuit on 12 May 2000, and on 26 October 2000 the Appeals Court upheld Judge Hall's decision. UTC was prevented from moving the work for the life of the contract.[46]

Preparing for a fight: job loss analyzed

Buoyed by their stunning court victory, District 91's leaders started preparations for what they felt would be bruising contract negotiations in the Fall of 2001. Unionists expected that Pratt would seek the removal of the job-security language. Eager to head off a new round of concessionary bargaining and determined to preserve existing jobs, unionists established a broad-based jobs preservation campaign under the banner "Grow Jobs in Connecticut". One component of the effort was a report District 91 commissioned on de-industrialization in Connecticut since the 1980s. As part of the report the Chicago-based Center for Labor & Community Research (CLCR) prepared an analysis of the projected financial and job losses in Connecticut should UTC curtail its manufacturing across the state. The report became the centerpiece for an educational campaign with union members, the state legislature, church and community groups, and other trade unions across the state.

CLCR determined that curtailed manufacturing would mean an end to 11,300 Connecticut UTC jobs – 6,100 production jobs and 5,200 support jobs. There would be a "ripple effect" cut of almost 21,000 additional jobs caused by the decreased wages and spending power; thus, total job losses would reach 32,400. For each production job eliminated just over four additional jobs would be lost. Jobs in retail trade (3,763), business services (3,608), health services (1,648), wholesale trade (1,034), and construction (1,024) would be the most severely impacted. Estimated costs for two years following the cessation of manufacturing included:[47] (1) The loss of

46. Court Brief, United States District Court, District of Connecticut. Civil Action No. 3:99-CV-1827 (JCH). Aeronautical Indus. Dist. Lodge 91 of the Int'l Ass'n of Machinists and Aerospace Workers, AFL-CIO Plaintiff, v. United Technologies Corp., Pratt & Whitney Defendant (n.p., 18 February 2000).

47. Ken Blum, *Social Cost Analysis of the Impact of Closing UTC's Aircraft Engine and Parts Plants in Connecticut* (Chicago, IL, 2001). For a discussion of employment multipliers and their calculation, see Dean Baker and Thea Lee, *Employment Multipliers in the US Economy*, Working

$304 million in local, state, and federal tax revenue along with an additional $119 million worth of expenditures to cover increased unemployment compensation. The two-year total cost to government would be $423 million. (2) Two years after job loss – based on Connecticut wage figures – a terminated production worker with a new job would earn just 76 per cent of his/her former income. Consideration was given to the fact that laid-off workers could receive severance wages and that many workers might receive some portion of their pension. (3) Based on March 2001 labor market information, it was estimated that 20 per cent of Pratt & Whitney and Hamilton Sundstrand workers (2,285 people) would remain unemployed for at least 26 weeks and that 4.6 per cent (521 people) would be unemployed after one year. Among the "ripple-effect" workers, an additional 699 people would be unemployed for at least one year. Thus, 1,220 people would be unemployed for at least one year.

The December 2001 strike

After waging a broad-based community campaign, at 12.01 a.m. on 3 December 2001 the first strike since 1960 at Pratt & Whitney began. The company's contract offer had included a 10 per cent pay raise and a $1,000 signing bonus, but, as anticipated, there were no job-security provisions. In fact, the proposed contract provided for the immediate removal of 500 East Hartford jobs out-of-state, with simply a nebulous promise to bring new work in. At the strike-vote meeting, Gary Allen, the IAM's national aerospace coordinator, told several thousand workers: "This is your defining moment as a union. You've got to send a message." Mike Stone, President of the East Hartford local added: "We can either die on the vine or fight to grow jobs in the state of Connecticut. Nothing is won without sacrifice. It is our time to sacrifice."

On the picket line 15-year Pratt worker, Greg Adorno, asked "What's the point of giving somebody a 10 per cent raise if they're not going to be here to benefit from it?" For James Parent, IAM District 91's chief negotiator, the issue appeared cut and dried. "We were at a point at the end of negotiations where we were close. It's not an issue of money. It's an issue of whether the jobs are going to be here. What good is a good package if you don't have a job?" With 63 per cent of the membership lost in the

Paper No. 107 (Washington DC, 1993). This study utilized an input–output model developed by the US Forest Service called Implan. The model produced multipliers showing sales, indirect business taxes, and jobs for all industries that produce inputs for the aircraft and missile engines and parts plants, and also industries producing goods and services consumed by UTC workers. The Center for Labor & Community Research was founded in 1982 as the Midwest Center for Labor Research and has been involved in research and worker/community organizing campaigns to stop de-industrialization and preserve working-class communities. It can be reached at: www.clcr.org.

past decade, Howard Haberern, with 34 years at Pratt, added "We're saying, leave the work in Connecticut. That's the crux of the whole thing."[48]

The IAM's national website reported,

> This is a strike to protect America's defense industrial base. This is a strike to keep good paying jobs and decent retirements available to the people of Connecticut. We seek a contract that keeps Pratt & Whitney successful and that keeps our members working. The company has illegally refused to provide information on subcontracted work inside the plants and on work they plan to send to outside vendors or overseas.

The union refused to abrogate the contract language it had so successfully used in federal court to block Pratt's earlier restructuring efforts. On the strike website, Gary Allen, head of IAM's aerospace division, remarked "The time has come to stand up and fight to save the best industrial jobs in Connecticut. IAM members and the people in our communities take this fight very seriously and we are committed to win."[49] Comments from the picket line reflected the strike's very high stakes. "I'm striking for the younger people", said fifty-four-year-old Mary Hurlburt, "They need a younger generation coming in to build these engines."[50]

Ten days into the strike, on 13 December 2001, workers ratified a new contract by a 75 per cent affirmative vote of the 4,000 votes cast. Pratt's prestrike wage offer remained unchanged. However, in an extremely important victory, Pratt agreed in writing to produce a new engine in Connecticut and work in the state remained subject to the court-tested Workplace Guarantee contract language. As a symbol of their commitment to "Grow Connecticut", Pratt agreed to start their very first joint Union/Company Apprenticeship Program. Finally, the company agreed to participate in the High Performance Work Organization training program at the IAM's New Technology Center.[51]

CLOSING THOUGHTS

At the turn of the new millennium, global market pressures and short-product life cycles have forced the corporate officers of many firms to consider worker intellect an asset, not a liability. But, as the evidence in this section demonstrates, in the drive to maximize production and

48. Barbara Nagy, "Union Votes to Strike at Pratt", *Hartford Courant* (3 December 2001), p. 1; John Moran and Barbara Nagy, "Job Security the Issue for Pratt Strikers", *Hartford Courant* (4 December 2001), p. 1.
49. www.goiam.org/news.
50. Barbara Nagy, "Pratt Negotiations May Resume Soon", *Hartford Courant* (5 December 2001), p. 1.
51. Barbara Nagy and John Moran, "Strike is Over at Pratt", *Hartford Courant* (14 December 2001), p. 1.

increase shareholder value, worker empowerment and team building still play second violin to the first chair occupied by output demand and "line speed-up". The delicate underpinnings of plant-level trust are threatened by the wherewithal of owners to arbitrarily shift production to gain even the slightest competitive advantages. Workers and their unions are thus squeezed between a rock and a hard place: they are condemned as backward thinkers should they refuse to consider management-proposed work changes that might give their plant a chance to prosper, yet they are equally doomed when they accede only to have managers "pick their brains" and transfer the work to plants in less expensive parts of the world, as occurred at Pratt & Whitney.

The aircraft-engine and engine-parts and components industry reflects several disturbing trends for workers and communities that mirror the socioeconomic downturns faced by defense workers in the US tossed out of work from 1987 to 1997. In an examination of what happened to the close to one million defense-related manufacturing jobs lost during these years, Ann Markusen and Laura Powers concluded that "a majority of workers did not, on average, experience rapid re-employment at wages comparable or better" than their lost jobs. A sizable minority experienced a drop in earnings of 50 per cent or more, which suggests that "many defense workers did not become re-employed in jobs that capitalized on their existing skills". With the wherewithal to manufacture around the globe, Pratt and GE continues shrewdly to play off workers from different unions, communities, and nations for "sweetheart" financial deals in return for jobs.[52] And as jobs exited Connecticut before the December 2001 strike and economic uncertainty intensified, UTC's CEO George David was handsomely rewarded for the corporation's "excellent financial results and long-term strategic accomplishments" with a salary and stock bonuses which topped $18 million.[53]

Over the years the state government and municipal governments have done little to protect the remainder of the state's manufacturing jobs. In the late 1980s and early 1990s, as manufacturers exited Connecticut and Massachusetts, the mayors of Hartford and Springfield engaged in a war of newspaper advertisements, each one trying to entice manufacturers from the other's city to their state. And while the Connecticut legislature has funded several programs to encourage business research in such areas as biotechnology and medical devices, these programs are not linked to any well-conceived plans for the transition of aerospace and other manufacturing workers losing jobs into new employment opportunities. And

52. Laura Powers and Ann Markusen, "A Just Transition? Lessons from Defense Worker Adjustment in the 1990s", *Economic Policy Institute Technical Paper*, 237 (Washington DC, 1999), pp. 3, 25; author interview with Jeff Crosby, union president at GE Lynn, Winter 1998.
53. Wypijewski, "GE Brings Bad Things"; Cowie, *Capital Moves*; Forrant, "Between a Rock".

twenty-year Pratt machinists are not going to be employed in financial services companies selling stocks and mutual funds, nor will they be able to make ends meet employed in the low-wage services and retail sectors. At the same time, the IAM and other unions are conspicuously absent from the myriad publicly-funded development agencies established to bring new jobs to Connecticut.

It is no geographical accident that highly skilled jet-engine and aerospace production took place in Connecticut for well over fifty years. Pratt & Whitney has a long history in the state, developing into leaders in their industry because the fertile skill base along the Connecticut River Valley provided engineering, innovation, and precision production skills.[54] But with ultramodern plants built elsewhere and fewer investments being made in Connecticut, management has "manufactured" the self-fulfilling prophecy that its Connecticut's factories are not productive enough. And as precision metalworking jobs disappear, the skill base cultivated up and down the Connecticut River Valley for over a century is disappearing.[55]

Economist Mary O'Sullivan describes innovation as the process through which productive resources are developed and utilized to generate higher quality and/or lower cost products than had previously been available.[56] At the enterprise level, strategic decisions are made that determine the performance of the firm and, at the same time, these decisions have effects on the economy as a whole. A work-removal strategy can generate high near-term returns for shareholders, as UTC's stock performance and handsome executive rewards indicates. Should this be the dominant strategy employed by a nation's corporations, the failure to invest in more efficient technologies and skills will eventually lead to a sharp decline in national productive capabilities. Communities that were formerly home to these industries will suffer years of falling living standards and sharp population losses, a trend clearly visible across Connecticut.

At Pratt & Whitney workers were educated in problem-solving techniques and encouraged to use these skills to continuously improve plant efficiencies, knowing full well that steadily deteriorating job security was likely to follow. To extend their global reach and achieve incomparable shopfloor control, managers have sought to capitalize on two conflicting predilections among workers: the first is the deep-seated fear of the loss of one's job; the second is the desire to contribute one's knowledge and skills in the work environment. It remains the case that the exigencies of global capitalism foster and impose decisions that are made far removed from individual factory floors, completely void of a collective

54. Almeida, "Linking Institutions".

55. Author interviews January and March 2001.

56. Mary O'Sullivan, "The Innovative Enterprise and Corporate Governance", *Cambridge Journal of Economics*, 24 (2000), pp. 393–416.

workers' voice. Thus, absent a consistent, concerted, and coordinated international labor voice, global production giants have the capacity to exercise significant bargaining leverage over their worldwide workforce and the power to worsen wages and working conditions for growing numbers of manufacturing workers as we have seen in Connecticut. The best hope for workers and their unions is to forge national and international bonds similar to the reach forged by global corporations. Plant closures and de-industrialization cannot be contested one factory at a time. Of course, this is easier said than done.[57]

In closing, consider remarks by UTC chairman George David before the Council on Foreign Relations. In discussing employment, he stated that Americans "don't want the jobs at the bottom of the economy, we want the jobs at the top, the issue is how to get there". Noting that UTC employed 201,000 people in 1990, and 148,000 in 2000 – with an announced additional 10 per cent cut coming – David urged American corporations to "guard against displacement" and to "establish and adhere to standards of performance and conduct internationally that are fair to employees everywhere".[58] For Pratt & Whitney machinist John Cloutier, working every day with the idea in the back of your mind, "How much longer will I have this job?" is extremely stressful. With gallows humor, unionist Ted Durkin gets the last words. "The old ethic that many companies had that their workforces really mattered is long gone. Now, when you leave the plant on Friday not laid off, you feel like you had a great week!" This is hardly the virtuous treatment David espoused before the Council on Foreign Relations.

57. Konzelmann and Forrant, "Creative Work Systems". For a discussion of a local union's corporate strategy, Andrew Jonas, "Investigating the Local-Global paradox: Corporate Strategy, Union Local Autonomy, and Community Action in Chicago", in Andrew Herod (ed.), *Organizing the Landscape: Geographical Perspectives on Labor Unionism* (Minneapolis, MN, 1998), pp. 325–350.

58. George David, "The Opportunity to Expand Skills and the Knowledge Base", speech before the Council on Foreign Relations, *City News Publishing Company Vital Speeches*, 66 (n.p., 15 March 2000), 14, p. 439.

IRSH 47 (2002), pp. 137–158 DOI: 10.1017/S0020859002000810

"Our Chronic and Desperate Situation": Anthracite Communities and the Emergence of Redevelopment Policy in Pennsylvania and the United States, 1945–1965

Gregory Wilson

On 3 May 1954, Lehigh Coal and Navigation Company announced that it would close its anthracite mining operations in Pennsylvania's Panther Valley. Company officials had hoped to keep some mines open but net losses in 1953 amounted to $1.4 million and the trend continued into early 1954. The company stated they would reopen the mines only if miners would work harder and produce more. All area locals of the United Mine Workers of America (UMW) voted to accept the program except one, Tamaqua Local 1571. Arguing that the new rules violated existing wage agreements, workers from this Local picketed the mines and called on miners across the anthracite region to join them. Tamaqua miners offered an alternative plan that called for workers to share control over management and production decisions. Lehigh managers refused and closed the mines, effective from 30 June. As other mining companies began to collapse in the 1950s and 1960s, local workers, business owners, union leaders, and politicians made efforts to either open mines or attract new industries. However, unemployment remained a difficult problem for the Panther Valley and for the entire anthracite region and the area still exhibits higher than average unemployment.

By the mid-1950s, what had seemed an isolated event in anthracite coal towns had begun to occur in communities dependent upon other industries key to Pennsylvania's economy, including bituminous coal mining, railroads, textiles, and steel. The process of de-industrialization, a term used in this essay to include the job loss, shutdowns, capital mobility, and resource depletion occurring in the anthracite mining industry, prompted calls for greater action at state level. In 1954 this helped George Leader become Pennsylvania's first Democratic Governor since George Earle's election twenty years earlier. The central program designed by the Leader administration to alleviate the effects of industrial change was the Pennsylvania Industrial Development Authority (PIDA). Created in 1956, PIDA authorized second mortgages on land and buildings for new industries in communities suffering from high unemployment.

Meanwhile, as Pennsylvanians were addressing these social and economic issues, federal policymakers had also begun attempts to pass similar legislation. Central to these efforts was the Depressed Areas Act, first introduced in 1955 by Democratic Senator Paul Douglas of Illinois and renamed the Area Redevelopment Act the following year. Douglas and his staff, which included Pennsylvania's Secretary of Labor William L. Batt, Jr, used the programs developed in Pennsylvania to craft their legislation. In addition, Pennsylvania's congressional leaders provided key support for the Douglas bill. Congress passed the Area Redevelopment Act in 1958 and 1960, but President Dwight D. Eisenhower – favoring Republican versions of redevelopment legislation – vetoed it both times. Following John F. Kennedy's victory in the 1960 election, Congress passed the Act again and Kennedy – who had co-sponsored the legislation while in the Senate – signed the bill on 1 May 1961, creating the Area Redevelopment Administration (ARA). This was Kennedy's first major domestic initiative and it both continued New-Deal ideas and served as an important precursor to later programs of the Great Society.

This article explores the intersection between de-industrialization and state building in postwar America, using developments in the anthracite region as a case study. Analyzing events in the region showcases how local citizens shaped both local and state policies, which in turn influenced actions in the federal arena. Pennsylvania was not the only state to have created economic development programs designed to create jobs. States in the South and in New England had done so by the time of PIDA's creation in 1956.[1] But the Pennsylvania program specifically targeted communities affected by de-industrialization, whose number grew in the decades following World War II as declines in employment occurred in many of the state's basic industries. As Table 1 shows, Pennsylvania exhibited high levels of structural unemployment in several industries, which occurs when workers' current skills do not match those demanded by employers and is caused primarily by technological change, the relocation of capital, and resource depletion.

Besides economic developments and politics, cultural concerns also shaped the context within which area redevelopment policy emerged. In letters and congressional testimony, local men and women expressed the need to provide jobs for men, to preserve a social system based upon a family economy of wage-earning fathers, sons, and daughters, with wives managing the household. Since fathers earned the majority of the income, de-industrialization was more than an economic crisis; it was also a crisis

1. See James C. Cobb, *The Selling of the South: The Southern Crusade for Industrial Development 1936–1990* (Urbana, IL, 1993), and William F. Hartford, *Where is Our Responsibility? Unions and Economic Change in the New England Textile Industry, 1870–1960* (Amherst, MA, 1996).

Table 1. *Employment by Industry, Pennsylvania, 1950–1970*

	1950	1955	1960	1965	1970
Anthracite coal	72,624	33,523	19,051	11,132	6,286
Bituminous coal	94,514	52,103	33,396	25,206	24,667
Fabricated metals	131,700	151,200	110,800	107,300	106,500
Non-electrical machinery	90,400	100,500	110,500	128,000	136,200
Electrical machinery	125,000	122,200	126,800	128,200	132,800
Primary metals	254,300	254,600	233,000	238,700	214,300
Apparel	180,100	193,000	172,000	185,700	161,900
Textiles	143,500	106,100	78,300	74,100	63,000

Source: *Pennsylvania Abstract* (1970, 1975).

of masculinity. Each of these threads – economics, politics, and culture – were part of the multifaceted state building process that began in communities, moved to the state level, and reached the federal arena. Events at each level interacted with the other to create a complex response to the problems of structural unemployment that healed some of the damage but did not halt the process of de-industrialization.

LNC AND ANTHRACITE'S POSTWAR COLLAPSE

For the anthracite region, the case of Lehigh Navigation Coal Company (LNC) illustrates the problem and response at the local level. LNC was the largest producer in the Panther Valley and one of the top mining companies in the anthracite region. The economic revival associated with World War II encouraged hopes among anthracite industry leaders for a permanent reversal of the decline that had characterized the industry in the 1920s and 1930s.[2] Running from northeast to east-central Pennsylvania, four anthracite coal fields contained 90 per cent of the American and 75 per cent of the world's supply. In post-World-War-II America, its major use was for home heating in the northeast, and firms looked to expand their market there. As LNC's 1946 annual report stated: "The coming year should be good for 'Old Company Lehigh' anthracite." LNC "is looking to the future with confidence". Such confidence fed into an intensive postwar marketing campaign to maintain and hopefully increase anthracite

2. On developments in the 1930s, see John Bodnar, *Worker's World: Kinship, Community, and Protest in an Industrial Society, 1900–1940* (Baltimore, MD, 1982); Thomas Dublin, "The Equalization of Work: An Alternative Vision of Industrial Capitalism in the Anthracite Region of Pennsylvania in the 1930s", *Canal History and Technology Proceedings*, 13 (1994), pp. 81–98; Melvyn Dubofsky and Warren Van Tine, *John L. Lewis: A Biography* (New York, 1977), pp. 187–97, 371–375; and Michael Kozura, "We Stood Our Ground: Anthracite Miners and the Expropriation of Corporate Property, 1930–1941", in Staughton Lynd (ed.), *"We Are All Leaders": The Alternative Unionism of the Early 1930s* (Urbana, IL, 1996), pp. 199–237.

demand. That year, anthracite operators created and funded the Anthracite Institute to conduct marketing, sales, and lobbying efforts.[3]

Three major factors ended those hopes: the switch to natural gas for home heating in the northeast; serious recessions in 1949 and 1953–1954; and a series of warm winters. LNC made profits during World War II and the Korean War, but in 1953 miners worked an average of only three days per week, and net losses for the firm amounted to $1.4 million. The trend continued into 1954, which prompted the company to adopt a drastic reorganization plan that consolidated underground operations, increased strip mining and mechanization, and called for increased productivity from miners. Although some miners staged brief walkouts, UMW President John L. Lewis and other UMW leaders met with the men and convinced them to accept the plan and return to work. Meanwhile, several smaller anthracite companies closed during the spring of 1954 and the number of unemployed in the region rose to over 50,000.[4] Although tonnage increased, financial losses continued, and on 3 May 1954, LNC's parent company, Lehigh Coal and Navigation Company (LC & N), announced it would end anthracite operations. To keep the mines open, LNC president and area native W. Julian Parton presented a five-point plan to both the parent company and the Panther Valley General Mine Committee. The Committee consisted of representatives of the area UMW locals. Parton followed this with an open letter published in the *Tamaqua Evening Courier* in which he urged miners to accept his new proposal. First, "each miner will have to produce all that he is capable of producing each day. He must work longer hours than in the past, and can only be excused where genuinely abnormal conditions exist." Second, Parton called for the end of consideration payments, which involved paying miners for fulfilling a contract even though abnormal mining conditions prevented them from doing so. Over time, the miners' and owners' definitions of "abnormal" had diverged greatly, resulting in increased production costs. Third, he demanded the increased use and diligent application of mechanized mining methods. Fourth, he called for double-shifting workplaces in order to increase production. Finally, Parton urged

3. 1946 Annual Report, box 4, Lehigh Coal and Navigation Company Records, PA State Archives (hereafter cited as LNC-PA). See also minutes, Pennsylvania Coal Company, various dates, box 1, Pennsylvania Coal Company Records, PA State Archives.

4. William J. Walton to Lewis (9 December 1953), and Lewis to Watson (10 December 1953), in folder 24, box 41, President/district correspondence, United Mine Workers Papers, Historical Collections and Labor Archives, Penn State University (hereafter UMW-HCLA). On LNC's losses see 1953 Annual Report, box 5, LNC-PA; W. Julian Parton, *The Death of a Great Company: Reflections on the Decline and Fall of the Lehigh Coal and Navigation Company* (Easton, PA?, 1986), p. 41; and "LNCC Suspends All Panther Valley Mines Indefinitely", *Hazleton Standard-Sentinel*, 4 May 1953, p. 1.

miners to adhere to this new contract strictly, without illegal strikes, so the mines could operate profitably.[5]

The offer challenged the miners' fundamental work practices and their deep sense of independence and control over their work. However, it also seemed to be the only way that some Panther Valley miners could stay employed in their trained profession. Divisions appeared as local union leaders contacted UMW officials and held the first of several mass meetings to consider Parton's offer. UMW Vice-President Thomas Kennedy supported Parton's plan as did District 7 President Martin Brennan. Kennedy urged "resumption of operations to the extent provided".[6] Miners in Tamaqua continued to hold out. Lewis, hoping to avoid a challenge to his authority, sent a blunt, tersely worded telegram to the General Committee, ordering the men to return to work. He argued that Parton's plan was not in violation of existing contracts. "The time for mass meetings is gone and it is now necessary for our members to comply with the policy recommended by the International District and General Mine Committee. There is no trespass upon the right of contract involved in this agreement."[7] While five of the six locals agreed, miners from the Tamaqua Local 1571 argued that the new arrangement was confusing and violated the 1952 wage agreement. Nevertheless, on Saturday 5 June, the General Committee met and agreed to return to work the next Monday under Parton's proposal.[8]

At 4 a.m., Monday 7 June, miners from Local 1571 created a thirty-five-car automobile caravan and drove through Tamaqua sounding their horns urging miners to join them in protesting the opening of the mines under the new agreement. The caravan also toured Coaldale before the carloads of miners established pickets around several Panther Valley collieries and mines. The majority surrounded the breaker at the Coaldale colliery. As the only one scheduled to operate, the company could process no coal.[9]

Over the next several days, Tamaqua workers attended mass rallies in high school athletic fields and urged the support of the UMW and the state and federal government. But Lewis remained steadfast and other miners in the region ignored the Tamaqua miners' call for a general strike.[10]

5. "Kennedy Met Valley Men", *Tamaqua Evening Courier*, 21 May 1954, p.1. Parton letter, *Tamaqua Evening Courier*, 29 May 1954, p. 4; Parton, *The Death of a Great Company*, pp. 86–87.
6. Kennedy quote in "Mine Locals Meeting Today to Discuss Return to Work", *Tamaqua Evening Courier*, 1 June 1954, p. 1.
7. Lewis to Erbe, 2 June 1954, folder 27, box 41, President/district correspondence, UMW-HCLA.
8. "General Mine Votes to Work Monday Under 'General Working Agreement' ", *Tamaqua Evening Courier*, 5 June 1954, p. 1.
9. "Pickets Halt Reopening of Mines", *Tamaqua Evening Courier*, 7 June 1954, p. 1.
10. Memo (15 June 1954), folder 27, box 41, President/district correspondence, UMW-HCLA. See also "Valley Group Meets Lewis in Hazleton", *Tamaqua Evening Courier*, 18 June 1954, p. 1, and "Local Will Get Report Tonight on Conference in Hazleton", *Tamaqua Evening Courier*, 19 June 1954, p. 1.

Undaunted, the workers presented a ten-point plan to save the company that demanded:

(1) no change in the working agreement between LNC and the UMW;
(2) the reopening of all mines;
(3) the discontinuance of buying coal from other sources;
(4) only LNC to process refuse from culm banks;
(5) lower company overheads by selling other interests including water and railroad firms;
(6) no restrictions on buying coal;
(7) all losses to be absorbed by miners and businesses in the Panther Valley;
(8) a committee of miners and citizens to have access to LNC financial records;
(9) the active assistance of all employees in making mining profitable; and
(10) active involvement from all citizens to increase the sale of coal.

In some ways, the plan echoed job equalization proposals of the 1930s, a decade when miners across the anthracite region staged protests and often seized control of mines and operated them independently of the mining companies. Micahel Kozura has argued that miners in the 1930s were not acting solely out of practical concerns for jobs and family, but sought to transform the social and political landscape through direct action.[11] John Bodnar, the leading historian of the anthracite region, suggests that "labor issues were essentially family issues" and that the actions of the 1930s were driven more by practical concerns for preserving jobs and family structure. Many of these men and women were of Slavic or East European heritage, and according to Bodnar they valued stability and security and stayed with mining as long as they could.[12]

It may be that a mixture of motives was involved, both in the 1930s as well as in the 1950s. Clearly, the Tamaqua plan was designed to preserve anthracite mining, and in turn protect a way of life and the miners' communities. Ezra Koch, a retired member of the Tamaqua Local, noted that "the men are determined to make a stand to preserve and not to destroy". He asserted that the recent attempts to alter work rules were evidence that LNC was "going into liquidation" and that the area needed a new company that would preserve the mines and make a profit.[13] The miners of Local 1571 fought for shared governance in company affairs as a

11. See Kozura, "We Stood Our Ground", pp. 199–237.
12. Bodnar, *Worker's World*, p. 178. An overview of the debate is in Kozura, "We Stood Our Ground".
13. "Valley Miners Will Seek Meeting With Pres. Eisenhower, Gov. Fine", *Tamaqua Evening Courier*, 21 June 1954, p. 1.

way to keep their jobs, at the same time they were also fighting to maintain their social and cultural traditions in the face of industrial transformation. Evidence outlined below on the nature of gender roles reinforces this point. These workers also challenged the authority of the UMW, which, like most major unions under the post-World-War-II "social contract" had given up a share in managerial decisions over production and investments in exchange for union recognition and the right to negotiate issues such as wages and benefits.[14] In 1954 the Tamaqua miners were doubly alone: neither their fellow anthracite miners nor the UMW leaders were willing to support the walkout and the alternative plan.

After a rally on 27 June, the Tamaqua miners asked Republican Governor John Fine to intervene on their behalf.[15] Fine did inform the company of the miners' plan, but to no avail. On 30 June the LC & N Board voted to dissolve LNC, terminating 5,000 employees, 4,500 of whom were miners. In a statement, the Board commented that the "request by the so-called citizens committee of Tamaqua was too tardy, however, to expect that the situation could be changed at that late date. Nothing of a tangible nature which the company could consider came from that meeting."[16] The conglomerate LC & N continued to maintain the mines in the hope that others would lease them and in the meantime restructured by investing in shipping, a resort, as well as bituminous coal mining. Some individuals and firms did lease the anthracite mines and many continued to mechanize, a policy sanctioned by the UMW leadership. While these operations continued into the 1960s, employment and profits in the industry dropped steadily.[17] Table 2 reflects these changes, showing that production, value, and employment declined while strip mining and mechanization allowed average tons per man-day to increase. Thus, by 1960, the economic situation of the anthracite industry had deteriorated so much that neither union nor company proposals would have saved miners' jobs. However, workers' economic and cultural concerns and appeals from union leaders such as Thomas Kennedy did help draw media and political

14. There are a number of sources outlining the creation of this social contract. Among them are: Alan Brinkley, *The End of Reform: New Deal Liberalism in Recession and War* (New York, 1995); Robert M. Collins, *The Business Response to Keynes, 1929–1964* (New York, 1981); David L. Stebenne, *Arthur J. Goldberg: New Deal Liberal* (New York, 1996); Robert Zeiger, *American Workers, American Unions, 1920–1985* (Baltimore, MD, 1986).

15. "Miners Offer New Proposal to Open Mines in Panther Valley", *Tamaqua Evening Courier*, 28 June 1954, p. 1.

16. "LNC Board Closes Affairs", *Tamaqua Evening Courier*, 1 July 1954, p. 1.

17. "Committee of 100 to Direct Fight to Get Valley Mines Opened", *Tamaqua Evening Courier*, 21 July 1954, p. 1; "New Firm Will Lease Lansford Mine District", *Tamaqua Evening Courier*, 6 August 1954, p. 1; "All Valley Local Unions Approve Leasing Lansford Mine District", *Tamaqua Evening Courier*, 10 August 1954, p. 1; Parton, *Death of a Great Company*, pp. 114–128; Annual Reports, 1954–1963, box 4, LNC-PA.

Table 2. *Pennsylvania anthracite production and employment, 1950–1965*

Year	Production (net tons)	Value of production	Employees	Average tons per man Day
1950	44,076,703	$392,398,006	72,624	2.88
1955	26,204,554	206,096,662	33,523	3.96
1960	18,817,441	147,116,250	19,051	5.60
1965	14,865,955	122,021,267	11,132	6.55

Source: *Pennsylvania Abstract* (1975).

attention to the anthracite region. This created further pressure for a political solution that resulted in a number of proposals at the state and eventually federal levels designed to alleviate unemployment. In this, workers contributed to state-building efforts in the 1950s and helped lay the groundwork for the poverty programs of the 1960s related to local and regional economic development, including the Area Redevelopment Administration, its successor the Economic Development Administration, and the Appalachian Regional Commission.

THE BUSINESS-DEVELOPMENT-GROUP MODEL

The shape the solution to industrial decline in Pennsylvania took resembled the business-development model created at the local level. As LNC and other anthracite companies began to fail, workers, labor leaders, business owners, and government officials sought further means to curb the effects of de-industrialization. Initially, they supported local private efforts through business-development groups, and these organizations served as a model that influenced both state and federal policies. Relying mostly on fund drives, local business leaders created industrial-development organizations that sought to attract new industries using various monetary incentives. Two examples from the region include the Scranton Lackawanna Industrial Building Company (SLIBCO), created in 1946, and the Lackawanna Industrial Fund Enterprise (LIFE), formed in 1950. Together, by 1951 SLIBCO and LIFE had raised $3.8 million, built 18 new plants themselves and attracted 22 companies to build their own. These new plants created 5,000 jobs with annual payrolls of about $18 million. New manufacturing industries included heating, cooling, and air conditioning equipment, metal cabinets, electrical equipment, textiles, and cigars. However, the gains did not offset the losses as coal firms continued their decline. At the same time, textile and apparel firms, which had moved into the area to tap the female labor force, also began closing plants, often moving their operations to the south or outside the country.[18]

As local efforts continued, regional-development groups emerged, the major one being the Northeast Pennsylvania Industrial Development Commission (NPIDC), which represented Carbon, Lackawanna, Luzerne, Northumberland, and Schuylkill counties. NPIDC president Victor Diehm, a radio and television executive, organized local conferences on redevelopment and created a special task force within NPIDC to publicize the region's economic difficulties and develop a program for regional development. In 1954 Diehm and task-force Chair Charles Weissman, a retail store executive, lobbied Governor Fine, Congressional representatives from the anthracite district, and President Eisenhower. As Diehm declared: "We feel [...] that we hold some kind of priority for federal emergency assistance. It is under this appraisal of our chronic and desperate situation that we gather our forces for the continuing campaign for regional economic relief."[19] However, Diehm's skills as a coalition builder and agent for change could not push either Governor Fine or President Eisenhower to craft a new policy for development. Fine preferred an indirect approach to industrial development, one that relied on state support for highway construction, public works, and mine drainage programs. For his part, Eisenhower expressed his interest in doing something and asked his economic advisor, Gabriel Hauge, to follow up. This eventually led to a Republican proposal introduced in Congress to counter Paul Douglas's Area Redevelopment Act.[20]

Although these local and regional groups worked hard to attract new industries, a political solution remained elusive as damaging socio-economic trends continued. During the late 1950s, unemployment in Scranton and Hazleton averaged between 11 and 16 per cent, while the national rate hovered between 4 and 6 per cent. A second prominent trend was outmigration. Between 1940 and 1960, the population in Scranton declined from 301,200 to 234,531, a 22 per cent drop. Over the same period, Wilkes-Barre–Hazleton witnessed a 21.4 per cent drop, from 441,500 to 346,972. Essentially, these declines reflected the loss of residents

18. "How a City Solves a Job Problem", *US News and World Report*, 28 December 1951, pp. 52–54; "Hard Times in the Hard Coal County", *Business Week*, 22 May 1952, pp. 108–112; US Department of Labor, *Area Manpower Guidebook* (n.p., 1957), pp. 265–266. Since 1914, the Scranton Industrial Development Company (SIDCO) had concentrated on providing capital for local industries that wanted to expand. These efforts met with limited success, and the group reorganized in 1946.

19. Quote in "Report Conference To Be Held By Development Commission", *Tamaqua Evening Herald*, 27 July 1954, p. 8.

20. Eisenhower to Hauge (n.d.), folder 3, box 632, OF, WHCF, Dwight D. Eisenhower Library (hereafter, DDEL).

between the prime working ages of 18 and 50, leaving the mining communities increasingly populated by older residents who, if not retired or medically unable, were less able to find high-paying jobs. Housing construction also remained below average in these communities. In 1950, housing built after 1945 averaged 10.23 per cent in the major eastern labor markets, but this figure was only 1.1 per cent in Scranton and 2.6 per cent in Wilkes-Barre–Hazleton. Furthermore, these latter figures were below even the 1950 average of 7.91 per cent for other major areas with chronic unemployment.[21] To reverse these trends, local business leaders joined with workers to demand that the state increase its responsibility for promoting economic development in their communities.

The combination of Fine's limited approach, a national recession, and a campaign contribution scandal hurt the Republicans during the 1954 gubernatorial election. In turn, Democratic candidate George Leader, a chicken farmer by trade, promised clean government and greater state involvement in social welfare and the economy. Leader called on and received support from the growing web of state and national Democratic resources, especially unions. Particularly active were the International Ladies Garment Workers' Union (ILGWU) and the United Steelworkers of America (USW). Leader won in Allegheny County, seat for Pittsburgh, in Philadelphia, and in all but one of the counties in the anthracite region; ironically, Schuylkill County, where Tamaqua lay, stayed with the Republicans. In addition, African-American voters in Philadelphia and Pittsburgh went with Leader. All of this was enough for him to defeat Lt Governor Lloyd Wood with 53.7 per cent of the vote. In the Pennsylvania General Assembly, Democrats gained control of the House by 14 seats, but Republicans held the Senate by 26 seats to 24. This meant that proposals for industrial development would have to pass some form of conservative litmus test. This was the nature of national politics as well: liberal Democrats gained in the 1954 congressional elections, but the coalition of Southern Democrats and conservative Republicans remained formidable.[22]

21. On unemployment and housing, see Lowell E. Gallaway, "Depressed Industrial Areas: A National Problem" (unpublished Ph.D. thesis, The Ohio State University, 1959), pp. 14–15, 63–64; and John R. Fernstrom, "A Community Attack Upon Chronic Unemployment – Hazleton, PA: A Case Study", in US Senate, Special Committee on Unemployment Problems, *Studies in Unemployment* (n.p., 1960), pp. 366–410. On population, see US Department of Labor, *Area Manpower Guidebook* (n.p., 1957), pp.263–265, and US Department of Commerce, *Population, Labor Force, and Unemployment in Chronically Depressed Areas* (n.p., 1964), p.13.

22. "Winner's 86,906 Margin in County Sets Record", *Pittsburgh Post-Gazette*, 4 November 1954, p. 6; "Negroes Win Election for Democrats", *Philadelphia Tribune*, 6 November 1954, p. 1; Roy R. Glashan (ed.), *American Governors and Gubernatorial Elections, 1775–1978* (Westport, CT, 1979), p. 262; Paul B. Beers, *Pennsylvania Politics Today and Yesterday: The Tolerable Accommodation* (University Park, PA, 1980), p. 216.

THE STATE LEVEL: GEORGE LEADER AND PIDA

Leader's inaugural address in January 1955 established the agenda for his administration. "Our great, our over-riding concern, is the economy of Pennsylvania." He noted how economic competition between states had accelerated in recent years and that Pennsylvania would have to revitalize its economy. It was necessary for the state and private citizens to support new industries and new energy resources. Echoing the rhetoric of FDR, Leader noted: "We will have a sober respect for experience and tradition, but we will be unafraid of experiment, willing to take risks, ready to adopt bold measures if they promise to advance the interests of the state."[23]

In developing his economic plan, Leader tapped a network of experts at the national and state levels. The most significant of these was William L. Batt, Jr, once active in implementing employment policy under the Truman administration and now head of the Toledo Industrial Development Council. Batt urged Leader to visit areas of high unemployment to secure the cooperation of local leaders, and create a statewide economic development program. As he helped Leader, Batt also assisted Senator Paul Douglas in drafting federal redevelopment legislation. Batt's work in 1954 led to his appointment as Pennsylvania's Secretary of Labor in 1957, which in turn led to his appointment as head of the Area Redevelopment Administration in 1961.[24]

Leader moved forward with a speech on 28 March 1955 in which he outlined his "Pennsylvania Plan" to the General Assembly. Like his inaugural, Leader's speech and proposals served as a bridge between the New Deal and later developments in the Kennedy and Johnson administrations.

> We are today declaring war against the shameful waste of human energy and human ability and human capacity to produce, which comes about when men and women find no work when they seek work; when marvelous energy sources like our Pennsylvania coals lie unmined in the ground; when whole communities and regions are seemingly condemned to chronic unemployment, deterioration, and hopelessly prolonged distress.[25]

Presaging many programs addressed at the federal level during the

23. Press release, "Inaugural Address of Governor George M. Leader" (18 January 1955), "Inauguration Address" folder, box 19, subject file, 1955–1959, George M. Leader Papers, Pennsylvania State Archives [hereafter Leader Papers].

24. Batt sent copies of his ideas to both Leader and the newly elected Democratic Governor of New York, Averill Harriman. Batt to Leader (12 November 1954), "Industrial Development Plan, Correspondence B" folder, box 19, subject files 1955–1959, Leader Papers. Batt replaced John Torquato after Leader ousted Torquato for maintaining state workers through a secret patronage fund. See Beers, *Pennsylvania Politics*, pp. 209–210.

25. "Speech Before the General Assembly" (28 March 1955), "Industrial Development Plan: Releases, 1955–58" folder, box 19, Leader Papers.

Kennedy and Johnson years, Leader sought to promote greater job opportunities, improve public health, welfare, and education, and provide efficient government, clean water, and unspoiled landscapes. Even with opposition from conservatives, Leader's administration saw a liberal swing in the relationship between the state and society. He appointed more blacks to government positions than any governor before him had, moving the total from 98 to 451 in four years. He succeeded in increasing appropriations for mental health, welfare, and school construction, and his other goals were established in subsequent administrations.[26]

But as he stated in his inaugural, fundamental to all these was a growing state economy and to promote this, Leader offered ten proposals. Key to the story of area redevelopment was his proposal for a $20 million State Industrial Development Authority that called for the state to purchase industrial sites, develop them for use, and lease them to companies with long-term employment potential.[27]

Immersed in debates over a tax increase, and opposed to government ownership of industrial sites, Republicans in the General Assembly blocked this initial plan. But in October 1955 Leader tried again and this time he followed Batt's suggestion and held town meetings in distressed communities prior to submitting a new proposal. Records of these meetings reveal broad support for a state program. In Wilkes-Barre, in the heart of the anthracite region, members of local development groups urged Leader to enact a program and called for federal aid. Workers and union officials echoed these desires. At a meeting in the western Pennsylvania city of Johnstown, business leaders, bituminous mine workers, UMW leaders, and representatives from the United Steelworkers (USW) expressed their support. This reflected the effects of technological unemployment in the soft coal industry and the early signs of problems in steel. As in the east, during the 1940s and 1950s, business, union, and civic leaders in western Pennsylvania had also begun to create development groups and to compete for new industries. For example, the Allegheny Conference on Community Development formed in 1944 and the Pittsburgh Regional Industrial Development Corporation formed in the summer of 1955. Led by elites in the Pittsburgh region, and fostered by an alliance between Democratic Mayor David Lawrence and Republican business executives, the two organizations aimed at both diversifying the

26. Beers, *Pennsylvania Politics*, pp. 225–230.

27. The other nine were: (1) a State Planning Agency to interpret future economic needs; (2) reorganization of the Department of Commerce; (3) an Economic Development Advisory Board; (4) a proposal to aid community groups working for industrial expansion; (5) a proposal to promote water protection and usage by working through Great Lakes Compact; (6) flood control in anthracite areas; (7) a coal research board; (8) support for highway construction; and (9) support for urban renewal.

area's economy, reducing air and water pollution, and promoting urban renewal.[28]

In addition to economic concerns and political battles, apprehension over shifting gender roles also emerged among redevelopment advocates. Preoccupation with gender roles was part of a national trend in the 1950s. In the anthracite region the concern rested on the interconnection between cultural tradition, often rooted in ethnicity, and the economic dependency upon an almost exclusively male industry. Given this, both men and women at the local level supported industrial development designed to attract or preserve jobs for men and national leaders expressed similar desires.[29]

One of the strongest supporters at the local level was Min Matheson, District Manager of the International Ladies Garment Workers Union (ILGWU) in Wilkes-Barre.[30] Matheson challenged the power of employers through union activities and efforts to improve workers' wages and benefits. She also worked to expand the welfare state and sought to diversify the economy of the anthracite region by supporting local, state and federal initiatives designed to create jobs there. Politically, she used her power and that of the ILGWU to support the Democratic Party and urged garment workers and others in the Wyoming Valley to do the same. Her work had both economic and social ends. While increasing women's wages and providing social welfare benefits grew more important as the mines closed, Matheson also hoped to empower women socially and spiritually through involvement in union activities.[31]

Although Matheson hoped to empower women in the Wyoming Valley, she remained concerned that improvements in women's lives might threaten traditional roles within the family, including males as primary

28. "Speech Before the General Assembly" (28 March 1955), "Industrial Development Plan: Releases, 1955–58" folder, box 19, Leader Papers; "Minutes of Conference on Governor's Industrial Development Plan" (25 October 1955), "Industrial Development Plan" folder, box 19, Leader Papers. See also R. Scott Fosler (ed.), *Local Economic Development: Strategies for a Changing Economy* (Washington, DC, 1991). Urban renewal met resistance from black and white working-class residents in Pittsburgh. See Louise Jezierski, "Political Limits to Development in Two Cities: Cleveland and Pittsburgh", in Michael Wallace and Joyce Rothschild (eds), *Deindustrialization and the Restructuring of American Industry* (Greenwich, CT, 1988), pp. 173–190.

29. On the nature of gender roles in the anthracite region see Kozura, "We Stood Our Ground", as well as John Bodnar, *Anthracite People: Families, Unions, and Work, 1900–1940* (Harrisburg, PA, 1983). On gender in 1950s America, see, among others, Elaine Tyler May, *Homeward Bound: American Families in the Cold War Era* (New York, 1988); Joanne Meyerowitz (ed.), *Not June Cleaver: Women and Gender in Postwar America, 1945–1960* (Philadelphia, PA, 1994); and Michael Kimmel, *Manhood in America: A Cultural History* (New York, 1996).

30. Kenneth C. Wolensky, "'We Are All Equal': Adult Education and the Transformation of Pennsylvania's Wyoming Valley District of the International Ladies' Garment Workers' Union, 1944–1963" (unpublished Ph.D. thesis, The Pennsylvania State University, 1996), pp. 69–77.

31. Wolensky, "We Are All Equal", pp. 104–185.

wage earners. This reflected local culture as well as the fact that men's position in the labor market had traditionally been more stable. Jobs available to women were in relatively low-paying, less secure sectors such as retail, or in textile or garment manufacturing. Given this, women lacked the relative security men possessed through either private or public welfare. As Matheson noted in congressional hearings during the late 1950s, "many of the women work in the garment factories only because the men in their homes [...] are unemployed and are at home doing the housework, the shopping and tending to the children – a complete reversal of the normal course of family life". Female garment workers echoed these concerns. A female ILGWU shop steward noted: "It's one thing to have an independent income if your husband is working, but it is no fun being the breadwinner." "What we need here", Matheson argued, "are industries that are primarily industries for men and schools that will train men for the tasks of those industries."[32]

Male workers, as well as state and federal leaders, expressed similar views of masculine and feminine identities. In the 1956 hearings, unemployed worker Stanley Chepel noted: "It is a shame for the woman of the house to be working and the man doing the housework. It is not right." To which Senator Matthew Neely (D-WV) responded: "We hope that this hearing will help to speed the solution of this problem." Daniel Flood, Democratic Representative from Pennsylvania's 11th district, centered in Wilkes-Barre, echoed similar concerns in 1959 hearings. "My men are in the kitchen. Do not tell me that is where they belong." He went on to connect traditional gender roles to the ethnic heritage of the miners and to the community itself. "And what that does to the heart and mind of Poles and Slovaks and Russians and Ukrainians and Irish and German and Welsh miners I leave to you. It is destroying us."[33] Here, Flood conflated the ethnic heritage of miners with beliefs in traditional gender roles, reinforcing ideas outlined earlier in connection with the Tamaqua protests.

These examples suggest that cultural issues such as gender and ethnicity, like politics and economics, were important to the history of both area redevelopment and state building in the years after World War II. In the anthracite region, de-industrialization became a crisis of masculinity that affected men's status as providers and diminished the pride coming from a lifetime of paid work. For women, the crisis meant that their new status as breadwinners, which provided a sense of independence, came amidst unemployment for their husbands, sons, and brothers. Such sentiments,

32. All quotes in US Congress, Senate, *Area Redevelopment: Hearings Before the Subcommittee on Labor on S. 2663*, 84th Congress, 2nd session (4, 6, 9, 23, 26 January and 3, 9, 10, 24 February 1956), Part 1, p. 71.

33. Flood quotation in US Congress, Senate, Committee on Banking and Currency, *Area Redevelopment Act*, Hearings, 86th Congress, 1st session (25, 26, 27 February 1959), Part 1, p. 81.

combined with the events surrounding the Tamaqua miners outlined above, reflect a certain irony that liberal means were used for essentially conservative ends, and highlight the complexity of de-industrialization.

George Leader heard many of these same concerns as he traversed the state for his town meetings on industrial development. In 1956 Leader tried again to create a policy response to de-industrialization. But while Leader had pledged bold initiatives in state policy, the institutional roadblocks present in the Senate meant that the outcome would be a moderate one. Introduced in the Pennsylvania Senate in February 1956 with the support of eight Republicans and eight Democrats, the new proposal requested $5 million for two years and established the Pennsylvania Industrial Development Authority (PIDA). Composed of both government officials and private, elite, citizens, the agency would offer second mortgage loans to private development groups located in areas of high unemployment, defined as a rate of 6 per cent for the preceding 3 years, or 9 per cent for the preceding 18 months. The bill required local groups to contribute 20 per cent of the project cost and a firm commitment from a tenant. Also, a new or upgraded facility could not be part of a company plan to relocate industry from one area of the state to another. The outcome of the bill reflected the political situation in Pennsylvania and highlights an important issue in policy formation. While the technological, economic, and cultural issues were critical for both generating a political response to industrial decline and establishing the context within which redevelopment emerged, those advocating a new program still needed to navigate the institutional structures of state government. In the case of Pennsylvania, while Leader and other liberals sought a broader program for communities facing industrial decline, conservative Republicans dominated the Assembly and thus had substantial power to shape the policy outcome. Having lost once on the issue, Leader and Democrats in the Assembly compromised. Conservatives limited the state's role through lower financing and increased local responsibility. Liberals made sure the state accepted some responsibility for aiding distressed areas and satisfied unions by inserting the measure against industrial relocation. After the bill passed unanimously in the House and with only two dissenting votes in the Senate, Leader signed it into law on 17 May 1956.[34]

The creation of PIDA represented an extension of the business-development-group model first introduced at the local level. Capital remained free to move, and PIDA acted as an inducement to attract firms and create jobs. With local solutions failing, would PIDA be enough to

34. Press release, "Industrial Development Plan: Releases, 1955–1958", 7 February 1956, folder, box 19, Leader Papers; "New State Industry-Aid Plan Offered", *Pittsburgh Post-Gazette*, 8 February 1956, p. 4.

Table 3. *National and redevelopment area unemployment rates, 1950–1960.*

Labor market	County	Labor market unemployment rate		
		1950 (national rate)	1955	1960
Altoona	Blair	4.8 (5.3%)	6.7 (4.4%)	10.4 (5.5%)
Erie	Erie	4.1	7.5	9.1
Johnstown	Cambria	6.7	10.1	11.9
Philadelphia	Philadelphia *et al.*	5.5	6.3	6.0
Pittsburgh	Allegheny *et al.*	6.0	5.5	9.3
Pottsville	Schuylkill	11.0	18.5	18.3
Scranton	Lackawanna	6.7	13.8	12.0
Wilkes-Barre/ Hazleton	Luzerne	7.2	12.5	14.6

Table 4. *PIDA loan information (1955–1965).*

Biennium & fiscal year	Appropriations	Number of projects	Amount of PIDA loans	Estimated project cost	Planned employment
1955–1957	$5,000,000	24	$3,904,329	$11,859,086	4,047
1957–1959	3,000,000	56	7,026,342	23,222,961	9,485
1959–1961	11,020,000	70	7,709,423	24,601,434	11,790
1961–1962	8,000,000	68	9,533,049	23,918,627	9,090
1962–1963	9,000,000	60	9,822,791	24,329,427	8,085
1963–1964	12,420,000	87	14,695,914	35,453,533	9,030
1964–1965	13,500,000	76	16,162,443	41,628,576	9,964
TOTALS	$61,940,000	441	$68,854,291	$185,013,644	61,491

Source: Commonwealth of Pennsylvania, *Pennsylvania Industrial Development Authority: 35 Years of Job Creating Loans* (1991).

halt de-industrialization? The evidence compiled in Tables 3 and 4 suggests a few minor successes amidst failure. According to PIDA records, between 1956 and 1965 the agency authorized nearly $62 million in loans with a planned employment of over 61,000 jobs. However, a study of 106 firms that received a PIDA loan between 1956 and 1965 found that only 66.5 per cent had reached their planned employment level between 3 and 6 years after receiving a loan. Why such difficulty? With aging populations and possessing a labor force with relatively fewer transferable skills, businesses were less likely to invest in such areas. Also, the industries PIDA managed to attract were in the service or light manufacturing sectors, which were typically lower paying and nonunionized areas of the economy. These jobs could not offset the continued de-industrialization of the older, union-dominated, core industries of Pennsylvania's economy and unemployment in eligible labor markets remained higher than the national average. For example, in 1960 Scranton and Wilkes-Barre had unemployment rates more than double the national rate of 5.5 per cent. The state offered other programs to help workers including unemployment benefits and job training, but the magnitude of the crisis overwhelmed these programs as it did PIDA. A similar story occurred in other distressed communities across Pennsylvania and across the country.[35]

TOWARDS NATIONAL LEGISLATION

National redevelopment legislation built on models developed at the local and state level in Pennsylvania as well as those created in New England to address the declines in the textile industry. After six years of sustained efforts in Congress, the federal Area Redevelopment Administration came into being in May 1961. It represented a limited financial contribution on the part of the federal government while at the same time addressing not only the effects of de-industrialization, but also poverty and unemployment among rural populations and on Native American reservations. These latter two mandates came as a result of political compromises with Southern Democrats as well as liberals representing Native American interests. Congress granted the ARA a four-year life and $390 million to promote both economic *redevelopment* in urban areas and economic *development* in rural ones across the United States. This amounted to approximately 0.39 per cent of an annual federal budget approaching $100 billion.[36] It is unclear whether a focused program like the original Douglas bill could have served as a basis for directly addressing de-industrialization in Pennsylvania and other states in the traditional manufacturing belt. What did happen was that the issue of de-industrialization became lost as the focus widened to address unemployment and poverty in both rural and urban communities throughout the United States.

In its four-year existence from 1961 to 1965, the ARA created 117,000 direct and indirect new jobs. It stimulated interest in the issue of structural unemployment and provided important links to programs developed during the Great Society, including job training, minority business programs, and regional development. The ARA also worked to use the

35. See Glenn H. Petry's "The Impact of the Pennsylvania Industrial Development Authority on Employment in Depressed Areas" (Honors Thesis, Pennsylvania, 1967).

36. On the history of the ARA see Sar Levitan, *Federal Aid to Depressed Areas: An Evaluation of the Area Redevelopment Administration* (Baltimore, MD, 1964) and Gregory Wilson, "Before the Great Society: Liberalism, Deindustrialization, and Area Redevelopment in the United States, 1933–1965", (unpublished Ph.D. thesis, The Ohio State University, 2001).

Table 5. *Approved ARA industrial/commercial loans by industry.*

Industry	Investment ($)	Projects	Employment potential	Investment per job ($)
Lumber and wood products	25,875,994	52	5,195	4,495
Hotels and motels	21,759,200	28	3,095	6,820
Food and kindred products	20,715,256	42	4,945	3,466
Stone, clay and glass	14,534,128	25	1,915	7,563
Rubber and miscellaneous plastics	14,204,154	27	3,185	4,433
Paper and allied products	12,423,410	12	1,265	9,821
Primary metal industries	8,030,417	15	1,455	5,208
Textile mill products	7,020,403	13	1,830	3,826
Retail trades, miscellaneous	6,432,180	4	1,300	4,948
Recreational services	6,350,267	21	1,305	4,866
Furniture and fixtures	5,159,209	17	1,525	2,109
Chemicals and allied products	5,134,136	12	1,270	4,026
Electrical machinery, equipment and supplies	4,184,162	15	1,345	3,111
Apparel and finished goods	3,555,785	24	3,315	1,065
Fabricated metal products	3,291,123	21	815	3,886
Miscellaneous manufacturing	3,006,650	5	440	6,561
Machinery (except electrical)	2,849,572	10	1,145	3,489

Transportation equipment	2,355,216	14	1,330	1,297
Medical and other health services	1,791,531	6	275	6,515
Professional, scientific, and controlling instruments	1,377,250	6	1,040	1,324
Motor freight transportation and warehousing	903,357	7	520	1,653
Petroleum refining and related industry	832,000	2	130	6,400
Printing and publishing	789,685	5	190	4,156
Wholesale trades	721,575	3	165	4,373
Miscellaneous business services (research and development, commercial)	576,450	3	160	3,603
Leather and leather products	529,353	2	415	1,276
Bituminous mining	406,360	2	35	9,286
Agriculture services	376,870	3	160	2,355
Tobacco manufacturers	225,000	1	375	600
Ordnance and accessories	195,000	1	60	3,250
Mining and quarrying of non-metallic metals	182,730	3	90	2,030
Services, personal	139,614	1	30	4,653
Miscellaneous repair service	87,750	1	10	8,775
Commercial farms (horticulture)	81,250	1	10	8,125
Retail trades	46,000	1	15	3,067
TOTALS	$176,143,037	405	40,355	$4,109

Compiled from ARA Reports.

Table 6. *Approved ARA public facility loans/grants.*

Type	Investment ($)	Number of projects	Employment potential
Recreational services	48,449,102	19	3,545
Electric, gas, and sanitary services	15,068,503	78	14,795
Medical and other health services	12,017,000	4	2,610
Industrial parks	11,295,280	37	7,265
Port facilities	8,796,000	8	1,310
Research and development/non-profit	4,933,000	2	–
Miscellaneous services	3,280,203	5	960
Airport facilities	233,624	3	585
Museums	25,580	1	15
TOTALS	104,098,292	157	31,085

Compiled from ARA Reports.

state to bring together various individuals and groups in an effort to eradicate unemployment and poverty and to make communities more livable. Its successor agency, the Economic Development Administration, continued these programs with a focus on smaller urban areas and rural communities. Hence, the ARA, drawing on experiences in Pennsylvania, presaged elements of the Great Society through programs designed to increase opportunities for individuals and communities to climb out of poverty. At the same time, the focus on economic planning and job training reflected aspects of the New Deal; thus, the ARA resembled both eras of liberal reform.

CONCLUSIONS

As this article suggests, local and state developments were important to the ARA's creation, especially those emanating in the anthracite region of Pennsylvania. There, workers, union leaders and mine owners struggled to create a response to de-industrialization. In the Panther Valley, miners of Tamaqua Local 1571 emphasized a shared governance while the UMW and owners of firms such as LNC preferred cost-cutting measures, including mechanization and longer work hours. LNC and the union won this battle, but the community and region lost the war as the market for hard coal collapsed and unemployment increased.

Local business leaders, with some union support, then sought further private solutions by creating development groups to compete for new industries against other communities. Although local citizens in Pennsylvania attracted new industries, they could not lower unemployment and reduce poverty to acceptable rates and turned to the state for help. The

Table 7. *ARA support by regions.*

ARA region	States	Number	Investment (in thousand $)	Potential jobs
Appalachia	KY, TN, VA, WV	326	76,834	13,975
Northeast	CT, DE, ME, MD, MA, NH, NJ, NY, PA, Puerto Rico, RI, VT	476 (499 incl. Puerto Rico)	66,105 (75,973)	20,050 (21,625)
Lake states	IL, IN, MI, MN, OH, WI	418	55,244	10,125
Southeast	AL, AR, FL, GA, LA, MS, NC, SC	306	53,851	15,915
Southwest	AZ, CA, CO, HI, KS, MO, NV, NM, OK, American Samoa, TX, UT	311 (316 incl. American Samoa)	38,875 (39,939)	7,475 (7,605)
Northwest	AK, ID, IA, MT, NB, ND, OR, SD, WA, WY	214	18,021	2,195

Compiled from ARA reports.

outcome was PIDA, which provided incentives to new industries but left the decisions regarding location in the hands of business owners. Like local efforts, PIDA could not bring unemployment rates down to national levels, prompting many Pennsylvanians to lobby for a federal solution to chronic unemployment.

The state building process related to the anthracite crisis moved simultaneously from local to national and from private to public arenas. In Pennsylvania, technological change and economic collapse led to rising unemployment and poverty, which mobilized citizens to demand solutions. Both private and public models emerged, involving business owners, labor leaders, political parties, experts, and workers in a complex and often ironic policy narrative. Developments in Pennsylvania influenced rising federal efforts to combat poverty and unemployment and shaped the nature of the programs developed. Besides technology and economics, gender was critical to state building efforts. By emphasizing jobs for men, redevelopment advocates framed the need for a new government program in a way that would appeal to conservatives and support traditional notions of gender. While technology, economics, and gender were all important for the creation of redevelopment policy, in the end the political process within government institutions remained the most decisive factor shaping the outcome. These events in postwar Pennsylvania reflect the complexity of state building and policy making in modern America by integrating the structural forces such as markets and technology with the concerns of various politically active groups, including male and female workers and labor leaders, business owners, experts, and politicians. Analyzing how these developments influenced the creation of federal policies aimed at promoting economic development in areas of poverty can provide a deeper understanding of de-industrialization and policymaking in between the New Deal and the Great Society.

IRSH 47 (2002), pp. 159–175 DOI: 10.1017/S0020859002000822

On "De-industrialization" and the Crisis of Male Identities

Chitra Joshi

The last two decades in India have seen the decline of traditional factory industries and a growing process of informalization and casualization of labour. The crisis of industries like textiles and steel has meant a virtual decimation of a working class in old industrial centres. This paper will look at the phenomenon of de-industrialization and its implications for a labouring population whose lives were intimately connected with industrial work.

I

De-industrialization at the end of twentieth century and the beginning of the twenty-first refers to a process quite different from de-industrialization in the nineteenth century. Nationalist accounts of a linear decline of Indian handicrafts under the onslaught of imported manufactures have long been questioned. Critics of nationalist frames have focused on the lack of statistical evidence showing a decline,[1] and critiqued the theoretical assumptions of the de-industrialization argument. Big industries, recent studies point out, have not always displaced the small: small-scale industries continued to survive and expand through a process of adaptation and innovation, and became in fact an integral feature of industrialization in India.[2] Despite differences, the protagonists of the debate have shared a common focus on the decline of small-scale industry. Today de-industrialization refers to another kind of process – one in which labour

1. For a discussion of de-industrialization within a nationalist paradigm, see B. Chandra, *Rise and Growth of Economic Nationalism in India* (New Delhi, 1966), chs 2 and 3; A.K. Bagchi, "Deindustrialization in India in the Nineteenth Century: Some Theoretical Implications", *Journal of Development Studies*, 12 (1976), pp. 135–164. For critiques questioning the statistical basis of de-industrialization, see Daniel and Alice Thorner, *Land and Labour in India* (New Delhi, 1962), ch. 6; J. Krishnamurthy, "Changes in the Composition of the Workforce in Manufacturing, 1901–1951: A Theoretical and Empirical Analysis", *Indian Economic and Social History Review*, 4 (1967), pp. 1–16.
2. For a critique on these lines, see Tirthankar Roy, *Artisans and Industrialization: Indian Weaving in the Twentieth Century* (Delhi, 1993); Konrad Specker, "Madras Handlooms in the Nineteenth Century", in Tirthankar Roy (ed.), *Cloth and Commerce: Textiles in Colonial India* (New Delhi, 1996), pp. 175–217.

in large factories is being displaced by casual and informal labour. A large network of informal labour, however, is not a new feature. It has always formed a part of the labour market in centres of large-scale industry like Bombay, Calcutta, Ahmedabad, and Kanpur. In cities like Kanpur, where the informal was closely tied to the formal, a decline in the latter has created a crisis for the informal economy.

What happens to urban lives in this context? What are the work and household strategies by which workers confront this situation? How do working-class men out of work perceive themselves and their lives? In trying to understand what processes of displacement and marginalization mean to working-class men, I begin by looking at the political culture of a city in north India, Kanpur, a major industrial centre.[3]

Kanpur, which was a trading centre connected with the East India Company trade since the late eighteenth century, became an important centre of the textile and leather industry in north India in the nineteenth century. Like Ahmedabad in western India, the city drew its labour supply largely from the surrounding countryside. In periods of famine and agrarian distress the influx into the city was much greater. The First and Second World Wars were major phases of expansion, with the Kanpur factories taking bulk orders for the British armies. Till the 1960s, textile and leather factories, and other small units in Kanpur employed over 80,000 workers. Apart from these, a host of small cottage units producing nuts, bolts, bearings, leather goods, furniture, and packing cases supplied materials to the large factories. Thousands were employed as daily labourers, loading and unloading goods coming into and going out of the city. Business for tea stalls, tobacco and betel nut shops, grocery, and other cloth shops outside the factory compounds was intimately connected with workers' pay day. Around shift times on pay day hundreds of workers milled around. Business was brisk.[4]

Today, smokeless mill chimneys, towering brick structures, and deserted mill compounds stand as silent reminders of the past of the city. Most textile mills are closed. Among the units managed by the nationalized British India Corporation, only the woollen mills run, but at less than a quarter of their former strength. Two other textile mills, Muir and New Victoria, which were controlled by the state-run National Textile Corporation, stopped production almost ten years ago, but they have a small number of workers on their payrolls. The daily routine for these workers consists of reporting for attendance at shift times, in the morning or afternoon. A large number of permanent employees of the

3. In looking at working-class worlds this essay draws heavily on two sets of oral narratives: (1) stories of individual lives collected between the late 1970s and early 1980s; and (2) narratives from more than 100 working-class households collected between between 1997 and 2002.

4. For more on Kanpur see C. Joshi, *Lost Worlds* (New Delhi, 2002), ch. 1.

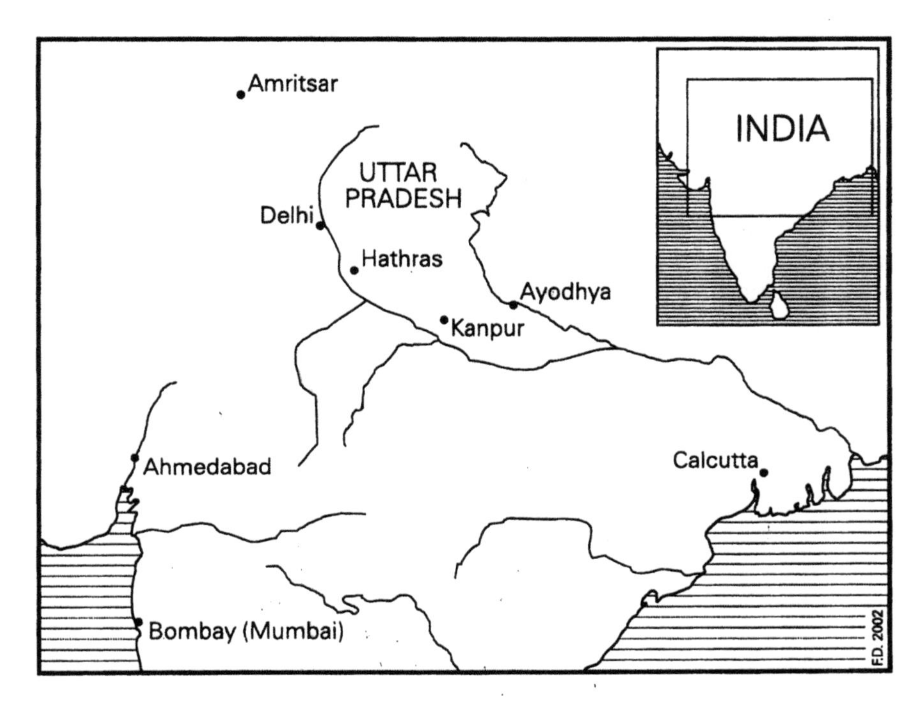

Figure 1. North India

closed units have left under voluntary retirement schemes (VRS). Outside the factory gates, teashops wear a deserted look, stalls have their shutters down, and no vendors line the roads, no people mill around. Earlier, petty vending was a recourse open to workers during spells of unemployment. Today, there are no clients for vendors, no noise and bustle at the Sunday markets in working-class neighbourhoods. Yet the flow of migrants to the city continues, adding to the scores of rickshaw pullers, vendors, casual labourers, and the unemployed. Old centres of industry like Kanpur remain predominantly working-class cities but with a labouring population that is increasingly invisible. The workforce is hidden in homes, in alleys and bye-lanes, working some days in the week, waiting other days, sometimes weeks on end. In a context when jobs for men in the "formal" sector are shrinking, women – never very visible in the factory labour force – form an important part of the invisible workforce in the city. Women sew, make brushes, and uppers for leather sandals, cut rubber straps for slippers, roll *bidis*, wrap toffees, and do a host of other small-waged jobs at home and in small workshops not enumerated as factories.[5]

5. It is virtually impossible to get figures of the numbers employed in these small establishments. Records are available only for registered units. And these understate the numbers employed and do not give the breakdown for men and women.

II

The closure of mills in Kanpur, and in other centres of large-scale industry in India, means more than an economic loss to workers – it has also meant the death of a political culture in industrial cities. In contrast to the present, when labour is increasingly invisibilized in the public sphere, the working class stamped the city with its presence through the militant struggles of the 1920s and 1930s. Industrial labour was an important constituency to which all political parties and leaders had to reach out. The politics of labour in Kanpur in the 1930s shaped the political context in the entire province. Local nationalists came into conflict with provincial leaders and eventually the strength of the local movement had a radical impact, pushing the provincial Congress into supporting working-class demands. In the eyes of colonial officials and the predominantly European entrepreneurs in the city the Congress was seen as taking a Left turn. Cartoons in contemporary newspapers capture the panic created by working-class militancy in 1937–1938.[6] In popular discourse, the city came to be known as "Red City" (*Lal Kanpur*). A history of the labour movement in Kanpur by a worker-militant chronicles the entire story of the city in terms of heroic struggles by workers.[7] The solidarities forged through collective struggles left their imprint on the political culture of the city in the decades to follow. For old trade unionists who lived through those times, the epithet *Lal Kanpur* remained fixed even in bleaker times. It was almost as if it was their city – it bore a name that they gave to it.

The world of radical trade-union politics was a male world. It reaffirmed and did not contest the masculinized nature of the public sphere in the city. Mass meetings during strikes were male affairs. If women formed a part of the audience, their presence goes unrecorded in official and unofficial reports. There were moments of inversion within this gendered sphere when women strikers appeared aggressively in the forefront, picketing mill gates during the strikes in 1938. Till the recent phase of decline of the labour movement, entry into the world of trade-union politics was valorized by young male workers. Recognition as leaders even at the factory and departmental level gave a new identity. Many workers who lived through those times remembered that as young workers they always yearned to become leaders.[8] Shriram, who worked in Kanpur factories in the 1930s and 1940s, recalled that the most important criteria for selecting factory-level leaders was their reputation for being fearless (*nidar*). In speeches at mill gates and outside during strikes, trade-union leaders openly attacked and abused managers and the government. Such acts that

6. See Joshi, *Lost Worlds*.
7. Sudarshan Chakr, *Kanpur Mazdur Andolan ka Itihaas* (Kanpur, 1986).
8. Interviews with workers like Shriram, Raghubir, and Moolchand who worked in the Kanpur factories in the 1920s and 1940s.

momentarily inverted hierarchies were empowering. Shriram himself was a secretary of the Muir Mills committee. The elevation to this post, he narrates, immediately brought him into fame. He proudly declares that after his militant role during strikes his name figured along with other important local and provincial leaders in the United Provinces.

Many workers who acquired recognition as trade-union leaders were not completely anonymous earlier. Long before he became a trade-union activist, Shriram was known and feared as a neighbourhood *dada*.[9] Tracing his early days in the city, Shriram recounted how he became a regular at a local *akhara* soon after he started work.[10] Sport and physical culture at the *akhara* were important both as entertainment and as an initiation into the male world of the city. In the street culture of the city, where violent affrays between muscle men could draw an entire neighbourhood into action, *dadas* could act both as protectors and predators for communities. A favourite pastime in his *dada* days, Shriram recollected, was drinking and engaging in brawls.[11] Like other local *dadas*, he moved around with a band of followers. *Dadas* like him had a style and appearance that marked them off – their fashionable clothes, their swagger, and their whole bearing was distinct.

Trade-union leaders both claimed their association with the masculinist *dada* world and distanced themselves from it. Typically the *dada* world is represented as an element of the distant past from which leaders emerged empowered, enriched by the experience of that world, but it was a past that they had to renounce. In his retrospective recounting of his life, Shriram seeks to distance himself from his *dada* past once he became a trade-union activist. Unlike a *dada*, who was distinguished by his capacity to consume, a communist militant in the 1930s was recognized by his austerity and acts of renunciation. After becoming a trade-union leader, Shriram tells us, he renounced drinking and the extravagance of his *dada* ways and vowed to remain celibate and virtuous.

Despite the clear demarcation drawn between the world of the trade-union activist and the *dada* in Shriram's narrative, his own experiences reflect the fluidity of the divisions between the two worlds in an industrial city like Kanpur. The visible hyper-masculinity of the *dada* world was in some ways characteristic of the culture of the city as a whole. To acquire a sense of power and control in the city as a trade-union leader or as a local *dada* required an aggressive masculinity. Even the minor leaders within mill departments were tough guys who could throw their weight around and bully other workers. Like local *dadas* who boasted about exploits

9. *Dada*: a tough aggressive male who could bully and threaten people in the neighbourhood. The term used for them in official and nonofficial discourse, *goonda*, has more pejorative connotations. Anyone categorized as a *goonda* was seen as a criminal.

10. *Akhara*: a centre for wrestling and various other forms of physical activity.

11. Shriram, *Ek Sarvahara ka Jivan Vritanta* (Kanpur, n.d.), p. 12.

against predators in the neighbourhood, trade-union leaders bragged about avenging strikebreakers. Shriram narrated how, as a trade-union leader, his main job was to fight back against anyone daring to break a strike.[12]

Such aggressiveness was an important survival strategy for working-class men in the city. To resist being bullied by foremen and supervisors, to find work in the daily coolie market for casual labour, to avoid being fleeced by corrupt moneylenders – all required street-smart ways. For fresh migrants, patronage by *dadas* in the neighbourhood was important to get a foothold in the labour market. For some, spaces like the *akhara* had a role to play in forging networks. Regular visitors to the *akhara* in the 1930s and the 1940s had their *addas* where they gathered.[13] Boastful talks about pugilistic exploits, one-upmanship, were an essential part of such *addas*. Once he became associated with them, a man tried to identify with the image of an *akhara pahalwan*.[14] Shriram soon became an object of envy for neighbourhood *dadas* and *pahalwans*. He was proud to earn the title of the *dada* of Colonelganj. Similarly, partridge fighting, a sport popular among some workers, was more than a source of entertainment.[15] Bets were placed on birds, which had been fed and trained to fight. Sports like wrestling and partridge fighting were both expressing as well as creating a culture of masculinity – of violence and aggression.

Various spaces in the city provided a space for bonding between male workers. The streets through which hundreds of workers walked in groups or rode on bicycles were spaces which the working class marked with its presence. During periods of working-class upsurge, and during major riots the numbers on the streets swelled to thousands. Today, when the mills are shut and hardly any men can be seen outside factory gates, workers nostalgically talk about the noise and bustle outside factories at shift times, during the day and in the middle of the night. Workers walking shoulder to shoulder, filling the streets created a sense of power and community.

Entry into the street culture of the city was not easy for migrants. However, despite the insecurities, the hardships – a common trope within which migration stories are written – the city acted as a powerful draw. Individual stories from the past of migration suggest how the desire to explore new places and commune with other young men in the city was attractive to migrants. Personal narratives of male migrants coming to work in the city emphasize specific representations of the rural and urban. For Shriram, who moved to the city when he was around twelve years old, the shift is a moment of self-discovery. Male tales of migration like his tend

12. Interview, Shriram.
13. *Adda*: meeting place.
14. *Pahalwan*: strong man; Shriram, *Ek Sarvahara ka Jivan*, p. 12.
15. A. Niehoff, *Factory Workers* (Milwaukee, WI, 1959), p. 95.

to represent men as self-conscious actors, fearlessly confronting problems. Shriram's account touches upon the initial insecurities of city life only to demonstrate how he was able to transcend these difficulties. Once he starts work as a *doffer* boy in the woollen mills, Shriram invokes a different experience of the city. A sense of adventure, a desire to move on and explore new places takes over. He enjoys the cameraderie (*yaraana dosti*) with other workers in the factory. But after two years of work in Kanpur, he yearns to travel further and explore new cities. Uncertainty and anxiety now gives way to the theme of mobility, of exploration. Stories are brought in by labour recruiters and others coming from distant places, and these feed into the fantasies of workers like him. Shriram and his friends travel and work in factories in Delhi, Hathras, and then Amritsar. He comes back to Kanpur, only to move again to Bombay.

In his story, Shriram projects himself as an actor willing to take risks: he can give up a secure job and move to another city; he is in control and can build networks and devise strategies to confront new challenges. His travels from city to city are motivated by a sense of curiosity and a desire to discover new places. Work in new cities allows him to move up to better-paid jobs – he is pleased to be promoted from a *doffer* boy to a machine man. Sriram is a male – new to the city but aware of the world, unwilling to be docile and gullible. His return to Kanpur is represented as a shift from a world of deceit and cunning to a world where he cannot be cheated. He feels a new sense of power on returning to Kanpur. His home – Kanpur – now becomes a space over which he has control. If there was any sense of powerlessness and insecurity in distant cities, his narrative elides the question. As a male, the theme of insecurity could not be openly acknowledged. We can only read it in his silence.

His story moves by constructing a series of contrasts between the city and country. In contrast to the stereotype picture of simple country folk and wily, deceitful townspeople, he offers an inverse imagery. His relatives in the village are greedy for money.[16] In the city, in contrast, he finds relatives who care and look after him. Times were good then – one earning member could support a whole family on factory wages. He felt proud of his earnings. Besides the factory he worked in was famous. [17] The job and wages gave him a new sense of self-esteem. Sriram was writing about the 1930s and 1940s, when factory jobs gave a different sense of security. His story continuously validates and reaffirms the urban. The urban becomes a metaphor for independence – from the past, from the constraints of the family; it stands for job and earning, male pride, and status.

16. "They were like vultures waiting to feed on a carcass", (*Jaise ki mare janvar ki khal nochne ke liye gidh baithe the* [...] *vaise vah kar rahe the*); Shriram, *Ek sarvahara ka Jivan Vritanta*, p. 5.
17. "I worked in a factory which was famous all over the country as Lalimli", (*Aisee mill mein kam karta tha jo Hindustan mein Lalimli ke nam se kaphi prasidh mill thi* [...]); *ibid.* pp. 8–9.

The nature of narratives of the past is defined by the context in which they are written. In a state of joblessness and insecurity today, when factories are closed, the security of the past is overstated. For male workers, factory work defined their masculinity and identity. Work gave them a sense of power, a status in the urban world.

III

With declining earnings in the city, the rural takes on a renewed significance for worker migrants. For the rural poor who migrated to the city earlier, factory jobs helped to pay back debts and free their land from mortgages. Today, the relationship is reversed and property in the village gives the security which factory jobs gave earlier in a different way. Workers like Ramcharan, who retained a close rural connection, longingly remembered the value of earnings from factory jobs in the past. In the old days, the British *zamana* (times), he recounted, workers were paid their bonus in silver coins. It was by putting aside these coins that he could buy six and a half acres of land in the village. While the cash value of the coins was not so much, its real value when invested in land seems incomparably greater. To Ramcharan, the incremental value embedded in the silver coins was realized in the phenomenal increase in the value of land. The land he bought for Rs 500 was now, in the 1990s, worth Rs 80,000.[18]

In the present context of joblessness and uncertainty, the security provided by factory jobs tends to be overstated, the analogy between land and urban jobs is overstretched. Factory jobs are represented in many worker narratives as an inheritance to be passed down generations. This inheritance ensured a continuity over generations, and a reproduction of skills, which was a basis of worker identity and could become a source of stable earnings for an entire family. The closure of mills, many argue therefore, renders not just the present generation but the future generations unemployed.[19]

Today, male narratives play on images of decay and ageing, drawing comparisons between their decrepit bodies and the worn-out machines in the factory. Work was physically empowering, nonwork created a sense of weariness, a slowing down of body rhythms. In worker narratives of the 1990s, there is a distancing from the travails and hardship of work in the past. Factory work is celebrated as enriching and fulfilling. There is a sense of bonding with the machines and the establishments they worked in. Many state proudly how the looms never stopped in their mills. The tight

18. Interview with Ramcharan who had worked in the Muir Mills since the mid-1940s.
19. Interview, Shriram Sharma, Elgin 2.

discipline within which they often had to work in the past is recounted by many with a sense of individual achievement and male pride.[20]

While accounts of old workers now amplify memories of work in the past, they tend to repress recollections of strikes, the past history of struggles. Till the early 1980s when the factories were still running, workers took pride in narrating stories of the *Lal Kanpur* days. Today, even those who were witness to the times find it difficult to focus on the experiences of worker militancy. The oral narratives of their past are broken – moving between fleeting recollections of a better time and coming back to the hardships of the present. Some returned to the past only to bring back memories of repression and defeat. In some accounts, time is telescoped, fusing a moment of struggle in the 1950s with stories of police repression and firing on workers in the 1920s.[21] Heroic moments of solidarity are layered in such accounts with the experience of despair and disunity in the present.

The decline in industrial employment in Kanpur is part of a wider crisis affecting all the major industrial centres in India.[22] This decline is different from earlier forms of de-industrialization when traditional crafts had to compete with factory industry. Today two kinds of shifts are perceptible. One, the modern factory sector is not dominated by industries like textiles, mining, iron and steel that were important earlier; second, there is shift from factory-based production to nonfactory, small-scale industrial production. Within textiles, two kinds of processes are at work. First, the demand for cotton textiles is being increasingly displaced by the growing market for synthetic fibres; second, production has shifted from factories to small power-loom units employing cheap unregulated labour, located away from the old centres.[23] In Kanpur, the decline can be traced to the 1980s, with private industrialists shifting from cotton textiles to other more profitable ventures. The large, state-owned spinning and

20. Interviews, Pramod Awasthi and Muhammad Said, Elgin Mills. Ramcharan of the Muir Mills, for instance, talked proudly of the times when the workers were not allowed to go to the lavatory during work.

21. On this see C. Joshi, "Hope and Despair: Textile Workers in Kanpur in 1937–38 and the 1990s", in J.P. Parry, J. Breman and K. Kapadia (eds), *The Worlds of Indian Industrial Labour* (New Delhi, 1999), pp. 197–199.

22. See for instance, Jan Breman, "An Informalised Labour System: End of Labour Market Dualism", *Economic and Political Weekly* [hereafter *EPW*], 36:52 (December–January 2002), pp. 4804–4821; Sharit Bhowmik Nitin More, "Ex-Textile Mill Workers in Central Mumbai", in *ibid.*, pp. 4822–4827; M. Vanamala, "Informalisation and Feministion of a Formal Sector Industry: A Case Study", *EPW*, 36:26 (June–July 2001), pp. 2378–2389; E. Noronha and R.N. Sharma, "Displaced Workers and the Withering of Welfare State", *EPW*, no.? (June 1999), pp. 1454–1460.

23. On the crisis in the textile industry, see C.P. Chandrashekhar, "Growth and Technical Change in Indian Cotton-Mill Industry" *EPW*, 19:4 (1984), pp. PE22–PE39; Omkar Goswami, "Sickness and Growth of India's Textile Industry: Analysis and Policy Options", *EPW*, 25:44, pp. 2429–2439, and 45 (1990), pp. 2496–2506; Tirthankar Roy, "Economic Reforms and Textile Industry in India", *EPW*, 33:32 (1998), pp. 2173–2182.

weaving factories accumulated huge losses in the face of a shrinking market. By the 1990s, pressures from the proliberalization lobby mounted and the state increasingly retreated from its welfarist commitments. Committees dominated by experts in favour of a liberal-market regime declared large textile units sick and beyond redemption. Apart from the woollen mills, all state-run units in Kanpur – those run by British India Corporation and others by the National Textile Corporation – stopped production in the early 1990s. Three units under the British India Corporation continued to keep workers on the rolls for almost ten years till 2001, and two under the National Textile Corporation are still not formally closed. Only a small proportion of the permanent employees opted for voluntary retirement schemes. Most workers considered the amount offered as compensation inadequate. Moreover, they preferred to remain employees even in fictional terms to early retirement.[24]

For those on the factory rolls, the daily routine for the past many years was to report at the mill gate at shift times. Men sat around, exchanged news, and then wearily traced their way home. Every two to three months workers would be stirred into some action – a sit-in or a demonstration to demand their wages and then hopes were lost again. But for many, being on the rolls and the fiction of work and was important. To take VRS and retire would mean the stamp of unemployment.

How do workers negotiate their lives in a shrinking job market? Working out strategies of survival involves finding ways that give some economic protection and preserve a sense of self and dignity. What are the kinds of strategies that workers devise in this context?

Workers entering their fifties seem the worst affected. After a decade of waiting for the factories to reopen, they feel a sense of tiredness and inertia. Many who worked as weavers in the mills for over thirty years appear bent with age and the vagaries of time. Not only is it difficult to find work but they feel it would never give the same satisfaction.[25] Families where the men worked as weavers were able to survive in the past on the earnings of one male member. The signs of their status and dignity in the past are now lost. They are dependent largely on the daily earnings of women and children. Being a *berozgar* (unemployed) is a situation male workers find hard to come to terms with. Not going to work means a diminished patriarchal presence in the household. At a loss, sitting vacant at home, they lurk in corners, shying away from visitors. Their body language, the look of despondency, the thick glasses after years at weaving sheds often tends to mark them out and makes them recognizable as former mill workers.

Unemployed men hang around *bastis* and *hatas*, with no fixed schedule.

24. Joshi, "Hope and Despair", pp. 171–204.
25. Interview, Niamat Rasul, Elgin Mills 2.

Notions of time change when leisure is unlimited: hours and days are whiled away at home or in the *gali* (alley) outside. Even in domesticity, women tend to have a different regime of time. There are meal times and fixed times when water must be fetched, or vegetables and household provisions bought. Many women are openly critical of men idle, unwashed, sleeping till midday.[26] Some quite freely make jibes at the men sitting around gambling and gossiping in the *hata* compound. Loss of work for men implies more than an economic loss. It means also a destabilization of authority within the household and loss of respect in the neigbourhood. Men not usefully occupied become objects of female laughter.[27]

Those who always worked as *badlis*, or substitute workers and contract workers in the factories, never had the security that permanent workers in the higher-income categories had. Yet there was a difference. Periods of uncertainty were followed by long spells of work. Besides, even as substitutes and contract labourers, they had a distinct identity that marked them off from ordinary casual labourers. Today, these distinctions are no longer valid. Even those with technical skills are levelled down to the ranks of ordinary coolies. Mahboob, for instance, was not a regular employee with any one factory.[28] He repaired boilers and worked on a contract basis. With scarcely any factories running, there is no work for boiler repairmen today. Mahboob now works as a *palledar* (porter), unloading goods from trucks coming to the leather market. He admits that as a boiler repairman he was respected in the factory. He interacted with engineers and important people. Now his earnings are reduced by half and his status has diminished. As a *palledar* he is anonymous – he is like any other porter in the leather market. Yet Mahboob was unwilling to dwell too much on his loss of status. He moved quickly from the question of hurt pride to the economics of his situation. He distinguished his position from a small vendor on the street – a *thelawala*. Unlike a *thelawala* who had no clients to sell to, Mahboob claimed he had work four days a week.

Others who were always a part of the casual labour force have an attitude of resignation. Their routine is fixed. They go to the coolie market in Moolganj every morning, and wait to be hired. If there is no work till noon they return home. Sometimes the ritual wait goes on for days together, with no work. This is the pattern for casual labourers like Durga Prasad, working in the city for thirty years. Sometimes four to five days go past without any work for him.[29] When there is work he earns Rs 40 at the end of the day.

26. Sameena, in her fifties living with her unemployed son, recounted how he never woke up till 11 to 12. "Is he human", she asked, "sleeping half the day?", (*Kya voh insaan hai. Adha din sota hai*); Interview Sameena , Fazalganj, Kanpur.

27. Interviews with Shyama and Krishna, Mathiya Vala Hatha, Kanpur.

28. Interview, Mahboob, Gwaltoli, Kanpur.

29. Interview, Durga Prasad, Cooperganj, Kanpur.

The lives of petty traders in bazaars in working-class neighbourhoods have always been intertwined with those of factory workers in the city. Many of them continue with their old trades but their conditions of work are not the same. Vegetable vendors roam around looking for the stray buyer for their dissipated, unattractive-looking products. With their poor returns they can barely buy any stocks. Some selling eatables – like cooked chickpeas and *puris*[30] – manage to put together a cartfull a few days a week. Even the small shopkeeper selling footwear – shoes and slippers of the cheapest kind – feels the difference. Describing their present plight, and how the factories touched their lives earlier, Abdul Parvez, a small-time shoe trader, made a short speech. Using dramatic gestures and bodily metaphors, Abdul elocuted: "The Elgin Mills were my hands, the Power House my stomach, the Muir Mills my eyes, I could see them and feel full and contented." And this he repeated twice over for effect.[31] For small traders like him, located in the earlier hub of working-class activity – Gwaltoli – the factories sustained different occupations in the city.[32] Now everything seemed lost.

Workers' experiences of the present phase of "de-industrialization" are also mediated by gender equations within the family and their caste background. In a labour market where jobs for men are declining, women's earnings are becoming increasingly important as a survival strategy. Yet women's work is a threat to entrenched patriarchal structures and there is continued resistance to it. But strategies of negotiation vary in different types of worker households.

In upper-caste labouring households, waged work by women has always been seen as a violation of family honour. In the present context of rapidly declining family income, they struggle to survive, but continue to seclude the women, resisting their entry into public spaces, seeking desperately to preserve existing gender equations in the household. But the partially employed/unemployed male breadwinner has a diminishing patriarchal presence in the household. With the decline of the male breadwinner, women's work has acquired increasing significance within the household economy.[33] In many lower-caste working-class households the prejudices against women's work were not so deep.[34] Yet factory employment for many generations of men, and an improved economic

30. *Puri*: a kind of bread fried in oil; interview, Hasan Ahmad, Maqbara, Kanpur.

31. Interview Abdul Parvez, Gwaltoli, Kanpur.

32. Gwaltoli was an area where some of the important mills were located and a centre from which important strikes began.

33. For an elaboration of this argument, see C. Joshi, "Notes on the Breadwinner Debate: Gender and Household Strategies in Working Class Families", *Studies in History*, 18 (2002), forthcoming.

34. These include castes like *Koris* and *Chamars*. *Koris* were traditionally engaged in weaving. Many women from a *Kori* background were engaged in occupations like *bidi*-making and sewing. *Chamars* were traditional leatherworkers.

position, had led to a gradual withdrawal of women from waged work, seclusion of women being seen as necessary for claims to higher status. But in a situation of declining male income, women in many such households are now engaged in waged activity at home. Ram Pyari, who makes a living through making *bidis*, emphasized that in the past when men in her marital household had factory jobs women did not work.[35] Some who went out to work tried to keep their work a secret from neighbours.[36]

In families where women are now the regular earning members and men are intermittently employed, power relationships at home are often fraught. Men in such families feel a double loss: a loss of their jobs and loss of male authority at home. Yet men struggle to retain their sense of self. Large numbers of labouring men have continued to define their masculinity through drink and their association with male *addas*.[37] Family-budget surveys suggest that the expenditure on drink among lower-caste households has been higher than among other castes.[38] Officials conducting such surveys doubt the reliability of such estimates because lower castes tend to exaggerate their expenditure on drink. Sweepers working in the city, for instance, saw a higher expenditure on drink as a sign of their status. Consumption of alcohol in a context of declining male earnings involved contests over domestic resources and conflicts between female notions of thrift and male prodigality. Many women asserted that the men had to provide for their own drink expenses.[39] It was common in many households for men to spend the day's earnings on drink, while women provided for the children. Improvidence in the face of adversity was to them an assertion of male pride.[40] Masculine self-assertion also took the form of increased aggression at home. Feelings of emasculation and lost pride are temporarily displaced

35. "My father-in-law worked in a mill so my mother-in law did not work"; interview, Ram Pyari, Chuna Bhatiya, Kanpur.

36. Interview with Asha who worked in a small hardware unit, Afim ki Kothi, Kanpur.

37. A study in the 1960s showed that liquor consumption was more common in industrial towns like Kanpur. About 70 per cent of the workers in Kanpur were believed to be "occasional drinkers" and 30 to 50 per cent "regular drinkers", who spent on an average around 20 to 25 per cent of their wages on liquor, the amount going up to 50 per cent in the case of single men; *Report of the Study Team on Prohibition*, vol. 2, (New Delhi, 1964), p. 227.

38. According a survey in the 1930s, the expenditure on drink among the "untouchable" sweepers was higher than among other castes. The investigators noted: "When we first began our survey we found that most of the sweepers prided themselves on the amount that they spent on intoxicants, this amount being regarded as a sort of index of social status." *Report of the Harijan Survey Committee 1933–34* (Kanpur, 1934), p. 30.

39. Interview, Shyama, Lachmipurwa; also Sunita, Tijiya and Rajkumari, Bisati ka hata. This last settlement was inhabited largely by families from the "untouchable" *Kureel* caste. *Kureel* men from this locality worked in leather establishments earlier and are now unemployed.

40. Women from many lower-caste households felt it was pointless asking men for money for the household. Sunita quipped: "If we complain that it is difficult to manage, the men tell us to go away with another man". Interview, Sunita, Bisati ka hata.

through a demonstration of physical power over women. Women in many lower-caste households were almost resigned to the idea of drunken men beating them up at night. The brute reality of everyday life ultimately structured relationships of power in the household. This is not to draw any necessary connection between feelings of emasculation and violence against women. However, I suggest that the domestic setting becomes a more embattled domain when spaces for affirmation of male selfhood which existed earlier are displaced. Established patterns of male aggression are intensified in a situation where the very identity of the male is under question.

IV

In what way were the issues of identity linked up with the politics of the times? In understanding the recent upsurge in communal strife between religious communities in old industrial centres, some social analysts have drawn a link between this form of violence and the marginalization of the industrial workforce and loss of earlier collectivities important to the working-class culture of the city.[41] I emphasize here that for large sections of the marginalized labouring poor an identification with militant Hindu and Islamic movements and a culture of violence becomes a way of recovering their emasculated selves.[42] The communal carnage in Ahmedabad beginning in February 2002 which continued for over four months,[43] the violence in Bombay and Kanpur in December 1992 after the demolition of the Babri Mosque in Ayodhya,[44] – all occurred in the context of a decline of old industries and the organized labour movement. In Bombay (now Mumbai) right-wing, fascistic organizations, like the Shiv Sena, acquired a wider mass base in the mid-1980s – a period which marked the collapse of the organized labour movement in the city.[45] In Kanpur, militant Hindu and Islamic organizations had a larger public presence in a period of collapse of the labour movement in the 1990s.

However, some nagging questions remain. Is there not a danger of a

41. See Jan Breman, "Communal Upheaval as a Resurgence of Social Darwinism", *EPW*, 37: 16 (April 2002), pp. 1485–1487.

42. Breman links the intensity of communal violence in working-class neighbourhoods in Ahmedabad with the shrinkage in the dialogic space for communion between communities; *ibid.*

43. Up to April the number of deaths according to official estimates were 700 while unofficial estimates recorded more than 2,000 deaths.

44. For a background to the Babri Masjid issue, see S. Gopal (ed.), *Anatomy of a Confrontation: the Babri Masjid-Ramjanmabhumi Issue* (New Delhi, 1991).

45. The decline of the labour movement in Bombay was preceded by an eighteen-month-long textile strike which resulted in virtually no concessions to labour. A detailed, area-by-area account of the Bombay riots is available in the Complete Report of the Srikrishna Commission on Riots in Bombay, www.altindia.net.

certain form of reductive logic in this argument? Are we to suggest that de-industrialization and unemployment create a situation which inevitably leads to communal violence? How do we conceptualize the connection between politics and the economic context in a way that resists reductive reading?

I argue here that this contextualist explanation of aggressive communal politics can be developed in nonreductive ways. It is not as if there is a large mass of unemployed waiting to be mobilized as mercenaries during communal violence. The point being emphasized is the absence or erasure of an alternative political culture welding wider solidarities cutting across vertical cleavages between communities. For large sections of the marginalized labouring poor, identification with fundamentalist militant Hindu and Islamic movements becomes a way of recovering their emasculated selves. Organizations like the Rashtriya Swayam Sevak Sangh, a militant Hindu outfit with close links with the ruling Bhartiya Janata Party, exhort Hindus to shed their docile, effeminate image and take up cudgels against Muslims.[46] In the violent events of December 1992 in Kanpur, the working classes – Hindu and Muslim – formed an important part of the rioting mobs. Lower-caste Hindus like *Pasis* and *Khatiks* were among those prominently involved in acts of violence against Muslims.[47] The mobilization of lower castes around communal movements is not entirely new. In the 1920s and 1930s *Khatiks* and other lower castes came together with upper-caste Hindus in revivalist activities, acquiring a new sense of status and identity through ties which cut across class lines.[48] The lines between the pure and impure momentarily blurred as different groups within the Hindu caste hierarchy united against Muslims. After the gruesome killings of both Hindus and Muslims during communal riots in March 1931,[49] Kanpur remained relatively free of such violence even when other regions were riven with strife.[50]

46. On the politics of the RSS, see Tapan Basu, Pradip Datta, Sumit Sarkar, Tanika Sarkar, Sambuddha Sen, *Khaki Shorts and Saffron Flags: A Critique of the Hindu Right* (New Delhi, 1993).

47. *Pasi*: a caste traditionally engaged in pastoral and agricultural activity; *Khatiks*: traditionally engaged in tending pigs and in Kanpur they were important in brush and bristle-making work. On the social composition of the rioters in 1992, see Paul Brass, *Theft of an Idol: Text and Context in the Representation of Collective Violence* (Calcutta, 1997). On the identity and politics of *Khatiks*, see also Maren Bellwinkel-Schempp, "The Khatiks of Kanpur and the Bristle Trade: Towards an Anthropology of Man and Beast", *Sociological Bulletin*, 47 (1998), pp. 185–206.

48. On the mobilization of low and intermediate castes around movements asserting a militant Hindu identity, see also Nandini Gooptu, *The Politics of the Urban Poor in Early Twentieth-Century India* (Cambridge, 2002), ch. 6.

49. In the riots in 1931 more than 400 people were killed and over 1,200 injured. A prominent nationalist trade-union leader in the city, Ganesh Shanker Vidyarthi, was brutally murdered. See N.G. Barrier (ed.), *Roots of Communal Politics* (New Delhi, 1976).

What is new today is not the fact of communal mobilization but the absence of alternative notions of community and identity. What is frightening about the present is not just the organized political manifestation of communal identity and communal violence but a deeper communalization of popular perceptions, the creation of mental structures that sustains the politics of violence. The shrinking of social and physical spaces which allowed for class solidarities both shape and reflect these changes. The increasing ghettoization of communities, the reorganization of social space in the city, the dispersal and informalization of work – all tend to erase memories of conviviality between communities and harden the lines of cleavage. These changes encode deeper changes in the private transcripts. Impassioned hatred against the other community builds up a palpable sense of threat in ways that were not so apparent at a day-to-day level earlier.

A reticence to talk about issues of communal conflict which characterized the public discourse of workers twenty years back has given way now to an eagerness to express feelings of bitterness and resentment against the "other" community. A separation is still made between spaces where such utterances are legitimate and where they are not. The factory and the mill-gate were sanitized spaces where the rhetoric of unity – "we are all one", "we live and work together" – are still repeated. Outside, in the security of the neighbourhood, emotions of anger are displayed more openly. Years after the violence following the demolition of Babri Masjid, a Muslim worker recounted in graphic detail the terror and fear of those days. Once he moved away from the mill-gate to his own neighbourhood his vitriolic speech was unstoppable: From time to time, his narrative was broken and recharged with a repetition of slogans which were shouted against Muslims those days: "*Katuon ke do sthan, Pakistan ya kabristan*"; (There are only two places for *katuon* or the circumscribed – Pakistan or the graveyard). Even the factory, he recalled, was heavy with tension with Muslims having to suffer taunts and shouts.

In times fraught with tension, stereotypes about the "other" take on new meanings. In lower-caste Hindu neighbourhoods of Kanpur, the image of the wily Muslim doing them out of work is often carried to bizarre lengths. Strangely, in a scenario when processes of "de-industrialization" have had a levelling impact on different categories of the informalized labouring poor, stories are repeated about the hidden wealth of Muslims. Workers making leather uppers for sandals in the Lachmipurwa area in Kanpur

50. Although tension in the city was palpable, there was no generalized violence in the days preceding Partition. On the sense of tension in the city in the 1940s, see Soumya Gupta, "The 'Vartman' and Pakistan: The Daily Reality of Partition", in Ravikant and Tarun K. Saint (eds), *Translating Partition* (New Delhi, 2001). It was in the 1980s that violence on the scale of 1931 was repeated; this time it was a pogrom against the Sikhs following the assassination of Indira Gandhi in November 1984.

attribute the decline in their earnings to the entry of Muslims into the leather trade. Muslims are represented as "making" the riots: "Hindus have no money, Muslims have the money, they create the riots", are statements commonly heard.[51] In the Chamanganj area, where the relative proportion of Muslims has increased in the last few decades, such feelings were widely shared in non-Muslim working-class households. To many it seemed that Chamanganj was being transformed into a Muslim fortress, a *garh*. The increase in the number of Muslims was seen as an evidence of Muslim wealth – wealth which was not visible was obviously coming from foreign lands: "Muslims get their money from Arabland", was an assertion which, to them, needed no corroboration – it was self-evident.[52]

Such representations of the other are not completely novel. They draw on pre-existing stereotypes. But they now seem to have a greater continuity in time, the anger that is expressed in private threatens every moment to spill over into the public. Acts of violence and aggressive postures against the other community are seen as legitimate assertions of male selfhood. In Gujarat in recent months, workers are among those providing muscle power for horrific acts of brutality. Despite an inherent fragility, such alliances between workers and others acquire a threatening resilience in a macabre present where other visions seem to fade and blur.

Processes of de-industrialization in the present context thus have deep cultural implications. The erosion of spaces around which the culture of work and leisure was built has created a crisis of male identities. The invisibilization of men in the workforce touches the inner space of the domestic – threatening male authority in the household, dislocating gender equations. Within this scenario, movements that mobilize around a politics of hatred and communal violence are gaining ground, tearing apart traditions of working-class solidarity and collectivity built up in the past.

51. *"Hindu ke pas paise nahi hai, Musalmano ke pas paisa hai vo larvate hain"*. Interview with leatherworkers in a small workshop in Lachmipurwa. Such statements were also made by many in areas like Chamanganj with a large Muslim population. Women talked of Muslims displacing Hindus in leatherwork, of Muslims buying off houses in this area because they had more money. One of them added: "Muslims are making Chamanganj their fortress. They get their money from Arab". Interviews with women workers in Chamanganj.

52. Interviews with women in Chamanganj.

For EU product safety concerns, contact us at Calle de José Abascal, 56–1°, 28003 Madrid, Spain or eugpsr@cambridge.org.

www.ingramcontent.com/pod-product-compliance
Ingram Content Group UK Ltd.
Pitfield, Milton Keynes, MK11 3LW, UK
UKHW020152060825
461487UK00017B/1360